MADE T
ST

Chip Heath is a Professor of   nal Behavior in the
Graduate School of Business at Sta   University. His research
examines why certain ideas – ranging from urban legends to folk
medical cures, from Chicken Soup for the Soul stories to business
strategy myths – survive and prosper in the social marketplace of ideas.
His research has appeared in a variety of academic journals, and
popular accounts of his research have appeared in *Scientific
American*, the *Financial Times*, the *Washington Post*, *BusinessWeek*,
Psychology Today, and *Vanity Fair*. He lives in Los Gatos, California.

Dan Heath is a Senior Fellow at Duke University's Center for the
Advancement of Social Entrepreneurship (CASE). Previously he was
a researcher at Harvard Business School, writing 10 cases on
entrepreneurship that are used in business school programmes, as
well as the co-founder of Thinkwell, a publishing company dedicated
to creating high-quality, multimedia university textbooks. Dan has an
MBA from Harvard Business School. He lives in Raleigh, North
Carolina.

Also by Chip Heath and Dan Heath

Switch: How to change things when change is hard
Decisive: How to make better decisions in life and work

MADE TO STICK

Why some ideas take hold and others come unstuck

• • •

CHIP HEATH

&

DAN HEATH

arrow books

20

Arrow Books
20 Vauxhall Bridge Road
London SW1V 2SA

Arrow Books is part of the Penguin Random House group of companies
whose addresses can be found at global.penguinrandomhouse.com

Copyright © Chip Heath and Dan Heath 2007

Chip Heath and Dan Heath have asserted their right to be identified
as the authors of this Work in accordance with the Copyright, Designs
and Patents Act 1988.

First published in Great Britain by Random House Books in 2007
First published in paperback by Arrow Books in 2008

www.penguin.co.uk

A CIP catalogue record for this book is available from the British Library

ISBN 9780099505693

Design by Stephanie Huntwork
Printed and bound by Clays Ltd, Elcograf S.p.A

Penguin Random House is committed to a sustainable future
for our business, our readers and our planet. This book is made
from Forest Stewardship Council® certified paper.

To Dad, for driving an old tan Chevette
while putting us through college.

To Mom, for making us breakfast
every day for eighteen years. Each.

INTRODUCTION
WHAT STICKS?
3

Kidney heist. Movie popcorn. Sticky = understandable, memorable, and effective in changing thought or behavior. Halloween candy. Six principles: SUCCESs. The villain: Curse of Knowledge. It's hard to be a tapper. Creativity starts with templates.

CHAPTER 1
SIMPLE
25

Commander's Intent. THE low-fare airline. Burying the lead and the inverted pyramid. It's the economy, stupid. Decision paralysis. Clinic: Sun exposure. Names, names, and names. Simple = core + compact. Proverbs. The Palm Pilot wood block. Using what's there. The pomelo schema. High concept: *Jaws* on a spaceship. Generative analogies: Disney's "cast members."

CHAPTER 2
UNEXPECTED
63

The successful flight safety announcement. The surprise brow. Gimmicky surprise and "postdictability." Breaking the guessing machine. "The Nordie who . . ." "No school next Thursday." Clinic: Too much on foreign aid? Saturn's rings. Movie turning points. Gap theory of curiosity. Clinic: Fund-raising. Priming the gap: NCAA football. Pocketable radio. Man on the moon.

MADE TO
STICK

WHAT STICKS?

A friend of a friend of ours is a frequent business traveler. Let's call him Dave. Dave was recently in Atlantic City for an important meeting with clients. Afterward, he had some time to kill before his flight, so he went to a local bar for a drink.

He'd just finished one drink when an attractive woman approached and asked if she could buy him another. He was surprised but flattered. Sure, he said. The woman walked to the bar and brought back two more drinks—one for her and one for him. He thanked her and took a sip. And that was the last thing he remembered.

Rather, that was the last thing he remembered until he woke up, disoriented, lying in a hotel bathtub, his body submerged in ice.

He looked around frantically, trying to figure out where he was and how he got there. Then he spotted the note:

DON'T MOVE. CALL 911.

A cell phone rested on a small table beside the bathtub. He picked it up and called 911, his fingers numb and clumsy from the ice. The operator seemed oddly familiar with his situation. She said, "Sir, I want you to reach behind you, slowly and carefully. Is there a tube protruding from your lower back?"

Anxious, he felt around behind him. Sure enough, there was a tube.

The operator said, "Sir, don't panic, but one of your kidneys has been harvested. There's a ring of organ thieves operating in this city, and they got to you. Paramedics are on their way. Don't move until they arrive."

You've just read one of the most successful urban legends of the past fifteen years. The first clue is the classic urban-legend opening: "A friend of a friend . . ." Have you ever noticed that our friends' friends have much more interesting lives than our friends themselves?

You've probably heard the Kidney Heist tale before. There are hundreds of versions in circulation, and all of them share a core of three elements: (1) the drugged drink, (2) the ice-filled bathtub, and (3) the kidney-theft punch line. One version features a married man who receives the drugged drink from a prostitute he has invited to his room in Las Vegas. It's a morality play with kidneys.

Imagine that you closed the book right now, took an hourlong break, then called a friend and told the story, without rereading it. Chances are you could tell it almost perfectly. You might forget that the traveler was in Atlantic City for "an important meeting with clients"—who cares about that? But you'd remember all the important stuff.

The Kidney Heist is a story that sticks. We understand it, we remember it, and we can retell it later. And if we believe it's true, it might change our behavior permanently—at least in terms of accepting drinks from attractive strangers.

Contrast the Kidney Heist story with this passage, drawn from a paper distributed by a nonprofit organization. "Comprehensive community building naturally lends itself to a return-on-investment rationale that can be modeled, drawing on existing practice," it begins, going on to argue that "[a] factor constraining the flow of resources to CCIs is that funders must often resort to targeting or categorical requirements in grant making to ensure accountability."

Imagine that you closed the book right now and took an hourlong break. In fact, don't even take a break; just call up a friend and retell that passage without rereading it. Good luck.

Is this a fair comparison—an urban legend to a cherry-picked bad passage? Of course not. But here's where things get interesting: Think of our two examples as two poles on a spectrum of memorability. Which sounds closer to the communications you encounter at work? If you're like most people, your workplace gravitates toward the nonprofit pole as though it were the North Star.

Maybe this is perfectly natural; some ideas are inherently interesting and some are inherently uninteresting. A gang of organ thieves—inherently interesting! Nonprofit financial strategy—inherently uninteresting! It's the nature versus nurture debate applied to ideas: Are ideas born interesting or made interesting?

Well, this is a nurture book.

So how do we nurture our ideas so they'll succeed in the world? Many of us struggle with how to communicate ideas effectively, how to get our ideas to make a difference. A biology teacher spends an hour explaining mitosis, and a week later only three kids remember what it is. A manager makes a speech unveiling a new strategy as the staffers nod their heads enthusiastically, and the next day the frontline employees are observed cheerfully implementing the old one.

Good ideas often have a hard time succeeding in the world. Yet the ridiculous Kidney Heist tale keeps circulating, with no resources whatsoever to support it.

Why? Is it simply because hijacked kidneys sell better than other topics? Or is it possible to make a *true*, *worthwhile* idea circulate as effectively as this false idea?

The Truth About Movie Popcorn

Art Silverman stared at a bag of movie popcorn. It looked out of place sitting on his desk. His office had long since filled up with fake-butter fumes. Silverman knew, because of his organization's research, that the popcorn on his desk was unhealthy. Shockingly unhealthy, in fact. His job was to figure out a way to communicate this message to the unsuspecting moviegoers of America.

Silverman worked for the Center for Science in the Public Interest (CSPI), a nonprofit group that educates the public about nutrition. The CSPI sent bags of movie popcorn from a dozen theaters in three major cities to a lab for nutritional analysis. The results surprised everyone.

The United States Department of Agriculture (USDA) recommends that a normal diet contain no more than 20 grams of saturated fat each day. According to the lab results, the typical bag of popcorn had 37 grams.

The culprit was coconut oil, which theaters used to pop their popcorn. Coconut oil had some big advantages over other oils. It gave the popcorn a nice, silky texture, and released a more pleasant and natural aroma than the alternative oils. Unfortunately, as the lab results showed, coconut oil was also brimming with saturated fat.

The single serving of popcorn on Silverman's desk—a snack someone might scarf down between meals—had nearly two days' worth of saturated fat. And those 37 grams of saturated fat were packed into a *medium*-sized serving of popcorn. No doubt a decent-sized bucket could have cleared triple digits.

The challenge, Silverman realized, was that few people know what "37 grams of saturated fat" means. Most of us don't memorize the USDA's daily nutrition recommendations. Is 37 grams good or bad? And even if we have an intuition that it's bad, we'd wonder if it was "bad bad" (like cigarettes) or "normal bad" (like a cookie or a milk shake).

Even the phrase "37 grams of saturated fat" by itself was enough to cause most people's eyes to glaze over. "Saturated fat has zero appeal," Silverman says. "It's dry, it's academic, who cares?"

Silverman could have created some kind of visual comparison — perhaps an advertisement comparing the amount of saturated fat in the popcorn with the USDA's recommended daily allowance. Think of a bar graph, with one of the bars stretching twice as high as the other.

But that was too scientific somehow. Too rational. The amount of fat in this popcorn was, in some sense, not rational. It was ludicrous. The CSPI needed a way to shape the message in a way that fully communicated this ludicrousness.

Silverman came up with a solution.

CSPI called a press conference on September 27, 1992. Here's the message it presented: "A medium-sized 'butter' popcorn at a typical neighborhood movie theater contains more artery-clogging fat than a bacon-and-eggs breakfast, a Big Mac and fries for lunch, and a steak dinner with all the trimmings — combined!"

The folks at CSPI didn't neglect the visuals — they laid out the full buffet of greasy food for the television cameras. An entire day's worth of unhealthy eating, displayed on a table. All that saturated fat — stuffed into a single bag of popcorn.

The story was an immediate sensation, featured on CBS, NBC, ABC, and CNN. It made the front pages of *USA Today*, the *Los Angeles Times*, and *The Washington Post*'s Style section. Leno and Letterman cracked jokes about fat-soaked popcorn, and headline writers trotted out some doozies: "Popcorn Gets an 'R' Rating," "Lights, Action, Cholesterol!" "Theater Popcorn is Double Feature of Fat."

The idea stuck. Moviegoers, repulsed by these findings, avoided popcorn in droves. Sales plunged. The service staff at movie houses grew accustomed to fielding questions about whether the popcorn was popped in the "bad" oil. Soon after, most of the nation's biggest theater chains—including United Artists, AMC, and Loews—announced that they would stop using coconut oil.

On Stickiness

This is an idea success story. Even better, it's a *truthful* idea success story. The people at CSPI knew something about the world that they needed to share. They figured out a way to communicate the idea so that people would listen and care. And the idea stuck—just like the Kidney Heist tale.

And, let's be honest, the odds were stacked against the CSPI. The "movie popcorn is fatty" story lacks the lurid appeal of an organ-thieving gang. No one woke up in an oil-filled bathtub. The story wasn't sensational, and it wasn't even particularly entertaining. Furthermore, there was no natural constituency for the news—few of us make an effort to "stay up to date with popcorn news." There were no celebrities, models, or adorable pets involved.

In short, the popcorn idea was a lot like the ideas that most of us traffic in every day—ideas that are interesting but not sensational, truthful but not mind-blowing, important but not "life-or-death." Unless you're in advertising or public relations, you probably don't have many resources to back your ideas. You don't have a multimillion-dollar ad budget or a team of professional spinners. Your ideas need to stand on their own merits.

We wrote this book to help you make your ideas stick. By "stick," we mean that your ideas are understood and remembered, and have a lasting impact—they change your audience's opinions or behavior.

At this point, it's worth asking why you'd *need* to make your ideas stick. After all, the vast majority of our daily communication doesn't require stickiness. "Pass the gravy" doesn't have to be memorable. When we tell our friends about our relationship problems, we're not trying to have a "lasting impact."

So not every idea is stick-worthy. When we ask people how often they need to make an idea stick, they tell us that the need arises between once a month and once a week, twelve to fifty-two times per year. For managers, these are "big ideas" about new strategic directions and guidelines for behavior. Teachers try to convey themes and conflicts and trends to their students — the kinds of themes and ways of thinking that will endure long after the individual factoids have faded. Columnists try to change readers' opinions on policy issues. Religious leaders try to share spiritual wisdom with their congregants. Nonprofit organizations try to persuade volunteers to contribute their time and donors to contribute their money to a worthy cause.

Given the importance of making ideas stick, it's surprising how little attention is paid to the subject. When we get advice on communicating, it often concerns our delivery: "Stand up straight, make eye contact, use appropriate hand gestures. Practice, practice, practice (but don't sound canned)." Sometimes we get advice about structure: "Tell 'em what you're going to tell 'em. Tell 'em, then tell 'em what you told 'em." Or "Start by getting their attention — tell a joke or a story."

Another genre concerns knowing your audience: "Know what your listeners care about, so you can tailor your communication to them." And, finally, there's the most common refrain in the realm of communication advice: Use repetition, repetition, repetition.

All of this advice has obvious merit, except, perhaps, for the emphasis on repetition. (If you have to tell someone the same thing ten times, the idea probably wasn't very well designed. No urban legend has to be repeated ten times.) But this set of advice has one glaring shortcoming: It doesn't help Art Silverman as he tries to figure out the best way to explain that movie popcorn is *really* unhealthful.

Silverman no doubt knows that he should make eye contact and practice. But what message is he supposed to practice? He knows his audience — they're people who like popcorn and don't realize how unhealthy it is. So what message does he share with them? Complicating matters, Silverman knew that he wouldn't have the luxury of repetition—he had only one shot to make the media care about his story.

Or think about an elementary-school teacher. She knows her goal: to teach the material mandated by the state curriculum committee. She knows her audience: third graders with a range of knowledge and skills. She knows *how* to speak effectively—she's a virtuoso of posture and diction and eye contact. So the goal is clear, the audience is clear, and the format is clear. But the design of the message itself is far from clear. The biology students need to understand mitosis—okay, now what? There are an infinite number of ways to teach mitosis. Which way will stick? And how do you know *in advance*?

What Led to Made to Stick

The broad question, then, is how do you design an idea that sticks?

A few years ago the two of us—brothers Chip and Dan—realized that both of us had been studying how ideas stick for about ten years. Our expertise came from very different fields, but we had zeroed in on the same question: Why do some ideas succeed while others fail?

Dan had developed a passion for education. He co-founded a start-up publishing company called Thinkwell that asked a somewhat heretical question: If you were going to build a textbook from scratch, using video and technology instead of text, how would you do it? As the editor in chief of Thinkwell, Dan had to work with his team to determine the best ways to teach subjects like economics, biology, calculus, and physics. He had an opportunity to work with some of the most effective and best-loved professors in the country: the calculus teacher who was also a stand-up comic; the biology teacher who was named national Teacher of the Year; the economics teacher who was also a chaplain and a playwright. Essentially, Dan enjoyed a crash course in what makes great teachers great. And he found that, while each teacher had a unique style, collectively their instructional *methodologies* were almost identical.

Chip, as a professor at Stanford University, had spent about ten years asking why bad ideas sometimes won out in the social market-place of ideas. How could a false idea displace a true one? And what made some ideas more viral than others? As an entry point into these topics, he dove into the realm of "naturally sticky" ideas such as urban legends and conspiracy theories. Over the years, he's become uncomfortably familiar with some of the most repulsive and absurd tales in the annals of ideas. He's heard them all. Here's a very small sampler:

- The Kentucky Fried Rat. Really, any tale that involves rats and fast food is on fertile ground.
- Coca-Cola rots your bones. This fear is big in Japan, but so far the country hasn't experienced an epidemic of gelati-nous teenagers.
- If you flash your brights at a car whose headlights are off, you will be shot by a gang member.
- The Great Wall of China is the only man-made object that is visible from space. (The Wall is really long but not very wide. Think about it: If the Wall were visible, then any in-terstate highway would also be visible, and maybe a few Wal-Mart superstores as well.)
- You use only 10 percent of your brain. (If this were true, it would certainly make brain damage a lot less worrisome.)

Chip, along with his students, has spent hundreds of hours col-lecting, coding, and analyzing naturally sticky ideas: urban legends, wartime rumors, proverbs, conspiracy theories, and jokes. Urban leg-ends are false, but many naturally sticky ideas are true. In fact, per-haps the oldest class of naturally sticky ideas is the proverb—a nugget of wisdom that often endures over centuries and across cultures. As an example, versions of the proverb "Where there's smoke there's fire" have appeared in more than fifty-five different languages.

In studying naturally sticky ideas, both trivial and profound, Chip has conducted more than forty experiments with more than 1,700 participants on topics such as:

- Why Nostradamus's prophecies are still read after 400 years
- Why *Chicken Soup for the Soul* stories are inspirational
- Why ineffective folk remedies persist

A few years ago, he started teaching a course at Stanford called "How to Make Ideas Stick." The premise of the course was that if we understood what made ideas naturally sticky we might be better at making our own messages stick. During the past few years he has taught this topic to a few hundred students bound for careers as managers, public-policy analysts, journalists, designers, and film directors.

To complete the story of the Brothers Heath, in 2004 it dawned on us that we had been approaching the same problem from different angles. Chip had researched and taught what made ideas stick. Dan had tried to figure out pragmatic ways to make ideas stick. Chip had compared the success of different urban legends and stories. Dan had compared the success of different math and government lessons. Chip was the researcher and the teacher. Dan was the practitioner and the writer. (And we knew that we could make our parents happy by spending more quality time together.)

We wanted to take apart sticky ideas—both natural and created—and figure out what made them stick. What makes urban legends so compelling? Why do some chemistry lessons work better than others? Why does virtually every society circulate a set of proverbs? Why do some political ideas circulate widely while others fall short?

In short, we were looking to understand what sticks. We adopted the "what sticks" terminology from one of our favorite authors, Malcolm Gladwell. In 2000, Gladwell wrote a brilliant book called *The Tipping Point*, which examined the forces that cause social phenomena to "tip," or make the leap from small groups to big groups, the way contagious diseases spread rapidly once they infect a certain critical mass of people. Why did Hush Puppies experience a rebirth? Why did crime rates abruptly plummet in New York City? Why did the book *Divine Secrets of the Ya-Ya Sisterhood* catch on?

The Tipping Point has three sections. The first addresses the need to get the right people, and the third addresses the need for the right context. The middle section of the book, "The Stickiness Factor," argues that innovations are more likely to tip when they're sticky. When *The Tipping Point* was published, Chip realized that "stickiness" was the perfect word for the attribute that he was chasing with his research into the marketplace of ideas.

This book is a complement to *The Tipping Point* in the sense that we will identify *the traits* that make ideas sticky, a subject that was beyond the scope of Gladwell's book. Gladwell was interested in what makes social epidemics epidemic. Our interest is in how effective ideas are constructed—what makes some ideas stick and others disappear. So, while our focus will veer away from *The Tipping Point*'s turf, we want to pay tribute to Gladwell for the word "stickiness." It stuck.

Who Spoiled Halloween?

In the 1960s and 1970s, the tradition of Halloween trick-or-treating came under attack. Rumors circulated about Halloween sadists who put razor blades in apples and booby-trapped pieces of candy. The rumors affected the Halloween tradition nationwide. Parents carefully examined their children's candy bags. Schools opened their doors at night so that kids could trick-or-treat in a safe environment. Hospitals volunteered to X-ray candy bags.

In 1985, an ABC News poll showed that 60 percent of parents worried that their children might be victimized. To this day, many parents warn their children not to eat any snacks that aren't prepackaged. This is a sad story: a family holiday sullied by bad people who, inexplicably, wish to harm children. But in 1985 the story took a strange twist. Researchers discovered something shocking about the candy-tampering epidemic: It was a myth.

The researchers, sociologists Joel Best and Gerald Horiuchi, studied every reported Halloween incident since 1958. They found no instances where strangers caused children life-threatening harm on Halloween by tampering with their candy.

Two children did die on Halloween, but their deaths weren't caused by strangers. A five-year-old boy found his uncle's heroin stash and overdosed. His relatives initially tried to cover their tracks by sprinkling heroin on his candy. In another case, a father, hoping to collect on an insurance settlement, caused the death of his own son by contaminating his candy with cyanide.

In other words, the best social science evidence reveals that taking candy from strangers is perfectly okay. It's your family you should worry about.

The candy-tampering story has changed the behavior of millions of parents over the past thirty years. Sadly, it has made neighbors suspicious of neighbors. It has even changed the laws of this country: Both California and New Jersey passed laws that carry special penalties for candy-tamperers. Why was this idea so successful?

Six Principles of Sticky Ideas

The Halloween-candy story is, in a sense, the evil twin of the CSPI story.

Both stories highlighted an unexpected danger in a common activity: eating Halloween candy and eating movie popcorn. Both stories called for simple action: examining your child's candy and avoiding movie popcorn. Both made use of vivid, concrete images that cling easily to memory: an apple with a buried razor blade and a table full of greasy foods. And both stories tapped into emotion: fear in the case of Halloween candy and disgust in the case of movie popcorn.

The Kidney Heist, too, shares many of these traits. A highly *unexpected* outcome: a guy who stops for a drink and ends up one kidney short of a pair. A lot of *concrete* details: the ice-filled bathtub, the weird tube protruding from the lower back. *Emotion:* fear, disgust, suspicion.

We began to see the same themes, the same attributes, reflected in a wide range of successful ideas. What we found based on Chip's research—and by reviewing the research of dozens of folklorists, psychologists, educational researchers, political scientists, and proverbhunters—was that sticky ideas shared certain key traits. There is no "formula" for a sticky idea—we don't want to overstate the case. But sticky ideas do draw from a common set of traits, which make them more likely to succeed.

It's like discussing the attributes of a great basketball player. You can be pretty sure that any great player has some subset of traits like height, speed, agility, power, and court sense. But you don't need all of these traits in order to be great: Some great guards are five feet ten and scrawny. And having all the traits doesn't guarantee greatness: No doubt there are plenty of slow, clumsy seven-footers. It's clear, though, that if you're on the neighborhood court, choosing your team from among strangers, you should probably take a gamble on the seven-foot dude.

Ideas work in much the same way. One skill we can learn is the ability to *spot* ideas that have "natural talent," like the seven-foot stranger. Later in the book, we'll discuss Subway's advertising campaign that focused on Jared, an obese college student who lost more than 200 pounds by eating Subway sandwiches every day. The campaign was a huge success. And it wasn't created by a Madison Avenue advertising agency; it started with a single store owner who had the good sense to spot an amazing story.

But here's where our basketball analogy breaks down: In the world of ideas, we can genetically engineer our players. We can *create* ideas with an eye to maximizing their stickiness.

As we pored over hundreds of sticky ideas, we saw, over and over, the same six principles at work.

PRINCIPLE 1: SIMPLICITY

How do we find the essential core of our ideas? A successful defense lawyer says, "If you argue ten points, even if each is a good point, when they get back to the jury room they won't remember any." To strip an idea down to its core, we must be masters of exclusion. We must relentlessly prioritize. Saying something short is not the mission—sound bites are not the ideal. Proverbs are the ideal. We must create ideas that are both simple *and* profound. The Golden Rule is the ultimate model of simplicity: a one-sentence statement so profound that an individual could spend a lifetime learning to follow it.

PRINCIPLE 2: UNEXPECTEDNESS

How do we get our audience to pay attention to our ideas, and how do we maintain their interest when we need time to get the ideas across? We need to violate people's expectations. We need to be counterintuitive. A bag of popcorn is as unhealthy as *a whole day's worth of fatty foods!* We can use surprise—an emotion whose function is to increase alertness and cause focus—to grab people's attention. But surprise doesn't last. For our idea to endure, we must generate *interest* and *curiosity*. How do you keep students engaged during the forty-eighth history class of the year? We can engage people's curiosity over a long period of time by systematically "opening gaps" in their knowledge—and then filling those gaps.

PRINCIPLE 3: CONCRETENESS

How do we make our ideas clear? We must explain our ideas in terms of human actions, in terms of sensory information. This is where so much business communication goes awry. Mission statements, synergies, strategies, visions—they are often ambiguous to the point of being meaningless. Naturally sticky ideas are full of concrete images—ice-filled bathtubs, apples with razors—because our brains are wired to remember concrete data. In proverbs, abstract truths are often encoded in concrete language: "A bird in hand is worth two in the bush." Speaking concretely is the only way to ensure that our idea will mean the same thing to everyone in our audience.

PRINCIPLE 4: CREDIBILITY

How do we make people believe our ideas? When the former surgeon general C. Everett Koop talks about a public-health issue, most people accept his ideas without skepticism. But in most day-to-day situations we don't enjoy this authority. Sticky ideas have to carry their own credentials. We need ways to help people test our ideas for themselves—a "try before you buy" philosophy for the world of ideas. When we're trying to build a case for something, most of us instinctively grasp for hard numbers. But in many cases this is exactly the wrong approach. In the sole U.S. presidential debate in 1980 between Ronald Reagan and Jimmy Carter, Reagan could have cited innumerable statistics demonstrating the sluggishness of the economy. Instead, he asked a simple question that allowed voters to test for themselves: "Before you vote, ask yourself if you are better off today than you were four years ago."

PRINCIPLE 5: EMOTIONS

How do we get people to care about our ideas? We make them *feel* something. In the case of movie popcorn, we make them feel disgusted by its unhealthiness. The statistic "37 grams" doesn't elicit any emotions. Research shows that people are more likely to make a charitable gift to a single needy individual than to an entire impoverished region. We are wired to feel things for people, not for abstractions. Sometimes the hard part is finding the right emotion to harness. For instance, it's difficult to get teenagers to quit smoking by instilling in them a fear of the consequences, but it's easier to get them to quit by tapping into their resentment of the duplicity of Big Tobacco.

PRINCIPLE 6: STORIES

How do we get people to act on our ideas? We tell stories. Firefighters naturally swap stories after every fire, and by doing so they multiply their experience; after years of hearing stories, they have a richer, more complete mental catalog of critical situations they might confront during a fire and the appropriate responses to those situations. Research shows that mentally rehearsing a situation helps us perform better when we encounter that situation in the physical environment. Similarly, hearing stories acts as a kind of mental flight simulator, preparing us to respond more quickly and effectively.

Those are the six principles of successful ideas. To summarize, here's our checklist for creating a successful idea: a Simple Unexpected Concrete Credentialed Emotional Story. A clever observer will note that this sentence can be compacted into the acronym SUCCESs. This is sheer coincidence, of course. (Okay, we admit, SUCCESs is a little corny. We could have changed "Simple" to "Core" and reordered a few letters. But, you have to admit, CCUCES is less memorable.)

No special expertise is needed to apply these principles. There are no licensed stickologists. Moreover, many of the principles have a commonsense ring to them: Didn't most of us already have the intuition that we should "be simple" and "use stories"? It's not as though there's a powerful constituency for overcomplicated, lifeless prose.

But wait a minute. We claim that using these principles is easy. And most of them do seem relatively commonsensical. So why aren't we deluged with brilliantly designed sticky ideas? Why is our life filled with more process memos than proverbs?

Sadly, there is a villain in our story. The villain is a natural psychological tendency that consistently confounds our ability to create ideas using these principles. It's called the Curse of Knowledge. (We will capitalize the phrase throughout the book to give it the drama we think it deserves.)

Tappers and Listeners

In 1990, Elizabeth Newton earned a Ph.D. in psychology at Stanford by studying a simple game in which she assigned people to one of two roles: "tappers" or "listeners." Tappers received a list of twenty-five well-known songs, such as "Happy Birthday to You" and "The Star-Spangled Banner." Each tapper was asked to pick a song and tap out the rhythm to a listener (by knocking on a table). The listener's job was to guess the song, based on the rhythm being tapped. (By the way, this experiment is fun to try at home if there's a good "listener" candidate nearby.)

The listener's job in this game is quite difficult. Over the course of Newton's experiment, 120 songs were tapped out. Listeners guessed only 2.5 percent of the songs: 3 out of 120.

But here's what made the result worthy of a dissertation in psychology. Before the listeners guessed the name of the song, Newton asked the tappers to predict the odds that the listeners would guess correctly. They predicted that the odds were 50 percent.

The tappers got their message across 1 time in 40, but they thought they were getting their message across 1 time in 2. Why?

When a tapper taps, she is *hearing the song in her head*. Go ahead and try it for yourself—tap out "The Star-Spangled Banner." It's impossible to avoid hearing the tune in your head. Meanwhile, the listeners can't hear that tune—all they can hear is a bunch of disconnected taps, like a kind of bizarre Morse Code.

In the experiment, tappers are flabbergasted at how hard the listeners seem to be working to pick up the tune. *Isn't the song obvious?* The tappers' expressions, when a listener guesses "Happy Birthday to You" for "The Star-Spangled Banner," are priceless: *How could you be so stupid?*

It's hard to be a tapper. The problem is that tappers have been given knowledge (the song title) that makes it impossible for them to imagine what it's like to *lack* that knowledge. When they're tapping, they can't imagine what it's like for the listeners to hear isolated taps rather than a song. This is the Curse of Knowledge. Once we know something, we find it hard to imagine what it was like not to know it. Our knowledge has "cursed" us. And it becomes difficult for us to share our knowledge with others, because we can't readily re-create our listeners' state of mind.

The tapper/listener experiment is reenacted every day across the world. The tappers and listeners are CEOs and frontline employees, teachers and students, politicians and voters, marketers and customers, writers and readers. All of these groups rely on ongoing communication, but, like the tappers and listeners, they suffer from enormous information imbalances. When a CEO discusses "unlocking shareholder value," there is a tune playing in her head that the employees can't hear.

It's a hard problem to avoid—a CEO might have thirty years of daily immersion in the logic and conventions of business. Reversing the process is as impossible as un-ringing a bell. You can't unlearn what you already know. There are, in fact, only two ways to beat the Curse of Knowledge reliably. The first is not to learn anything. The second is to take your ideas and transform them.

This book will teach you how to transform your ideas to beat the Curse of Knowledge. The six principles presented earlier are your best weapons. They can be used as a kind of checklist. Let's take the CEO who announces to her staff that they must strive to "maximize shareholder value."

Is this idea simple? Yes, in the sense that it's short, but it lacks the useful simplicity of a proverb. Is it unexpected? No. Concrete? Not at all. Credible? Only in the sense that it's coming from the mouth of the CEO. Emotional? Um, no. A story? No.

Contrast the "maximize shareholder value" idea with John F. Kennedy's famous 1961 call to "put a man on the moon and return him safely by the end of the decade." Simple? Yes. Unexpected? Yes. Concrete? Amazingly so. Credible? The goal seemed like science fiction, but the source was credible. Emotional? Yes. Story? In miniature.

Had John F. Kennedy been a CEO, he would have said, "Our mission is to become the international leader in the space industry through maximum team-centered innovation and strategically targeted aerospace initiatives." Fortunately, JFK was more intuitive than a modern-day CEO; he knew that opaque, abstract missions don't captivate and inspire people. The moon mission was a classic case of a communicator's dodging the Curse of Knowledge. It was a brilliant and beautiful idea—a single idea that motivated the actions of millions of people for a decade.

Systematic Creativity

Picture in your mind the type of person who's great at coming up with ideas. Have a mental image of the person? A lot of people, when asked to do this, describe a familiar stereotype—the "creative genius," the kind of person who thinks up slogans in a hot advertising agency. Maybe, like us, you picture someone with gelled hair and hip clothing, carrying a dog-eared notebook full of ironies and epiphanies, ready to drop everything and launch a four-hour brainstorming session in a room full of caffeine and whiteboards. Or maybe your stereotype isn't quite so elaborate.

There's no question that some people are more creative than others. Perhaps they're just born that way. So maybe you'll never be the Michael Jordan of sticky ideas. But the premise of this book is that creating sticky ideas is something that can be learned.

In 1999, an Israeli research team assembled a group of 200 highly regarded ads—ads that were finalists and award winners in the top advertising competitions. They found that 89 percent of the award-winning ads could be classified into six basic categories, or *templates*. That's remarkable. We might expect great creative concepts to be highly idiosyncratic—emerging from the whims of born creative types. It turns out that six simple templates go a long way.

Most of these templates relate to the principle of unexpectedness. For example, the *Extreme Consequences* template points out unexpected consequences of a product attribute. One ad emphasizes the power of a car stereo system—when the stereo belts out a tune, a bridge starts oscillating to the music, and when the speakers are cranked up the bridge shimmies so hard that it nearly collapses. This same template also describes the famous World War II slogan devised by the Ad Council, a nonprofit organization that creates public-service campaigns for other nonprofits and government agencies: "Loose Lips Sink Ships." And speaking of extreme consequences, let's not forget the eggs sizzling in the 1980s commercial "This is your brain on drugs" (also designed by the Ad Council). The template also pops up spontaneously in naturally sticky ideas—for example, the legend that Newton discovered gravity when an apple fell on his head. (For the other templates, see the endnotes.)

The researchers also tried to use their six templates to classify 200 other ads—from the same publications and for the same types of products—that had not received awards. Amazingly, when the researchers tried to classify these "less successful" ads, they could classify only 2 percent of them.

The surprising lesson of this story: Highly creative ads are more predictable than uncreative ones. It's like Tolstoy's quote: "All happy families resemble each other, but each unhappy family is unhappy in its own way." All creative ads resemble one another, but each loser is uncreative in its own way.

But if creative ads consistently make use of the same basic set of templates, perhaps "creativity" can be taught. Perhaps even novices— with no creative experience—could produce better ideas if they understood the templates. The Israeli researchers, curious about the ability to teach creativity, decided to see just how far a template could take someone.

They brought in three groups of novices and gave each group some background information about three products: a shampoo, a diet-food item, and a sneaker. One group received the background information on the products and immediately started generating ads, with no training. An experienced creative director, who didn't know how the group had been trained, selected its top fifteen ads. Then those ads were tested by consumers. The group's ads stood out: Consumers rated them as "annoying." (Could this be the long-awaited explanation for the ads of local car dealerships?)

A second group was trained for two hours by an experienced creativity instructor who showed the participants how to use a free-association brainstorming method. This technique is a standard method for teaching creativity; it's supposed to broaden associations, spark unexpected connections, and get lots of creative ideas on the table so that people can select the very best. If you've ever sat in a class on brainstorming great ideas, this method is probably the one you were taught.

Again, the fifteen best ads were selected by the same creative director, who didn't know how the group had been trained, and the ads were then tested by consumers. This group's ads were rated as less annoying than those of the untrained group but no more creative.

The final group was trained for two hours on how to use the six creative templates. Once again, the fifteen best ads were selected by the creative director and tested with consumers. Suddenly these novices sprouted creativity. Their ads were rated as 50 percent more creative and produced a 55 percent more positive attitude toward the products advertised. This is a stunning improvement for a two-hour investment in learning a few basic templates! It appears that there are indeed systematic ways to produce creative ideas.

What this Israeli research team did for advertisements is what this book does for your ideas. We will give you suggestions for tailoring your ideas in a way that makes them more creative and more effective with your audience. We've created our checklist of six principles for precisely this purpose.

But isn't the use of a template or a checklist confining? Surely we're not arguing that a "color by numbers" approach will yield more creative work than a blank-canvas approach?

Actually, yes, that's exactly what we're saying. If you want to spread your ideas to other people, you should work within the confines of the rules that have allowed other ideas to succeed over time. You want to invent new ideas, not new rules.

This book can't offer a foolproof recipe. We'll admit it up front: We won't be able to show you how to get twelve-year-olds to gossip about mitosis around the campfire. And in all likelihood your process-improvement memo will not circulate decades from now as a proverb in another culture.

But we can promise you this: Regardless of your level of "natural creativity," we will show you how a little focused effort can make almost any idea stickier, and a sticky idea is an idea that is more likely to make a difference. All you need to do is understand the six principles of powerful ideas.

CHAPTER 1

SIMPLE

Every move an Army soldier makes is preceded by a staggering amount of planning, which can be traced to an original order from the president of the United States. The president orders the Joint Chiefs of Staff to accomplish an objective, and the Joint Chiefs set the parameters of the operation. Then the orders and plans begin to cascade downward—from generals to colonels to captains.

The plans are quite thorough, specifying the "scheme of maneuver" and the "concept of fires"—what each unit will do, which equipment it will use, how it will replace munitions, and so on. The orders snowball until they accumulate enough specificity to guide the actions of individual foot soldiers at particular moments in time.

The Army invests enormous energy in its planning, and its processes have been refined over many years. The system is a marvel of communication. There's just one drawback: The plans often turn out to be useless.

"The trite expression we always use is *No plan survives contact with the enemy*," says Colonel Tom Kolditz, the head of the behavioral sciences division at West Point. "You may start off trying to fight your plan, but the enemy gets a vote. Unpredictable things happen—the weather changes, a key asset is destroyed, the enemy responds in a way you don't expect. Many armies fail because they put all their emphasis into creating a plan that becomes useless ten minutes into the battle."

The Army's challenge is akin to writing instructions for a friend to play chess on your behalf. You know a lot about the rules of the game, and you may know a lot about your friend and the opponent. But if you try to write move-by-move instructions you'll fail. You can't possibly foresee more than a few moves. The first time the opponent makes a surprise move, your friend will have to throw out your carefully designed plans and rely on her instincts.

Colonel Kolditz says, "Over time we've come to understand more and more about what makes people successful in complex operations." He believes that plans are useful, in the sense that they are proof that *planning* has taken place. The planning process forces people to think through the right issues. But as for the plans themselves, Kolditz says, "They just don't work on the battlefield." So, in the 1980s the Army adapted its planning process, inventing a concept called Commander's Intent (CI).

CI is a crisp, plain-talk statement that appears at the top of every order, specifying the plan's goal, the desired end-state of an operation. At high levels of the Army, the CI may be relatively abstract: "Break the will of the enemy in the Southeast region." At the tactical level, for colonels and captains, it is much more concrete: "My intent is to have Third Battalion on Hill 4305, to have the hill cleared of enemy, with only ineffective remnants remaining, so we can protect the flank of Third Brigade as they pass through the lines."

The CI never specifies so much detail that it risks being rendered obsolete by unpredictable events. "You can lose the ability to execute the original plan, but you never lose the responsibility of executing the intent," says Kolditz. In other words, if there's one soldier left in the Third Battalion on Hill 4305, he'd better be doing something to protect the flank of the Third Brigade.

Commander's Intent manages to align the behavior of soldiers at all levels without requiring play-by-play instructions from their leaders. When people know the desired destination, they're free to improvise, as needed, in arriving there. Colonel Kolditz gives an example: "Suppose I'm commanding an artillery battalion and I say, 'We're going to pass this infantry unit through our lines forward.' That means something different to different groups. The mechanics know that they'll need lots of repair support along the roads, because if a tank breaks down on a bridge the whole operation will come to a screeching halt. The artillery knows they'll need to fire smoke or have engineers generate smoke in the breech area where the infantry unit moves forward, so it won't get shot up as it passes through. As a commander, I could spend a lot of time enumerating every specific task, but as soon as people know what the *intent* is they begin generating their own solutions."

The Combat Maneuver Training Center, the unit in charge of military simulations, recommends that officers arrive at the Commander's Intent by asking themselves two questions:

If we do nothing else during tomorrow's mission, we must

_____.

The single, most important thing that we must do tomorrow is

_____.

No plan survives contact with the enemy. No doubt this principle has resonance for people who have no military experience whatsoever. *No sales plan survives contact with the customer. No lesson plan survives contact with teenagers.*

It's hard to make ideas stick in a noisy, unpredictable, chaotic environment. If we're to succeed, the first step is this: Be simple. Not simple in terms of "dumbing down" or "sound bites." You don't have to speak in monosyllables to be simple. What we mean by "simple" is *finding the core of the idea.*

"Finding the core" means stripping an idea down to its most critical essence. To get to the core, we've got to weed out superfluous and tangential elements. But that's the easy part. The hard part is weeding out ideas that may be really important but just aren't *the most important* idea. The Army's Commander's Intent forces its officers to highlight the most important goal of an operation. The value of the Intent comes from its singularity. You can't have five North Stars, you can't have five "most important goals," and you can't have five Commander's Intents. Finding the core is analogous to writing the Commander's Intent—it's about discarding a lot of great insights in order to let the most important insight shine. The French aviator and author Antoine de Saint-Exupéry once offered a definition of engineering elegance: "A designer knows he has achieved perfection not when there is nothing left to add, but when there is nothing left to take away." A designer of simple ideas should aspire to the same goal: knowing how much can be wrung out of an idea before it begins to lose its essence.

In fact, we'll follow our own advice and strip this book down to its core. Here it is: There are two steps in making your ideas sticky—Step 1 is to find the core, and Step 2 is to translate the core using the SUCCESs checklist. That's it. We'll spend the next half chapter on Step 1, and the remainder of the book on Step 2. The first step in unpacking these ideas is to explore why Southwest Airlines deliberately ignores the food preferences of its customers.

Finding the Core at Southwest Airlines

It's common knowledge that Southwest is a successful company, but there is a shocking performance gap between Southwest and its competitors. Although the airlines industry as a whole has only a passing acquaintance with profitability, Southwest has been consistently profitable for more than thirty years.

The reasons for Southwest's success could (and do) fill up books, but perhaps the single greatest factor in the company's success is its dogged focus on reducing costs. Every airline would like to reduce costs, but Southwest has been doing it for decades. For this effort to succeed, the company must coordinate thousands of employees, ranging from marketers to baggage handlers.

Southwest has a Commander's Intent, a core, that helps to guide this coordination. As related by James Carville and Paul Begala:

> Herb Kelleher [the longest-serving CEO of Southwest] once told someone, "I can teach you the secret to running this airline in thirty seconds. This is it: We are THE low-fare airline. Once you understand that fact, you can make any decision about this company's future as well as I can.
>
> "Here's an example," he said. "Tracy from marketing comes into your office. She says her surveys indicate that the passengers might enjoy a light entrée on the Houston to Las Vegas flight. All we offer is peanuts, and she thinks a nice chicken Caesar salad would be popular. What do you say?"
>
> The person stammered for a moment, so Kelleher responded: "You say, 'Tracy, will adding that chicken Caesar salad make us THE low-fare airline from Houston to Las Vegas? Because if it doesn't help us become the unchallenged low-fare airline, we're not serving any damn chicken salad.'"

Kelleher's Commander's Intent is "We are THE low-fare airline." This is a simple idea, but it is sufficiently useful that it has guided the actions of Southwest's employees for more than thirty years.

Now, this core idea—"THE low-fare airline"—isn't the whole story, of course. For instance, in 1996 Southwest received 124,000 applications for 5,444 openings. It's known as a great place to work, which is surprising. It's not supposed to be fun to work for penny-pinchers. It's hard to imagine Wal-Mart employees giggling their way through the workday.

Yet somehow Southwest has pulled it off. Let's think about the ideas driving Southwest Airlines as concentric circles. The central circle, the core, is "THE low-fare airline." But the very next circle might be "Have fun at work." Southwest's employees know that it's okay to have fun so long as it doesn't jeopardize the company's status as THE low-fare airline. A new employee can easily put these ideas together to realize how to act in unscripted situations. For instance, is it all right to joke about a flight attendant's birthday over the P.A.? Sure. Is it equally okay to throw confetti in her honor? Probably not—the confetti would create extra work for cleanup crews, and extra clean-up time means higher fares. It's the lighthearted business equivalent of the foot soldier who improvises based on the Commander's Intent. A well-thought-out simple idea can be amazingly powerful in shaping behavior.

A warning: In the future, months after you've put down this book, you're going to recall the word "Simple" as an element of the SUC-CESs checklist. And your mental thesaurus will faithfully go digging for the meaning of "Simple," and it's going to come back with associations like dumbing down, shooting for the lowest common denominator, making things easy, and so on. At that moment, you've got to remind your thesaurus of the examples we've explored. "THE low-fare airline" and the other stories in this chapter aren't simple because they're full of easy words. They're simple because they reflect the Commander's Intent. It's about elegance and prioritization, not dumbing down.

Burying the Lead

News reporters are taught to start their stories with the most important information. The first sentence, called the lead, contains the most essential elements of the story. A good lead can convey a lot of information, as in these two leads from articles that won awards from the American Society of Newspaper Editors:

A healthy 17-year-old heart pumped the gift of life through 34-year-old Bruce Murray Friday, following a four-hour transplant operation that doctors said went without a hitch.

JERUSALEM, Nov. 4—A right-wing Jewish extremist shot and killed Prime Minister Yitzhak Rabin tonight as he departed a peace rally attended by more than 100,000 in Tel Aviv, throwing Israel's government and the Middle East peace process into turmoil.

After the lead, information is presented in decreasing order of importance. Journalists call this the "inverted pyramid" structure—the most important info (the widest part of the pyramid) is at the top.

The inverted pyramid is great for readers. No matter what the reader's attention span—whether she reads only the lead or the entire story—the inverted pyramid maximizes the information she gleans. Think of the alternative: If news stories were written like mysteries, with a dramatic payoff at the end, then readers who broke off in midstory would miss the point. Imagine waiting until the last sentence of a story to find out who won the presidential election or the Super Bowl.

The inverted pyramid also allows newspapers to get out the door on time. Suppose a late-breaking story forces editors to steal space from other stories. Without the inverted pyramid, they'd be forced to do a slow, careful editing job on all the other articles, trimming a word here or a phrase there. With the inverted pyramid structure, they simply lop off paragraphs from the bottom of the other articles, knowing that those paragraphs are (by construction) the least important.

According to one account, perhaps apocryphal, the inverted pyramid arose during the Civil War. All the reporters wanted to use military telegraphs to transmit their stories back home, but they could be cut off at any moment; they might be bumped by military personnel, or the communication line might be lost completely—a common occurrence during battles. The reporters never knew how much time they would get to send a story, so they had to send the most important information first.

Journalists obsess about their leads. Don Wycliff, a winner of prizes for editorial writing, says, "I've always been a believer that if I've got two hours in which to write a story, the best investment I can make is to spend the first hour and forty-five minutes of it getting a good lead, because after that everything will come easily."

So if finding a good lead makes everything else easy, why would a journalist ever fail to come up with one? A common mistake reporters make is that they get so steeped in the details that they fail to see the message's core—what readers will find important or interesting. The longtime newspaper writer Ed Cray, a professor of communications at the University of Southern California, has spent almost thirty years teaching journalism. He says, "The longer you work on a story, the more you can find yourself losing direction. No detail is too small. You just don't know what your story is anymore."

This problem of losing direction, of missing the central story, is so common that journalists have given it its own name: Burying the lead. "Burying the lead" occurs when the journalist lets the most important element of the story slip too far down in the story structure.

The process of writing a lead—and avoiding the temptation to bury it—is a helpful *metaphor* for the process of finding the core. Finding the core and writing the lead both involve *forced prioritization*. Suppose you're a wartime reporter and you can telegraph only one thing before the line gets cut, what would it be? There's only one lead, and there's only one core. You must choose.

Forced prioritization is really painful. Smart people recognize the value of all the material. They see nuance, multiple perspectives—and because they fully appreciate the complexities of a situation, they're often tempted to linger there. This tendency to gravitate toward complexity is perpetually at war with the need to prioritize. This difficult quest—the need to wrestle priorities out of complexity—was exactly the situation that James Carville faced in the Clinton campaign of 1992.

"If You Say Three Things, You Don't Say Anything."

A political campaign is a breeding ground of decision angst. If you think your organization has problems, imagine this challenge: You must build a nationwide organization from scratch, using primarily unpaid and largely unskilled workers. You've got about a year to pull the team together and line up an endless supply of doughnuts. Everyone in the organization needs to sing from the same hymnal, but you don't have much time to rehearse the choir. And the media prod you to sing a new song every day. To make matters worse, you must constantly contend with opponents who will seize on every errant word.

Bill Clinton's 1992 campaign was a classic example of sticky ideas at work in a difficult environment. Not only did the campaign have the normal set of complexities, Clinton himself added a few new wrinkles. First, there were the "bimbo eruptions," which need not be reexamined here. Second, Clinton was a policy wonk by nature, which meant that he was inclined to pontificate on virtually every issue that he was asked about, instead of staying focused on a few key principles.

As his key political adviser, James Carville had to cope with this complexity. One day, struggling to maintain his focus, he wrote three phrases on a whiteboard for all the campaign workers to see. One of the phrases on the impromptu list was "It's the economy, stupid." This message would become the core of Clinton's successful campaign.

The word "stupid" was added as a taunt to the campaign workers themselves, reminding them not to lose focus on what was important. "It was simple and it was self-effacing," Carville explained. "I was trying to say, 'Let's don't be too clever here, don't come down here thinking we're too smart. Let's just remember the basics.'"

The need for focus extended to Bill Clinton himself, perhaps especially to Clinton himself. At one point, Clinton was frustrated that he'd been advised to stop talking about balanced budgets despite the fact that Ross Perot, the third-party candidate for president in 1992, was getting positive attention for his stand on the balanced budget. Clinton said, "I've been talking about these things for two years, why should I stop talking about them now because Perot is in?" Clinton's advisers had to tell him, "There has to be message triage. If you say three things, you don't say anything."

"It's the economy, stupid" was the lead of the Clinton story—and it was a good one, because in 1992 the U.S. economy was mired in a recession. But if "It's the economy, stupid" is the lead, then the need for a balanced budget can't also be the lead. Carville had to stop Clinton from burying the lead.

Decision Paralysis

Why is prioritizing so difficult? In the abstract, it doesn't sound so tough. You prioritize important goals over less important goals. You prioritize goals that are "critical" ahead of goals that are "beneficial."

But what if we can't tell what's "critical" and what's "beneficial"? Sometimes it's not obvious. We often have to make decisions between one "unknown" and another. This kind of complexity can be paralyzing. In fact, psychologists have found that people can be driven to irrational decisions by too much complexity and uncertainty.

In 1954, the economist L. J. Savage described what he perceived as a basic rule of human decision-making. He called it the "sure-thing principle." He illustrated it with this example: A businessman is thinking about buying a piece of property. There's an election coming up soon, and he initially thinks that its outcome could be relevant to the attractiveness of the purchase. So, to clarify his decision, he thinks through both scenarios. If the Republican wins, he decides, he'll buy. If the Democrat wins, he'll do the same. Seeing that he'd buy in either scenario, he goes forward with the purchase, despite not knowing the outcome. This decision seems sensible—not many people would quibble with Savage's logic.

Two psychologists quibbled. Amos Tversky and Eldar Shafir later published a paper proving that the "sure-thing principle" wasn't always a sure thing. They uncovered situations where the mere existence of uncertainty seemed to alter how people made decisions— even when the uncertainty was irrelevant to the outcome, as with the businessman's purchase. For instance, imagine that you're in college and you've just completed an important final exam a couple of weeks before the Christmas holidays. You'd been studying for this exam for weeks, because it's in a subject that's important to your future career.

You've got to wait two days to get the exam results back. Meanwhile, you see an opportunity to purchase a vacation during the holidays to Hawaii at a bargain-basement price. Here are your three options: You can buy the vacation today, pass on it today, or pay a five-dollar fee to lock in the price for two days, which would allow you to make your decision *after* you got your grade. What would you do?

You may feel some desire to know the outcome of your exam before you decide, as did the students who faced this choice in the original experiment. So Tversky and Shafir simply removed this uncertainty for two groups of participants. These groups were told up front how they did on the exam. Some students were told that they passed the exam, and 57 percent of them chose to go on the trip (after all, it makes for a good celebration). Other students were told that they failed the exam, and 54 percent of them chose to go on the trip (after all, it makes for good recuperation). Both those who passed and those who failed wanted to go to Hawaii, pronto.

Here's the twist: The group of students who, like you, didn't know their final exam results behaved completely differently. The majority of them (61 percent) paid five dollars to wait for two days. Think about that! If you pass, you want to go to Hawaii. If you fail, you want to go to Hawaii. If you don't know whether you passed or failed, you . . . wait and see? This is not the way the "sure-thing principle" is supposed to behave. It's as if our businessman had decided to wait until after the election to buy his property, despite being willing to make the purchase regardless of the outcome.

Tversky and Shafir's study shows us that uncertainty—even irrelevant uncertainty—can paralyze us. Another study, conducted by Shafir and a colleague, Donald Redelmeier, demonstrates that paralysis can also be caused by *choice*. Imagine, for example, that you are in college and you face the following choice one evening. What would you do?

1. Attend a lecture by an author you admire who is visiting just for the evening, or
2. Go to the library and study.

Studying doesn't look so attractive compared with a once in a lifetime lecture. When this choice was given to actual college students, only 21 percent decided to study.

Suppose, instead, you had been given three choices:

1. Attend the lecture.
2. Go to the library and study.
3. Watch a foreign film that you've been wanting to see.

Does your answer differ? Remarkably, when a different group of students were given the three choices, 40 percent decided to study—

double the number who did before. Giving students two good alternatives to studying, rather than one, paradoxically makes them less likely to choose either. This behavior isn't "rational," but it is human.

Prioritization rescues people from the quicksand of decision angst, and that's why finding the core is so valuable. The people who listen to us will be constantly making decisions in an environment of uncertainty. They will suffer anxiety from the need to choose—even when the choice is between two good options, like the lecture and the foreign film.

Core messages help people avoid bad choices by reminding them of what's important. In Herb Kelleher's parable, for instance, someone had to choose between chicken salad and no chicken salad—and the message "THE low-fare airline" led her to abandon the chicken salad.

Idea Clinics

The goal of this book is to help you make your ideas stick. So, periodically throughout the book, we will present "Idea Clinics," which illustrate, in practical terms, how an idea can be made stickier. The Clinics were inspired by the classic "before and after" photos used by weight-loss centers—visible evidence that the diet works. Like patients trying a new diet, the initial ideas in the Clinics vary in their need for change; some need dramatic help, like a stomach-stapling and liposuction, and some only need to lose a few pounds around the waistline.

The point of the Clinics is not to wow you with our creative genius, and it's fortunate for readers and authors alike that this is not the goal, because we are not creative geniuses. The point is simply to model *the process* of making ideas stickier. In contrast to traditional disclaimers, this *is* something you should try at home. Think about each message and consider how you would improve it using the principles in the book.

You can safely skip the Clinics—they are intended as sidebars to the text, rather than as building blocks—but we hope you'll find them useful.

Warning: Sun Exposure Is Dangerous

THE SITUATION: *Health educators at Ohio State University want to inform the academic community about the risks of sun exposure.*

• • •

MESSAGE 1: Here's a Web page with facts about sun exposure from Ohio State University. We've added numbers to each paragraph so that we can analyze the message later:

Sun Exposure: Precautions and Protection

(1) A golden, bronze tan is often considered a status symbol. Perhaps this supports the idea that people who have time to lie in the sun long enough to develop a deep tan, or who can travel to warm climates during winter, have more money or leisure time than "common folk." Nevertheless, the goal of many is a deep tan early in spring or to return from vacation with that hearty, healthy glow. Whether a tan suggests status or not, careless exposure to the sun can be harmful. Ultraviolet rays from the sun will damage skin but can also create vision problems, allergic reactions, and depressed immune systems.

(2) Tanning and burning are caused by ultraviolet rays from the sun. These rays cannot be seen or felt, but penetrate the skin and stimulate cells containing a brownish pigment called melanin. Melanin protects the skin by absorbing and scattering ultraviolet rays. People with dark skins have high amounts of melanin, have greater natural protection from ultraviolet rays, and tan more easily. Blondes, redheads, and people with fair skins have less melanin and, therefore, burn more quickly.

(3) As melanin is stimulated by ultraviolet rays, it rises to the skin's surface as a tan and provides protection against future sun exposure. Individuals with dark skins such as olive, brown, or black are not immune to burning and skin damage caused by careless exposure to the sun.

(4) Two types of ultraviolet rays (UV) from the sun exist: UVA and UVB. UVB cause burning of the skin or the red associated with sunburn, skin cancer, and premature aging of skin. UVA rays stimulate tanning but are also linked to other problems such as impaired vision, skin rashes, and allergic or other reactions to drugs.

(5) Skin damage from overexposure to the sun is cumulative over the years and cannot be reversed. Once damage occurs, it cannot be undone. Most serious and lasting damage occurs before age 18. Protection should start early, particularly with children who enjoy outdoor play on sunny days.

Before you read our comments below, go back and reread Message 1. What can you do to improve it?

COMMENTS ON MESSAGE 1: What's the lead here? What's the core? The first paragraph dives into tanned skin as a status symbol, which is simply an interesting red herring. (In fact, the text acknowledges as much when it says, "Whether a tan suggests status or not . . .") To us, Paragraph 5 flashes in neon lights as the core: *Skin damage . . . is cumulative over the years and cannot be reversed.* Wow. Isn't that the single most important thing we'd want to tell sun-worshippers? By contrast, Paragraphs 2–4 provide superfluous mechanics. As an analogy, do smokers really need to understand the workings of the lungs in order to appreciate the dangers of smoking?

• • •

MESSAGE 2: In the text below, we have reordered the points and tinkered with the prose a bit in the hope of unburying the lead.

Sun Exposure: How to Get Old Prematurely

(5) Skin damage from overexposure to the sun is like getting older: It is cumulative over the years and cannot be reversed. Once damage occurs, it cannot be undone. Most serious and lasting damage occurs before age 18. Fortunately, unlike aging, skin damage can be prevented. Sun protection should start early, particularly with children who enjoy playing outdoors on sunny days.

(2, 3, 4) Tanning and burning are caused by ultraviolet rays from the sun. Ultraviolet rays cause sunburn, which is a temporary sign of deeper underlying skin damage. Sunburns eventually disappear, but the underlying damage persists and may eventually cause premature aging or skin cancer.

(1) Ironically, a golden, bronze tan is often considered a sign of good health. But ultraviolet rays not only damage skin, they can also create vision problems, allergic reactions, and depressed immune systems. So instead of a "healthy tan," perhaps we should call it a "sickly tan."

COMMENTS ON MESSAGE 2: The core of this message is that skin damage is cumulative and irreversible. So we've rewritten the message to stress that point and eliminate nonessential information. We've done this to illustrate the process of forced prioritization; we've had to eliminate some interesting stuff (such as the references to melanin) in order to let the core shine through.

We've tried to emphasize the core in a couple of ways. First, we've unburied the lead—putting the core right up front. Second, we've added the analogy to aging to hammer home the idea that damage is irreversible. Third, we've added a concrete and perhaps unexpected image: Sunburns are a signal of damage; they may disappear, but the underlying damage does not.

SCORECARD

Checklist	Message 1	Message 2
Simple	-	✓
Unexpected	-	✓
Concrete	-	✓
Credible	-	-
Emotional	-	-
Story	-	-

PUNCH LINE: Avoid burying the lead. Don't start with something interesting but irrelevant in hopes of entertaining the audience. Instead, work to make the core message itself more interesting.

Names, Names, and Names

Dunn, North Carolina, is a small town about forty miles south of Raleigh. It has 14,000 residents and its workforce is primarily blue collar. The local diner is packed in the morning with people eating big breakfasts and drinking coffee. Waitresses call you "hon." The town recently got a Wal-Mart.

All in all, Dunn is a pretty normal place, except for one fact: Almost everyone there reads the local paper, the *Daily Record*. As a matter of fact, *more than everyone* in Dunn reads the paper.

The *Daily Record*'s penetration in the Dunn community is 112 percent, which is the highest penetration of any newspaper in the country. For a community penetration to exceed 100 percent, one of two things must be true: (1) People from outside Dunn—perhaps people commuting to jobs in Dunn—are buying the paper; or (2) some households are buying more than one paper. Maybe it's hard for some couples in Dunn to share.

What's the explanation for this remarkable success? The people of Dunn certainly have plenty of options for their news: *USA Today*, the Raleigh *News & Observer*, CNN, the Internet, and hundreds of other outlets. So why is the *Daily Record* so popular?

The Dunn *Daily Record* was founded in 1950 by Hoover Adams. Adams was born with ink in his blood. He got his first byline by sending dispatches from his Boy Scout camp. By the time he was in high school he was serving as a stringer—a freelance reporter—for the Raleigh paper. After World War II, Adams became the editor of the Dunn *Dispatch*. Eventually, he grew restless at the *Dispatch* and decided to start his own paper, the *Daily Record*. In 1978, after twenty-eight years of head-to-head competition, the *Dispatch* finally gave up and sold out to him.

Across the fifty-five years of his tenure as publisher, Adams has had a remarkably consistent editorial philosophy. He believes that newspapers should be relentlessly local in their coverage. In fact, he's a zealot about community coverage.

In 1978, frustrated by what he felt was insufficient focus on local issues in the paper, he wrote a memo to his staff, explaining his views:

"All of us know that the main reason anybody reads a local newspaper is for local names and pictures. That's the one thing we can do better than anybody else. And that's the thing our readers can't get anywhere else. Always remember, the mayor of Angier and the mayor of Lillington are just as important to those towns as the mayor of New York is to his people."

Let's be clear: Adams's focus on local coverage is not a revolutionary sentiment. In fact, among publishers of small newspapers it would be utterly uncontroversial. Yet it's easy enough to see that the idea has not become a reality at most papers. The average local newspaper is loaded with wire stories, analyses of pro sports teams, and spot photos with nary a person in sight.

In other words, finding the core isn't synonymous with communicating the core. Top management can *know* what the priorities are but be completely ineffective in *sharing* and *achieving* those priorities. Adams has managed to find *and* share the core. How did he do it?

Sharing the Core

Adams found the core of his newspaper operations: local focus. Then he turned his attention to sharing his core message—making it stick with his staff. For the rest of the chapter—in fact, the rest of the book—we will discuss ways to get core messages to stick. And we will start by studying the way Adams has made his "local focus" message stick.

While many publishers pay lip service to the value of local focus,

Adams is an extremist about it. He's willing to hurt the bottom line for local focus:

> The fact is, a local newspaper can never get enough local names. I'd happily hire two more typesetters and add two more pages in every edition of each paper if we had the names to fill them up.

He's willing to be boring for local focus:

> I'll bet that if the *Daily Record* reprinted the entire Dunn telephone directory tonight, half the people would sit down and check it to be sure their name was included. . . . When somebody tells you, "Aw, you don't want all those names," please assure them that's exactly what we want, *most of all!*

He gleefully exaggerates in order to emphasize the value of local focus, quoting a saying of a friend, Ralph Delano, who runs the local paper in Benson:

> If an atomic bomb fell on Raleigh, it wouldn't be news in Benson unless some of the debris and ashes fell on Benson.

In fact, asked why the *Daily Record* has been so successful, Adams replies, "It's because of three things: Names, names, and names."

What's going on here? Adams has found the core idea that he wants to communicate—that local focus is the key to his newspaper's success. That's Step 1. Step 2 is to communicate the core to others. And he does that brilliantly.

Look at the techniques Adams uses to communicate his seriousness about local focus. He uses an analogy: comparing the mayor of Angier to the mayor of New York. (We'll have more to say about analogy later in this chapter.) He says he'd hire more typesetters if the reporters could generate enough names. This is forced prioritization: Local focus is more important than minimizing costs! (Not a common sentiment among small-town papers. See the "Unexpected" chapter.)

He also speaks in clear, tangible language. What does he want? Names. He wants lots of individual names in the newspaper every day. (See the "Concrete" chapter.) This idea is concrete enough that everyone in the organization can comprehend and use it. Is there any room for misunderstanding? Is there a staffer who won't understand what Adams means by "names"?

"Names, names, and names" is a simple statement that is symbolic of a core truth. It's not just that names are helpful. In Adams's mind, names trump costs. Names trump well-written prose. Names trump nuclear explosions in neighboring communities.

For fifty-five years, since Adams founded the paper, his core value of community focus has helped hundreds of people at the paper, in thousands of circumstances, make good decisions. As a publisher, Adams has presided over close to 20,000 issues. And each of those issues involved countless decisions: Which stories do we cover? What's important in the stories? Which photos do we run? Which do we cut out to save space?

Adams can't possibly be personally involved in the vast majority of these hundreds of small decisions. But his employees don't suffer from decision paralysis, because Adams's Commander's Intent is clear: "Names, names, and names." Adams can't be everywhere. But by finding the core and communicating it clearly, *he has made himself everywhere*. That's the power of a sticky idea.

Simple = Core + Compact

Adams is a clever wordsmith, but his most useful bit of wordplay is probably his least clever: "Names, names, and names." This phrase is useful and memorable because it is highly concrete, but also because it is highly succinct. This example illustrates a second aspect of simplicity: Simple messages are core and *compact*.

At one level, the idea of compactness is uncontroversial. Rarely will you get advice to make your communications lengthy and convoluted, unless you write interest-rate disclosures for a credit card company. We know that sentences are better than paragraphs. Two bullet points are better than five. Easy words are better than hard words. It's a bandwidth issue: The more we reduce the amount of information in an idea, the stickier it will be.

But let's be clear: Compactness alone isn't enough. We could latch on to a compact message that isn't core; in other words, a pithy slogan that doesn't reflect our Commander's Intent. Compact messages may be sticky, but that says nothing about their *worth*. We can imagine compact messages that are lies ("The earth is flat"), compact messages that are irrelevant ("Goats like sprouts"), and compact messages that are ill-advised ("Never let a day pass without a shoe purchase").

In other cases, compactness itself can come to seem an unworthy goal. Lots of us have expertise in particular areas. Becoming an expert in something means that we become more and more fascinated by nuance and complexity. That's when the Curse of Knowledge kicks in, and we start to forget what it's like *not* to know what we know. At that point, making something simple can seem like "dumbing down." As an expert, we don't want to be accused of propagating sound bites or pandering to the lowest common denominator. Simplifying, we fear, can devolve into oversimplifying.

So if we're going to define "simple" as core *and* compact, we need to assure ourselves that compactness is worth striving for. We've already got core, why do we need compact? Aren't "stripped-down" ideas inherently less useful than fully elaborated ideas? Suppose we took compactness to its most extreme form. Is it possible to say something meaningful in the span of a sound bite?

"A Bird in the Hand"

For thousands of years, people have exchanged sound bites called proverbs. Proverbs are simple yet profound. Cervantes defined proverbs as "short sentences drawn from long experience." Take the English-language proverb: "A bird in the hand is worth two in the bush." What's the core? The core is a warning against giving up a sure thing for something speculative. The proverb is short and simple, yet it packs a big nugget of wisdom that is useful in many situations.

As it turns out, this is not just an English-language proverb. In Sweden, the saying is "Rather one bird in the hand than ten in the woods." In Spain: "A bird in the hand is better than a hundred flying birds." In Poland: "A sparrow in your hand is better than a pigeon on the roof." In Russia: "Better a titmouse in the hand than a crane in the sky."

Other variants can be found in Romanian, Italian, Portuguese, German, Icelandic, and even medieval Latin. The first documented case in English is from John Bunyan's *Pilgrim's Progress* in 1678. But the proverb may be much older still. In one of Aesop's fables, a hawk seizes a nightingale, who pleads for its life, arguing that it is too tiny a morsel to satisfy the hawk. The hawk replies, "I would be foolish to release the bird I have in my hand to pursue another bird that is not even in sight." This story dates from 570 B.C.

The "bird in hand" proverb, then, is an astoundingly sticky idea. It has survived for more than 2,500 years. It has spread across continents, cultures, and languages. Keep in mind that nobody funded a "bird in hand" advertising campaign. It spreads on its own. Many other proverbs share this longevity. In fact, a repertoire of proverbs has been found in almost every documented culture. Why? What is their purpose?

Proverbs are helpful in guiding individual decisions in environments with shared standards. Those shared standards are often ethical or moral norms. Proverbs offer rules of thumb for the behavior of individuals. The Golden Rule, "Do unto others as you would have them do unto you," is so profound that it can influence a lifetime of behavior. The Golden Rule is a great symbol of what we're chasing in this chapter: ideas that are compact enough to be sticky and meaningful enough to make a difference.

Great simple ideas have an elegance and a utility that make them function a lot like proverbs. Cervantes's definition of "proverbs" echoes our definition of Simple ideas: *short sentences* (compact) *drawn from long experience* (core). We are right to be skeptical of sound bites, because lots of sound bites are empty or misleading— they're compact without being core. But the Simple we're chasing isn't a sound bite, it's a proverb: compact *and* core.

Adams managed to turn his core idea—the need to focus relentlessly on local issues—into a journalistic proverb. "Names, names, and names" is an idea that helps guide individual decision-making in a community of shared standards. If you're a photographer, the proverb has no value as a literal statement, unless you plan to shoot name tags. But when you know that your organization thrives on names— i.e., the specific actions taken by specific members of the local community—that knowledge informs the kinds of photo ops you look for. Do you shoot the boring committee deliberations or the gorgeous sunset over the park? Answer: the boring committee deliberations.

Palm Pilot and the Visual Proverb

Compact ideas help people learn and remember a core message. But they may be even more important when it comes time to help people act properly, particularly in an environment where they have to make lots of choices.

Why do remote controls have more buttons than we ever use? The answer starts with the noble intentions of engineers. Most technology and product-design projects must combat "feature creep," the tendency for things to become incrementally more complex until they no longer perform their original functions very well. A VCR is a case in point.

Feature creep is an innocent process. An engineer looking at a prototype of a remote control might think to herself, "Hey, there's some extra real estate here on the face of the control. And there's some extra processing capacity on the chip. Rather than let it go to waste, what if we give people the ability to toggle between the Julian and Gregorian calendars?"

The engineer is just trying to help — to add another gee-whiz feature that will improve the remote control. The other engineers on the team, meanwhile, don't particularly care about the calendar-toggle. Even if they think it's lame, they probably don't care enough to stage a protest: "Either the calendar-toggle button goes or I quit!" In this way, slowly and quietly, remote controls — and, by extension, other types of technologies — are featured to death.

The Palm Pilot team, aware of this danger, took a hard line against feature creep. When the team began its work, in the early 1990s, personal digital assistants (PDAs) had an unblemished record of failure. Apple's famous debacle with its Newton PDA had made other competitors gun-shy.

One of the competitors on the PDA market in 1994 looked like a malnourished computer. It was a bulky device with a keyboard and multiple ports for peripherals. Jeff Hawkins, the Palm Pilot team leader, was determined that his product would avoid this fate. He wanted the Palm Pilot to be simple. It would handle four things: calendars, contacts, memos, and task lists. The Palm Pilot would do only four things, but it would do them well.

Hawkins fought feature creep by carrying around a wooden block the size of the Palm. Trae Vassallo, a member of the Palm V design team, says, "The block was dumb, which resonated with the simple technological goals of the product, but it was also small, which made the product elegant and different." Hawkins would pull out the wooden block to "take notes" during a meeting or "check his calendar" in the hallway. Whenever someone suggested another feature, Hawkins would pull out the wooden block and ask them where it would fit.

Vassallo said that the Palm Pilot became a successful product "almost because it was defined more in terms of what it was not than in terms of what it was." Tom Kelley, from IDEO, a prominent Silicon Valley design firm, made a similar point: "The real barrier to the initial PDAs . . . was the idea that the machine had to do nearly everything."

Hawkins knew that the core idea of his project needed to be elegance and simplicity (and a tenacious avoidance of feature creep). In sharing this core idea, Hawkins and his team used what was, in essence, a visual proverb. The block of wood became a visual reminder to do a few things and do them well.

There is a striking parallel between the development of the Palm Pilot and the Clinton campaign led by James Carville. In both cases, the teams were composed of people who were knowledgeable and passionate about their work. Both teams boasted plenty of people who had the *capability* and the *desire* to do a lot of different things—argue every issue and engineer every feature. Yet in both cases the team needed a simple reminder to fight the temptation to do too much. When you say three things, you say nothing. When your remote control has fifty buttons, you can't change the channel anymore.

Using What's There

Our messages have to be compact, because we can learn and remember only so much information at once. But suppose we've assessed the core of our message and we have too much information to aspire to the compactness of a proverb. How do we convey lots of information when we need to? The following exercise is designed to reinforce the need for compactness and to provide a hint about how to cram more information into a compact message.

Here are the rules of this exercise: Spend ten to fifteen seconds, no more, studying the letters below. Then close the book, pull out a sheet of paper, and write down as many letters as you can remember. Spoiler alert: Don't turn the page until you've finished the exercise.

J   FKFB   INAT   OUP   SNA   SAI   RS

If you're like most people, you probably remembered about seven to ten letters. That's not much information. Compactness is essential, because there's a limit to the amount of information we can juggle at once.

Now turn the page and try the exercise again.

There's a twist this time. We haven't changed the letters or the sequence. All we've done is change the way the letters are grouped. Once again, study the letters for ten to fifteen seconds, then close the book and test your recall.

JFK   FBI   NATO   UPS   NASA   IRS

Chances are you did much better the second time. Suddenly the letters meant something, which made them easier to remember. In Round 1, you were trying to remember raw data. In Round 2, you were remembering concepts: John F. Kennedy, the FBI, the North Atlantic Treaty Organization, UPS, NASA, the IRS.

But wait a second. Why is it easier to remember "John F. Kennedy" than the random letters F, J, K? Surely John F. Kennedy is a bigger bundle of information than the three random letters! Think of all the associations with JFK—politics, relationships, his assassination, and his famous family. If remembering was like weight lifting, it would be ridiculous to think we could "lift" JFK easier than three little letters!

The secret, of course, is that we're *not* "lifting" JFK. All the remembering work related to JFK has already been done. We've already built those muscles—the concept of JFK, and all its associations, is already embedded in our memories. What we're remembering is simply a pointer to this information—we're posting a little flag on the terrain of our memory. With the raw letters, we're posting three separate flags. In the end, it's one bit of information (or one flag) versus three, and it's no surprise that one is easier to remember.

So what? Is this just neat brain trivia? Here's where we're going: We've seen that compact ideas are stickier, but that compact ideas alone aren't valuable—only ideas with *profound* compactness are valuable. So, to make a profound idea compact you've got to pack a lot of meaning into a little bit of messaging. And how do you do that? You use flags. You tap the existing memory terrain of your audience. You use what's already there.

The Pomelo Schema

So far we have presented situations in which one simple idea, or a handful of simple ideas, were useful in guiding behavior. But, let's face it, most people in the world do complicated things. It's not our intention to argue that complicated things—law, medicine, construction, programming, teaching—can be pared down to two or three compact messages. We obviously can't replace a school of architecture with a single compact idea ("Keep the building from falling down").

This leads us to an important issue that we haven't discussed yet: *How do you turn a freshman into an architect?* How does complexity emerge from simplicity? We will argue that it is possible to create complexity through the artful use of simplicity. If simple ideas are staged and layered correctly, they can very quickly become complex.

Let us teach you what a "pomelo" is. (If you already know what a pomelo is, be a good sport and feign ignorance.) Here is one way that we can explain to you what a pomelo is:

EXPLANATION 1: A pomelo is the largest citrus fruit. The rind is very thick but soft and easy to peel away. The resulting fruit has a light yellow to coral pink flesh and can vary from juicy to slightly dry and from seductively spicy-sweet to tangy and tart.

Quick question: Based on this explanation, if you mixed pomelo juice half and half with orange juice, would it taste good? You might make a guess, but the answer is probably a bit ambiguous. Let's move on to an alternative explanation:

EXPLANATION 2: A pomelo is basically a supersized grapefruit with a very thick and soft rind.

Explanation 2 sticks a flag on a concept that you already know: a grapefruit. When we tell you that a pomelo is *like* a grapefruit, you call up a mental image of a grapefruit. Then we tell you what to change about it: It's "supersized." Your visualized grapefruit grows accordingly.

We've made it easier for you to learn a new concept by tying it to a concept that you already know. In this case, the concept is "grapefruit." "Grapefruit" is a *schema* that you already have. ("Schema" is a bit of technical jargon from psychology, but it's so useful that we think it's worth carrying through the book.)

Psychologists define schema as a collection of generic properties of a concept or category. Schemas consist of lots of prerecorded information stored in our memories. If someone tells you that she saw a great new sports car, a picture immediately springs to mind, filled with generic properties. You know what "sports cars" are like. You picture something small and two-door, with a convertible top perhaps. If the car in your picture moves, it moves fast. Its color is almost certainly red. Similarly, your schema of "grapefruit" also contains a cluster of generic properties: yellow-pink color, tart flavor, softball-sized, and so on.

By calling up your grapefruit schema, we were able to teach you the concept of pomelo much faster than if we had mechanically listed all the attributes of a pomelo. Note, too, that it's easier to answer the question about the blend of pomelo and orange juice. You know that grapefruit juice blends well with OJ, so the pomelo schema *inherits* this property from the grapefruit schema. (By the way, to be complete, Explanation 1 is itself full of schemas. "Citrus fruit" is a schema, "rind" is a schema, and "tangy" is a schema. Explanation 2 is easier to parse only because "grapefruit" is a higher-level schema — a schema composed of other schemas.)

By using schemas, Explanation 2 improves both our comprehension and our memory. Let's think about the two definitions of "pomelo" in terms of the inverted pyramid structure. What's the lead? Well, with Explanation 1 the lead is: citrus fruit. After the lead, there is no clear hierarchy; depending on what catches people's attention, they might remember the rind info ("very thick but soft and easy to peel away") or the color info ("light yellow to coral pink") or the juiciness info or the taste info.

With Explanation 2, the lead is: grapefruit-like. The second paragraph is: supersized. The third paragraph is: very thick and soft rind.

Six months from now, people will remember—at best!—the lead of our story. That means that with one story they'd remember "fruit" or "citrus fruit." With the other story they'd remember "grapefruit." The second story is clearly better—it isn't a judgment call.

This concludes what will probably be the last psychological discussion of citrus fruit you'll ever encounter. But though the concept of "pomelo" may not be worth the neurons you just burned on it, the underlying concept—that schemas *enable* profound simplicity—is critical.

Good teachers intuitively use lots of schemas. Economics teachers, for instance, start with compact, stripped-down examples that can be understood by students who have no preexisting economics schemas. "Let's say that you grow apples and I grow oranges. We're the only two people around. Let's also say that we'd prefer to eat some of both fruits rather than all of either. Should we trade? If so, how do we go about doing it?"

Students are initially taught how trade works in this simplified context. This knowledge, in turn, becomes a basic trade schema for them. Once learned, this schema can be called up and stretched along some dimension. For example, what happens if you suddenly get better at growing apples? Do we still trade the same way we did before? To solve this problem, we're calling up a schema and adapting it, just as we did in making a pomelo out of our grapefruit schema.

Complexity from Simplicity

Schemas help us create complex messages from simple materials. In school, lots of science courses are taught by clever uses of schemas. Introductory physics deals with simple, idealized situations: pulleys, inclines, objects moving at constant rates along frictionless paths. As students become familiar with the "pulley" schema, it can be stretched in some way or merged with other schemas to solve more complicated problems.

Another nice use of a schema is the solar system model of the atom, which many of us were taught as kids. This model posits that electrons orbit the nucleus, much as planets orbit the sun. This analogy gives students a quick, compact insight into how the atom works.

The planetary analogy also provides an insight into the reason that many people avoid compact schemas ("a supersized grapefruit") in favor of exhaustive description ("a citrus fruit with a soft, thick rind, blah blah blah . . ."). The use of schemas can sometimes involve a somewhat slower route to the "real truth." For instance, physicists now know that electrons don't orbit the nucleus the way that planets do. In reality, electrons move in "probability clouds." So what do you tell a sixth grader? Do you talk about the motion of planets, which is easy to understand and nudges you closer to the truth? Or do you talk about "probability clouds," which are impossible to understand but accurate?

The choice may seem to be a difficult one: (1) accuracy first, at the expense of accessibility; or (2) accessibility first, at the expense of accuracy. But in many circumstances this is a false choice for one compelling reason: If a message can't be used to make predictions or decisions, it is without value, no matter how accurate or comprehensive it is.

Herb Kelleher could tell a flight attendant that her goal is to "maximize shareholder value." In some sense, this statement is more accurate and complete than that the goal is to be "THE low-fare airline." After all, the proverb "THE low-fare airline" is clearly incomplete—Southwest could offer lower fares by eliminating aircraft maintenance, or by asking passengers to share napkins. Clearly, there are additional values (customer comfort, safety ratings) that refine

Southwest's core value of economy. The problem with "maximize shareholder value," despite its accuracy, is that it doesn't help the flight attendant decide whether to serve chicken salad. An accurate but useless idea is still useless.

We discussed the Curse of Knowledge in the introduction—the difficulty of remembering what it was like not to know something. Accuracy to the point of uselessness is a symptom of the Curse of Knowledge. To a CEO, "maximizing shareholder value" may be an immensely useful rule of behavior. To a flight attendant, it's not. To a physicist, probability clouds are fascinating phenomena. To a child, they are incomprehensible.

People are tempted to tell you everything, with perfect accuracy, right up front, when they should be giving you just enough info to be useful, then a little more, then a little more.

Schemas in Hollywood: High-concept Pitches

A great way to avoid useless accuracy, and to dodge the Curse of Knowledge, is to use analogies. Analogies derive their power from schemas: A pomelo is like a grapefruit. A good news story is structured like an inverted pyramid. Skin damage is like aging. Analogies make it possible to understand a compact message because they invoke concepts that you already know.

A good analogy can wield a lot of power. In fact, in Hollywood $100 million movies can be green-lighted based largely on the strength of a one-sentence analogy.

The average Hollywood studio considers hundreds of pitches or screenplays for every movie it makes. It may be hard to muster sympathy for the life of studio execs, but let's try for a moment. Imagine the terrifying decisions they must make. When they invest in a movie, they are essentially betting millions of dollars—and their own reputations—on an intangible idea.

Contrast a movie pitch with the blueprint for a home. If an architect creates a nifty blueprint for a home, and someone puts up the money for construction, you can feel pretty confident that, nine months later, you'll have a home that realizes the architect's original vision.

A movie pitch, on the other hand, is destined to change. When a screenwriter is hired, the story will change. When a director is hired, the artistic feel of the movie will change. When stars are hired to play the parts, their personalities will change how we perceive the characters in the story. When producers are hired, the storytelling will become subject to financial and logistical constraints. And when the movie is completed, months or years later, the marketing team will need to find a way to explain the plot to the public in about thirty seconds—without giving away too much.

Imagine investing millions in an idea that will change as it is filtered through the consciousness of a succession of individuals with giant egos: directors, stars, producers, marketers. That idea had better be good.

In Hollywood, people use core ideas called "high-concept pitches." You've probably heard some of them. *Speed* was "*Die Hard* on a bus." *13 Going on 30* was "*Big* for girls." *Alien* was "*Jaws* on a spaceship."

The high-concept pitches don't always reference other movies. *E.T.*, for instance, was pitched as "Lost alien befriends lonely boy to get home." But a lot of pitches do invoke past movies. Why is that? Is it because Hollywood is full of cynical execs who shamelessly recycle old ideas?

Well, yes, but that's only part of the reason. The concept of the movie *Speed*, before it was pitched, obviously did not exist in the minds of the execs. It was like the word "pomelo," before you knew what it meant. The compact, five-word phrase "*Die Hard* on a bus" pours a breathtaking amount of meaning into the previously nonex-

istent concept of *Speed*. To see this, think of all the important decisions you could make, just on the strength of those five words. Do you
hire an action director or an indie director? Action. Do you budget
$10 million for the movie or $100 million? $100 million. Big star or
ensemble cast? Big star. Target a summer release or a Christmas release? Summer.

As another example, imagine that you were just hired to be the
production designer on the new film *Alien*. It will be your job to design the spaceship where most of the movie takes place. What does it
look like? If you knew nothing at all about the movie, you might sen-
sibly start by looking at old spaceship designs. For instance, think of
the cool, immaculate interior of the *Enterprise* on *Star Trek*.

Then your boss tells you that the vision for the movie is "*Jaws* on
a spaceship." That changes everything. *Jaws* was not cool or immaculate. Richard Dreyfus navigated around on a rickety old boat. Decisions were rushed, slapdash, claustrophobic, anxiety-ridden. The
environment was sweaty. As you think about what made *Jaws* tick,
your ideas start to take shape: The ship will be underdeveloped,
dingy, and oppressive. The crew members will not wear bright Lycra
uniforms. The rooms will not be well lit and lintless.

High-concept pitches are Hollywood's version of core proverbs.
Like most proverbs, they tap the power of analogy. By invoking
schemas that already exist (e.g., what the movie *Jaws* is like), the proverbs radically accelerate the learning process for people working on a
brand-new movie.

Obviously, a good pitch is not synonymous with a good movie.
"*Jaws* on a spaceship" could have turned into a terrible movie if it
weren't for the contributions of hundreds of talented people over a
period of years. On the other hand, a bad pitch—a bad proverb—is
plenty to ruin a movie. No director could save "*Terms of Endearment*
on a spaceship."

If high-concept pitches can have this power in the movie world—

an environment filled with forty times the normal density of egos—we should feel confident that we can harness the same power in our own environments.

Generative Analogies

Some analogies are so useful that they don't merely shed light on a concept, they actually become platforms for novel thinking. For example, the metaphor of the brain as a computer has been central to the insights generated by cognitive psychologists during the past fifty years. It's easier to define how a computer works than to define how the brain works. For this reason it can be fruitful for psychologists to use various, well-understood aspects of a computer—such as memory, buffers, or processors—as inspiration to locate similar functions in the brain.

Good metaphors are "generative." The psychologist Donald Schon introduced this term to describe metaphors that generate "new perceptions, explanations, and inventions." Many simple sticky ideas are actually generative metaphors in disguise. For example, Disney calls its employees "cast members." This metaphor of employees as cast members in a theatrical production is communicated consistently throughout the organization:

- Cast members don't *interview* for a job, they *audition* for a *role*.
- When they are walking around the park, they are *onstage*.
- People visiting Disney are *guests*, not customers.
- Jobs are *performances*; uniforms are *costumes*.

The theater metaphor is immensely *useful* for Disney employees. It is so useful that just by reading the last few paragraphs you can probably predict how cast members should behave in situations we haven't discussed. For instance, you can probably guess that employees are not allowed to be on break while in costume and in a public area. (An actor would never have a chat and a cigarette in mid-scene.) You might guess that street sweepers are evaluated on criteria other than the cleanliness of their sidewalks. Indeed, street sweepers are some of the most highly trained cast members, since their very visible public presence—coupled with the fact that they are clearly Disney employees—makes them an obvious target for customers' questions about rides, parades, and restroom locations. Having them think of their role as performance, rather than maintenance, is a key part of the park's success. "Employees as cast members" is a generative metaphor that has worked for Disney for more than fifty years.

Contrast Disney with Subway. Like Disney, Subway has created a metaphor for its frontline employees. They are "sandwich artists." This metaphor is the evil twin of Disney's "cast members." It is utterly useless as a guide to how the employee should act. Disney expects its cast members to behave like actors, but Subway does not expect its counter help to behave like artists. The defining trait of an "artist" is individual expression. We wonder how long an employee would last at Subway if she exhibited a lot of individual expression—in dress, in interaction, in the presentation of sandwiches. No doubt Subway's sandwich artists are trusted to place a handful of onions on a twelve-inch sub, and it's true that this is a certain kind of liberty. But one suspects that the counter person's "artistry" can't extend to adding an extra slice of turkey.

The Power of Simplicity

Generative metaphors and proverbs both derive their power from a clever substitution: They substitute something easy to think about for something difficult. The proverb "A bird in hand is worth two in the bush" gives us a tangible, easily processed statement that we can use for guidance in complex, emotionally fraught situations. Generative metaphors perform a similar role. The "cast members" at Disney might find it easier to tackle a new situation from the perspective of a hired actor than from their own unique individual perspective.

Proverbs are the Holy Grail of simplicity. Coming up with a short, compact phrase is easy. Anybody can do it. On the other hand, coming up with a profound compact phrase is incredibly difficult. What we've tried to show in this chapter is that the effort is worth it—that "finding the core," and expressing it in the form of a compact idea, can be enduringly powerful.

CHAPTER 2

UNEXPECTED

By FAA edict, a flight attendant must make a safety announcement before a passenger plane takes off. We've all heard it: where the exits are, what to do in case of a "sudden change in cabin pressure," how to use your seat as a flotation device, and why you shouldn't smoke in the lavatories (or tinker with the smoke alarm).

Flight-safety announcements might be labeled a tough message environment. No one cares about what's being communicated. The flight attendant doesn't care. The passengers don't care. Filibusters are fascinating by comparison.

What if you were asked to make the safety announcement? Worse, what if you actually needed people to listen to you? How would you handle it?

A flight attendant named Karen Wood faced exactly this situation and solved it with creativity. On a flight from Dallas to San Diego, she made the following announcement:

> If I could have your attention for a few moments, we sure would love to point out these safety features. If you haven't been in an automobile since 1965, the proper way to fasten your seat belt is

to slide the flat end into the buckle. To unfasten, lift up on the buckle and it will release.

And as the song goes, there might be fifty ways to leave your lover, but there are only six ways to leave this aircraft: two forward exit doors, two over-wing removable window exits, and two aft exit doors. The location of each exit is clearly marked with signs overhead, as well as red and white disco lights along the floor of the aisle.

Made ya look!

It didn't take long for passengers to tune into Wood's comic spiel. When she wrapped up her announcement, scattered applause broke out. (And if a well-designed message can make people applaud for a safety announcement there's hope for all of us.)

The first problem of communication is getting people's attention. Some communicators have the authority to demand attention. Parents are good at this: "Bobby, look at me!" Most of the time, though, we can't demand attention; we must attract it. This is a tougher challenge. People say, "You can't make people pay attention," and there is a commonsense ring to that. But wait a minute: That's exactly what Karen Wood did. She made people pay attention, and she didn't even need to raise her voice.

The most basic way to get someone's attention is this: Break a pattern. Humans adapt incredibly quickly to consistent patterns. Consistent sensory stimulation makes us tune out: Think of the hum of an air conditioner, or traffic noise, or the smell of a candle, or the sight of a bookshelf. We may become consciously aware of these things only when something changes: The air conditioner shuts off. Your spouse rearranges the books.

Wood got people's attention in a message-hostile environment by avoiding the same generic safety spiel that her passengers had heard many times. She told jokes, which not only got people's attention but kept it. But if *getting* attention had been Wood's only concern, she wouldn't have needed to be so entertaining. She could have gotten passengers' attention just as easily by starting the announcement and then suddenly pausing in midsentence. Or switching to Russian for a few seconds.

Our brain is designed to be keenly aware of changes. Smart product designers are well aware of this tendency. They make sure that, when products require users to pay attention, something *changes*. Warning lights blink on and off because we would tune out a light that was constantly on. Old emergency sirens wailed in a two-note pattern, but modern sirens wail in a more complex pattern that's even more attention-grabbing. Car alarms make diabolical use of our change sensitivity.

This chapter focuses on two essential questions: *How do I get people's attention?* And, just as crucially, *How do I keep it?* We can't succeed if our messages don't break through the clutter to *get* people's attention. Furthermore, our messages are usually complex enough that we won't succeed if we can't *keep* people's attention.

To understand the answers to these two questions, we have to understand two essential emotions—surprise and interest—that are commonly provoked by naturally sticky ideas.

- *Surprise* gets our attention. Some naturally sticky ideas propose surprising "facts": The Great Wall of China is the only man-made structure visible from space! You use only 10 percent of your brain! You should drink eight glasses of water a day! Urban legends frequently contain surprising plot twists.
- *Interest* keeps our attention. There are classes of sticky ideas that maintain our interest over time. Conspiracy theories keep people ravenously collecting new information. Gossip keeps us coming back to our friends for developments.

Naturally sticky ideas are frequently unexpected. If we can make our ideas more unexpected, they will be stickier. But can you generate "unexpectedness"? Isn't "planned unexpectedness" an oxymoron?

GETTING PEOPLE'S ATTENTION

No One Ever Does

The television commercial for the new Enclave minivan opens with the Enclave sitting in front of a park. A boy holding a football helmet climbs into the minivan, followed by his two younger sisters. "Introducing the all-new Enclave," begins a woman's voice-over. Dad is behind the wheel and Mom is in the passenger seat. Cup holders are everywhere. Dad starts the car and pulls away from the curb. "It's a minivan to the max."

The minivan cruises slowly through suburban streets. "With features like remote-controlled sliding rear doors, 150 cable channels, a full sky-view roof, temperature-controlled cup holders, and the six-point navigation system . . . It's the minivan for families on the go."

The Enclave pulls to a stop at an intersection. The camera zooms in on the boy, gazing out a side window that reflects giant, leafy trees. Dad pulls into the intersection.

That's when it happens.

A speeding car barrels into the intersection and broadsides the minivan. There is a terrifying collision, with metal buckling and an explosion of broken glass.

The screen fades to black, and a message appears: "Didn't see that coming?"

The question fades and is replaced by a statement: "No one ever does."

With the sound of a stuck horn blaring in the background, a few final words flash across the screen: "Buckle up . . . Always."

There is no Enclave minivan. This ad was created by the Ad

Council. (The Enclave spot was sponsored by the U.S. Department of Transportation.) The Ad Council, founded in 1942, has launched many successful campaigns, from the World War II–era "Loose Lips Sink Ships" to the more recent "Friends Don't Let Friends Drive Drunk." The Enclave ad, like many other Council ads, capitalizes on the second characteristic of sticky ideas: Unexpectedness.

The Enclave ad is unexpected because it violates our schema for car commercials. We know how car commercials are supposed to behave. Pickups climb mountains of boulders. Sports cars zip along vacant curvy roads. SUVs carry yuppies through forests to waterfalls. And minivans deliver kids to soccer practice. No one dies, ever.

The ad is unexpected in a second way: It violates our schema of real-life neighborhood trips. We take thousands of trips in our neighborhoods, and the vast majority of them end safely. The commercial reminds us that accidents are inherently unexpected—we ought to buckle up, just in case.

Our schemas are like guessing machines. Schemas help us predict what will happen and, consequently, how we should make decisions. The Enclave asks, "Didn't see that coming?" No, we didn't. Our guessing machines failed, which caused us to be surprised.

Emotions are elegantly tuned to help us deal with critical situations. They prepare us for different ways of acting and thinking. We've all heard that anger prepares us to fight and fear prepares us to flee. The linkages between emotion and behavior can be more subtle, though. For instance, a secondary effect of being angry, which was recently discovered by researchers, is that we become more certain of our judgments. When we're angry, we *know* we're right, as anyone who has been in a relationship can attest.

So if emotions have biological purposes, then what is the biological purpose of surprise? Surprise jolts us to attention. Surprise is triggered when our schemas fail, and it prepares us to understand why the failure occurred. When our guessing machines fail, surprise grabs our attention so that we can repair them for the future.

The Surprise Brow

Surprise is associated with a facial expression that is consistent across cultures. In a book called *Unmasking the Face*, Paul Ekman and Wallace Friesen coined a term, "the surprise brow," to describe the distinctive facial expression of surprise: "The eyebrows appear curved and high. . . . The skin below the brow has been stretched by the lifting of the brow, and is more visible than usual."

When our brows go up, it widens our eyes and gives us a broader field of vision—the surprise brow is our body's way of forcing us to see more. We may also do a double take to make sure that we saw what we thought we saw. By way of contrast, when we're angry our eyes narrow so that we can focus on a known problem. In addition to making our eyebrows rise, surprise causes our jaws to drop and our mouths to gape. We're struck momentarily speechless. Our bodies temporarily stop moving and our muscles go slack. It's as though our bodies want to ensure that we're not talking or moving when we ought to be taking in new information.

So surprise acts as a kind of emergency override when we confront something unexpected and our guessing machines fail. Things come to a halt, ongoing activities are interrupted, our attention focuses involuntarily on the event that surprised us. When a minivan commercial ends in a bloodcurdling crash, we stop and wonder, *What is going on?*

Unexpected ideas are more likely to stick because surprise makes us pay attention and think. That extra attention and thinking sears unexpected events into our memories. Surprise gets our attention. Sometimes the attention is fleeting, but in other cases surprise can lead to enduring attention. Surprise can prompt us to hunt for underlying causes, to imagine other possibilities, to figure out how to avoid surprises in the future.

Researchers who study conspiracy theories, for instance, have noted that many of them arise when people are grappling with unexpected events, such as when the young and attractive die suddenly. There are conspiracy theories about the sudden deaths of JFK, Marilyn Monroe, Elvis, and Kurt Cobain. There tends to be less conspiratorial interest in the sudden deaths of ninety-year-olds.

Surprise makes us want to find an answer—to resolve the question of why we were surprised—and big surprises call for big answers. If we want to motivate people to pay attention, we should seize the power of big surprises.

Avoiding Gimmickry

Going for a big surprise, though, can cause a big problem. It's easy to step over the line into gimmickry.

The late 1990s was the heyday of the dot-com bubble. Venture-backed start-ups poured millions of dollars into advertising to establish their brands. With increasing amounts of money chasing a finite amount of consumer attention, ads had to work harder and harder to provoke surprise and interest.

During the Super Bowl of 2000, an ad ran that opened with a college marching band practicing on a football field. We're shown close-ups of the band members as they execute their precision movements. Then we cut to the stadium tunnel, which leads out onto the field—and suddenly a dozen ravenous wolves rush onto the field. Band members scatter in terror as the wolves hunt them down and attack.

What was this advertisement for? We have no idea. There's no question that this ad was surprising and memorable. To this day, we remember the tastelessly comic image of the wolves chasing the terrified band members. But because the surprise was utterly non-germane to the message that needed to be communicated, it was worthless. If the product being advertised had been "mauling-proof band uniforms," on the other hand, the ad could have been an award winner.

In this sense, the wolves ad is the opposite of the Enclave ad. Both ads contain powerful surprises, but only the Enclave ad uses that surprise to reinforce its core message. In Chapter 1 we discussed the importance of finding the core in your ideas. Using surprise in the service of a core message can be extremely powerful.

Hension and Phraug

Below is a list of four words. Read each one and take a second to determine whether it's a real English word.

HENSION
BARDLE
PHRAUG
TAYBL

According to Bruce Whittlesea and Lisa Williams, the researchers who developed this task, "PHRAUG and TAYBL often cause raised eyebrows, and an 'Oh!' reaction. HENSION and BARDLE often cause a frown."

PHRAUG and TAYBL cause the surprise brow because they *look* unfamiliar but *sound* familiar. The "Oh!" reaction comes when we realize that PHRAUG is just a funny way to spell FROG.

HENSION and BARDLE are more troubling. They seem oddly familiar, because they borrow letter combinations from common words. They have the look of SAT words—fancy vocabulary that we should probably know but don't. But HENSION and BARDLE are made-up words. When we realize that we've been struggling to find a nonexistent solution, we get frustrated.

HENSION and BARDLE provide an example of surprise without insight. So far, we've talked a lot about the power of surprise, and how surprise can make our ideas stickier. But although HENSION and BARDLE are surprising, they aren't sticky; they're just frustrating. What we see now is that surprise isn't enough. We also need *insight*.

To be surprising, an event can't be predictable. Surprise is the opposite of predictability. But, to be satisfying, surprise must be "postdictable." The twist makes sense after you think about it, but it's not something you would have seen coming. PHRAUG is post-dictable, but HENSION isn't. Contrast the feeling you get from TV shows or films, such as *The Sixth Sense*, that have great surprise endings— endings that unite clues that you've been exposed to all along—with the feeling you get from gimmicky, unforeseeable endings ("It was all a dream").

We started the chapter by pointing out that surprise happens when our guessing machines fail. The emotion of surprise is designed to focus our attention on the failure, so that we can improve our guessing machines for the future. Then we drew a distinction between gimmicky surprise, like dot-com ads, and meaningful postdictable surprise.

Here is the bottom line for our everyday purposes: If you want your ideas to be stickier, you've got to break someone's guessing machine and then fix it. But in surprising people, in breaking their guessing machines, how do we avoid gimmicky surprise, like the wolves? The easiest way to avoid gimmicky surprise and ensure that your unexpected ideas produce insight is to make sure you target an aspect of your audience's guessing machines that relates to your core message. We've already seen a few examples of this strategy.

In Chapter 1, we discussed Hoover Adams, the newspaper publisher whose mantra is "Names, names, and names." To most local newspaper reporters, this mantra will seem like common sense. Certainly, their schemas of "good local news" involve community-focused stories.

But that wasn't Adams's point. He had something much more radical in mind. So he broke their schema by saying, essentially, "If I could, I'd publish pages from the phone book to get names. In fact, if I could gather up enough names I'd hire more typesetters to lay out more pages so they'd fit." Suddenly the reporters realized that

"Names, names, and names" was *not* consistent with their schemas. Whereas their previous schema might have been "Try to emphasize local angles when you can," Adams had replaced that with "Names come before everything else, even my own profitability." That's a message that draws power from its unexpectedness.

Another example we discussed in Chapter 1 was Southwest Airlines' proverb "THE low-cost airline." Again, most Southwest staffers and customers know that Southwest is a discount airline. In that context, the proverb seems intuitive. It was only when Kelleher put teeth in the proverb—refusing to offer chicken salad to customers even if they really wanted it—that its meaning sank in. Before Kelleher, an average staffer's guessing machine might have predicted, "We want to please our customers in a low-cost way." After Kelleher, the guessing machine was refined to "We will be THE low-cost airline, even if it means intentionally disregarding some of our customers' preferences."

So, a good process for making your ideas stickier is: (1) Identify the central message you need to communicate—find the core; (2) Figure out what is counterintuitive about the message—i.e., What are the unexpected implications of your core message? Why isn't it already happening naturally? (3) Communicate your message in a way that breaks your audience's guessing machines along the critical, counterintuitive dimension. Then, once their guessing machines have failed, help them refine their machines.

Common sense is the enemy of sticky messages. When messages sound like common sense, they float gently in one ear and out the other. And why shouldn't they? If I already intuitively "get" what you're trying to tell me, why should I obsess about remembering it? The danger, of course, is that what *sounds* like common sense often *isn't*, as with the Hoover Adams and Southwest examples. It's your job, as a communicator, to expose the parts of your message that are uncommon sense.

Tire Chains at Nordstrom

Nordstrom is a department store known for outstanding customer service. That extra service comes at a price: Nordstrom can be an expensive place to shop. Yet many people are willing to pay higher prices precisely because Nordstrom makes shopping so much more pleasant.

For Nordstrom's strategy to work, it must transform its frontline employees into customer-service zealots. And they do not walk in the door that way. Most people with service experience come from environments where managers spend much of their energy trying to minimize labor costs. The prevailing schema of customer service might be, roughly, "Get customers in and out the door as fast as possible, and try to smile."

Job applicants at Nordstrom will likely have years of experience acting on this schema. But Nordstrom has a different philosophy: Make customers happy even at the expense of efficiency. How does Nordstrom break down one schema and replace it with another?

The company solves this problem, in part, through unexpected stories. Jim Collins and Jerry Porras, in their book *Built to Last*, describe stories told at Nordstrom about unexpected service by employees, who are known within the firm as "Nordies":

The Nordie who ironed a new shirt for a customer who needed it for a meeting that afternoon;

the Nordie who cheerfully gift wrapped products a customer bought at Macy's;

the Nordie who warmed customers' cars in winter while they finished shopping;

the Nordie who made a last-minute delivery of party clothes to a frantic hostess;

and even the Nordie who refunded money for a set of tire chains—although Nordstrom doesn't sell tire chains.

You can imagine the surprise, if not shock, that these stories provoke in new Nordstrom employees. "Wrap a gift from Macy's! I don't get it. What's in it for us?" These stories attack the unspoken assumptions of customer service, such as: Service stops at the door of the store. Don't waste your time on someone who's not buying. Once you close a sale, move on to the next prospect.

To new employees, the idea of wrapping a gift bought at a competitor's store is so absurd, so far outside the bounds of their existing notion of "service," that the story stops them in their tracks. Their guessing machines have been broken. Their old "good service" guessing machine would never have produced the idea of altruistic gift-wrapping. The stories provide the first step toward replacing a new employee's schema of "good service" with the Nordstrom service schema.

In this way, Nordstrom breaks through the complacency of common sense. Instead of spreading stories about "Nordies," Nordstrom could simply tell its employees that its mission is to provide "the best customer service in the industry." This statement may be true, but, unfortunately, it sounds like something that JCPenney or Sears might also tell its employees. To make a message stick, you've got to push it beyond common sense to uncommon sense. "Great customer service" is common sense. Warming customers' cars in the winter is uncommon sense.

Note that these stories would be even more unexpected—and even less commonsensical—if they were told about a 7-Eleven employee. "Yeah, I went in to get a pack of smokes and the counter clerk *ironed my shirt!*" The value of the stories does not come from unexpectedness in and of itself. The value comes from the perfect alignment between Nordstrom's goals and the content of the stories. These stories could just as easily be destructive in another context. The 7-Eleven management does not want to face an epidemic of gift-wrapping clerks.

Nordstrom's stories are a classic example of the power of unexpectedness. There's no danger that the stories will feel gimmicky, because the surprise is followed by insight—the stories tell us what it means to be a good Nordstrom employee. It's uncommon sense in the service of a core message.

Journalism 101

Nora Ephron is a screenwriter whose scripts for *Silkwood*, *When Harry Met Sally*, and *Sleepless in Seattle* have all been nominated for Academy Awards. Ephron started her career as a journalist for the *New York Post* and *Esquire*. She became a journalist because of her high school journalism teacher.

Ephron still remembers the first day of her journalism class. Although the students had no journalism experience, they walked into their first class with a sense of what a journalist does: A journalists gets the facts and reports them. To get the facts, you track down the five Ws—who, what, where, when, and why.

As students sat in front of their manual typewriters, Ephron's teacher announced the first assignment. They would write the lead of a newspaper story. The teacher reeled off the facts: "Kenneth L. Peters, the principal of Beverly Hills High School, announced today that the entire high school faculty will travel to Sacramento next Thursday for a colloquium in new teaching methods. Among the speakers will be anthropologist Margaret Mead, college president Dr. Robert Maynard Hutchins, and California governor Edmund 'Pat' Brown."

The budding journalists sat at their typewriters and pecked away at the first lead of their careers. According to Ephron, she and most of the other students produced leads that reordered the facts and condensed them into a single sentence: "Governor Pat Brown, Margaret Mead, and Robert Maynard Hutchins will address the Beverly Hills High School faculty Thursday in Sacramento . . . blah, blah, blah."

The teacher collected the leads and scanned them rapidly. Then he laid them aside and paused for a moment.

Finally, he said, "The lead to the story is *'There will be no school next Thursday.'*"

"It was a breathtaking moment," Ephron recalls. "In that instant I realized that journalism was not just about regurgitating the facts but about figuring out the point. It wasn't enough to know the who, what, when, and where; you had to understand what it meant. And why it mattered." For the rest of the year, she says, every assignment had a secret—a hidden point that the students had to figure out in order to produce a good story.

This idea should be in the Sticky Hall of Fame. This teacher had a huge impact not because he was a dynamic speaker or a caring mentor—though he may have been both—but because he crafted a brilliant idea. It was an idea that, in a matter of seconds, rewrote the schema of journalism in the minds of his students. An idea that changed a student's career plans and stuck with her thirty years later.

What made this idea work? First, the teacher knew that the students had a defective schema of journalism, and he knew *how* it was defective. Second, he made them publicly commit to their defective models with the "write the lead" assignment. Then he pulled the rug out from under them with a well-structured surprise. By revealing the right lead—"There will be no school next Thursday"—he took their mental models, gave them a swift kick, and made them work better.

Does America Spend Too Much. on Foreign Aid?

THE SITUATION: *Over the years, polls have shown that the majority of Americans think the federal government spends too much on foreign aid. The ratio has dropped toward fifty/fifty since 9/11, but half of Americans still think we overspend. Let's look at two arguments that try to persuade people that we spend too little, not too much.*

◆ ◆ ◆

MESSAGE 1: Here is a message from the Intercommunity Peace and Justice Center, a Catholic advocacy group:

Americans persist in thinking we spend too much on foreign aid despite honest efforts to inform the public by the State Department and other government agencies. Even President Bush's proposed increases, though welcome, will not make the United States generous in its foreign assistance. In fiscal year 2003, the Bush administration will spend about $15-billion in foreign aid, but over $7-billion of this amount—almost half—will be military, not economic assistance. The $8-billion in foreign economic assistance is, according to a recent estimate by the Congressional Budget Office, less than the cost of one month of war with Iraq. Of all the industrialized nations, the U.S. spends proportionally the least amount on foreign aid, and has for many years. All of sub-Saharan Africa receives just over $1-billion of economic assistance, about the cost of a B-2 bomber. Our foreign aid programs do not support our belief that we are a nation known for its good works around the world.

COMMENTS ON MESSAGE 1: First, notice that the lead has been buried. The last sentence is the most effective argument. Americans' schema of the United States is that it is a generous, caring country—"known for its good works around the world." The way to break that schema is to lay out the blunt fact that the United States "spends proportionally the least amount on foreign aid, and has for many years."

The numbers in billions are unlikely to stick—huge numbers are difficult to grasp and hard to remember. One effective part of the message, in combating this "big-number problem," is the analogy comparing our sub-Saharan Africa aid to the cost of a single B-2 bomber. We really like this comparison, because it puts the reader in a decision-making mode: "Would I trade one B-2 bomber for the chance to *double* aid to sub-Saharan Africa?"

To make this message stickier, let's try two things. First, let's just reshuffle the great raw materials that are already there while downplaying the numbers in the billions. Second, let's choose a concrete comparison that has a better emotional resonance. Some people might think B-2 bombers are a reasonable expense. Let's try to create a comparison that would be more unexpected because it's clearly frivolous.

• • • •

MESSAGE 2: Our foreign-aid programs do not support our belief that we are a nation known for its good works around the world. The public believes we spend a great deal more money helping other countries than we actually do. Polls suggest that most Americans think the federal government spends about 10 to 15 percent of its budget on foreign aid. The truth is that we spend less than 1 percent, the lowest of any industrialized nation.

All of sub-Saharan Africa receives just over $1 billion in economic aid. If everyone in the United States gave up one soft drink a month, we could double our current aid to Africa. If everyone gave up one movie a year, we could double our current aid to Africa *and* Asia.

COMMENTS ON MESSAGE 2: Here's what we tried to do to make this message stickier: First, we built interest by quickly and directly breaking our schema of a "generous America." We also shifted the conversation to percentages, which are easier to understand than billions. Second, we tried to make the B-2 analogy more concrete by replacing it with soft drinks and movies. Soft drinks and movies are more tangible—does anyone really have a "gut feel" for what a B-2 bomber costs, or what it's worth? Soft drinks and movies, because they are frivolous expenses, also provide an emotional contrast to the critical human needs present in Africa.

SCORECARD

Checklist	Message 1	Message 2
Simple	-	✓
Unexpected	✓ (B-2 comparison)	✓✓ (intro & comparison)
Concrete	✓	✓
Credible	✓	✓
Emotional	-	✓
Story	-	-

PUNCH LINE: The best way to get people's attention is to break their existing schemas directly.

KEEPING PEOPLE'S ATTENTION

The Mystery of the Rings

We began this chapter with two questions: How do we get people's attention? And how do we keep it? So far, most of our unexpected ideas represent relatively simple, quick adjustments to a model. They may be profound—as with Nora Ephron's journalism teacher—but they happen rapidly, so they only need to get people's attention for a short time. Sometimes, though, our messages are more complex. How do we get people to stick with us through a more complex message? How do we *keep* people's attention?

A few years ago, Robert Cialdini, a social psychologist at Arizona State University, set out to improve the way he talked about science in his writing and in his classes. For inspiration, he went to the library. He pulled down every book he could find in which scientists were writing for an audience of nonscientists. He photocopied sections of prose that he liked. Later, flipping through his stack of copied passages, he hunted for consistencies.

In passages that weren't interesting, he found mostly what he expected. The purpose wasn't clear, and the prose was too formal and riddled with jargon. He also found a lot of predictable virtues in the good passages: The structure was clear, the examples vivid, and the language fluid. "But," says Cialdini, "I also found something I had not expected—the most successful of these pieces all began with a mystery story. The authors described a state of affairs that seemed to make no sense and then invited the reader into the material as a way of solving the mystery."

One example that stuck in his mind was written by an astronomer, who began with a puzzle:

How can we account for what is perhaps the most spectacular planetary feature in our solar system, the rings of Saturn? There's nothing else like them. What *are* the rings of Saturn made of anyway?

And then he deepened the mystery further by asking, "How could three internationally acclaimed groups of scientists come to wholly different conclusions on the answer?" One, at Cambridge University, proclaimed they were gas; another group, at MIT, was convinced they were made up of dust particles; while the third, at Cal Tech, insisted they were comprised of ice crystals. How could this be, after all, each group was looking at the same thing, right? So, what *was* the answer?

The answer unfolded like the plot of a mystery. The teams of scientists pursued promising leads, they hit dead ends, they chased clues. Eventually, after many months of effort, there was a breakthrough. Cialdini says, "Do you know what the answer was at the end of twenty pages? Dust. Dust. Actually, ice-covered dust, which accounts for some of the confusion. Now, I don't care about dust, and the makeup of the rings of Saturn is entirely irrelevant to my life. But that writer had me turning pages like a speed-reader."

Mysteries are powerful, Cialdini says, because they create a need for closure. "You've heard of the famous *Aha!* experience, right?" he says. "Well, the *Aha!* experience is much more satisfying when it is preceded by the *Huh?* experience."

By creating a mystery, the writer-astronomer made dust interesting. He sustained attention, not just for the span of a punch line but for the span of a twenty-page article dense with information on scientific theories and experimentation.

Cialdini began to create mysteries in his own classroom, and the power of the approach quickly became clear. He would introduce the mystery at the start of class, return to it during the lecture, and reveal the answer at the end. In one lecture, though, the end-of-class bell rang before he had time to reveal the solution. He says, "Normally five to ten minutes before the scheduled end time, some students start preparing to leave. You know the signals—pencils are put away, notebooks folded, backpacks zipped up." This time, though, the class was silent. "After the bell rang, no one moved. In fact, when I tried to end the lecture without revealing the mystery, I was pelted with protests." He said he felt as if he'd discovered dynamite.

Cialdini believes that a major benefit of teaching using mysteries is that "the process of resolving mysteries is remarkably similar to the process of science." So, by using mysteries, teachers don't just heighten students' interest in the day's material; they train them to think like scientists.

Science doesn't have a monopoly on mysteries. Mysteries exist wherever there are questions without obvious answers. Why is it so hard to get pandas at the zoo to breed? Why don't customers like our new product? What's the best way to teach kids about fractions?

Notice what is happening here: We have now moved to a higher level of unexpectedness. In the Nordstrom example, the Nordie stories had a punchy immediacy: *Nordies warm up customers' cars!* When you hear this, your past schema of customer service is called up, contradicted, and refined, all in a short period of time. Mysteries act differently. Mystery is created not from an unexpected moment but from an unexpected *journey*. We know where we're headed—we want to solve the mystery—but we're not sure how we'll get there.

A schema violation is a onetime transaction. Boom, something has changed. If we were told that the rings of Saturn were made of dryer lint, a schema would be violated. We could call it "first-level" unexpectedness. But the actual "rings of Saturn mystery" is more extended and subtle. We are told that scientists do not know what Saturn's rings are made of, and we're asked to follow on a journey whose ending is unpredictable. That's second-level unexpectedness. In this way, we jump from fleeting surprise to enduring interest.

Curiosity in Hollywood Screenplays

Early in the movie *Trading Places*, Billy Ray Valentine (played by Eddie Murphy), an apparently legless beggar, is using his arms to push himself around on a skateboardish contraption in a public park. He begs for money from passersby and harasses an attractive woman for a date. A couple of cops approach. As they jerk him up, his legs— perfectly normal legs—are exposed. Valentine is a con artist.

Later in the movie, the Duke brothers—two elderly business-men—intervene to get Valentine out of jail, persuading the cops to release him into their custody. A couple of scenes later, Valentine appears, dressed in a three-piece suit, in a wood-paneled office. The Duke brothers have turned him into a commodities trader.

Robert McKee, the screenwriting guru, uses this example to illustrate the concept of a "Turning Point." McKee knows something about how to hold an audience's attention. His screenwriting seminars play to packed auditoriums of aspiring screenwriters, who pay five hundred dollars a head to listen to his thoughts. *The Village Voice* described his course as "damned near indispensable not only for writers, but also for actors, directors, reviewers, and garden-variety cinephiles." His students have written, directed, or produced television shows such as *E.R.*, *Hill Street Blues*, and *The X-Files*, and movies ranging from *The Color Purple* to *Forrest Gump* and *Friday the 13th*.

McKee says, "*Curiosity* is the intellectual need to answer questions and close open patterns. *Story* plays to this universal desire by doing the opposite, posing questions and opening situations." In *Trading Places*, the Turning Point with Billy Ray and the Duke brothers makes the audience curious. How will Valentine, the street-smart con man, fare as a trader?

In McKee's view, a great script is designed so that every scene is a Turning Point. "Each Turning Point hooks curiosity. The audience wonders, *What will happen next?* and *How will it turn out?* The answer to this will not arrive until the Climax of the last act, and so the audience, held by curiosity, stays put." McKee notes that the *How will it turn out?* question is powerful enough to keep us watching even when we know better. "Think of all the bad films you've sat through just to get the answer to that nagging question."

What will happen next? How will it turn out? We want to answer these questions, and that desire keeps us interested. It keeps us watching bad movies — but it might also keep us reading long scientific articles. McKee and Cialdini have come up with similar solutions to very different problems.

Yet there are other domains where people can be rabidly interested in something that lacks this sense of mystery. Kids who obsessively memorize Pokémon characters and their traits are motivated by something, but it isn't *What will happen next?* It isn't a sense of an unfolding mystery that keeps car buffs plowing through every issue of *Car & Driver*. But, as we'll discover, Pokémon fans and car buffs have something in common with movie viewers and students in an intriguing lecture.

Psychologists have studied this question — *What makes people interested?* — for decades. The holy grail of research on interest is to find a way to describe situational interest. In other words, what features of a situation spark and elevate interest? What makes situations interesting? As it turns out, Cialdini and McKee were pretty close to the mark.

The "Gap Theory" of Curiosity

In 1994, George Loewenstein, a behavioral economist at Carnegie Mellon University, provided the most comprehensive account of situational interest. It is surprisingly simple. Curiosity, he says, happens when we feel a gap in our knowledge.

Loewenstein argues that gaps cause pain. When we want to know something but don't, it's like having an itch that we need to scratch. To take away the pain, we need to fill the knowledge gap. We sit patiently through bad movies, even though they may be painful to watch, because it's too painful not to know how they end.

This "gap theory" of interest seems to explain why some domains create fanatical interest: They naturally create knowledge gaps. Take movies, for instance. McKee's language is similar to Loewenstein's: McKee says, "*Story* works by posing questions and opening situations." Movies cause us to ask, *What will happen?* Mystery novels cause us to ask, *Who did it?* Sports contests cause us to ask, *Who will win?* Crossword puzzles cause us to ask, *What is a six-letter word for "psychiatrist"?* Pokémon cards cause kids to wonder, *Which characters am I missing?*

One important implication of the gap theory is that we need to *open* gaps before we *close* them. Our tendency is to tell people the facts. First, though, they must realize that they need these facts. The trick to convincing people that they need our message, according to Loewenstein, is to first highlight some specific knowledge that they're missing. We can pose a question or puzzle that confronts people with a gap in their knowledge. We can point out that someone else knows something they don't. We can present them with situations that have unknown resolutions, such as elections, sports events, or mysteries. We can challenge them to predict an outcome (which creates two knowledge gaps—*What will happen?* and *Was I right?*).

As an example, most local news programs run teaser ads for upcoming broadcasts. The teasers preview the lead story of the evening, usually in laughably hyperbolic terms: "There's a new drug sweeping the teenage community—and it may be in your own medicine cabinet!" "Which famous local restaurant was just cited—for *slime in the ice machine*?" "There's an invisible chemical in your home—and it may be killing you right now!"

These are sensationalist examples of the gap theory. They work because they tease you with something that you don't know—in fact, something that you didn't care about at all, until you found out that you didn't know it. "Is my daughter strung out on one of my old prescriptions? I wonder if I ate at the restaurant with the slime?"

A little dollop of the news-teaser approach can make our communications a lot more interesting, as we'll see in the Clinic.

An Internal Presentation on Fund-raising

THE SITUATION: *Imagine that you're the fund-raising manager for a local theater company. Your job is to help raise donations to support the theater. It's now the end of the year, and you're preparing a summary presentation for the theater's board of directors.*

* * * *

MESSAGE 1: (Both messages in this Clinic are made up.)

This year we targeted support from theatergoers under thirty-five. Our goal is to increase donations from younger patrons, who have traditionally composed a much greater percentage of our audience than of our donor base. To reach them, we implemented a phone-based fund-raising program. Six months into the program, the response rate has been almost 20 percent, which we consider a success.

COMMENTS ON MESSAGE 1: This message is a classic summary approach. I know the facts. I've put the facts in a logical order and I will spoon-feed them to you. As a presentation format, it's safe and normal and thoroughly nonsticky.

In improving this message, we need to think about how to elicit interest rather than force-feeding facts. We'll try to add a dash of the news-teaser approach.

* * *

MESSAGE 2: This year we set out to answer a question: Why do people under thirty-five, who make up 40 percent of our audience, provide only 10 percent of our donations? Our theory was that they didn't realize how much we rely on charitable donations to do our work, so we decided to try calling them with a short overview of our business and our upcoming shows. Going into the six-month test, we thought a 10 percent response rate would be a success. Before I tell you what happened, let me remind you of how we set up the program.

COMMENTS ON MESSAGE 2: This approach is inspired by the gap theory. The goal is not to summarize; it's to make you care about knowing something, and then to tell you what you want to know. Like the Saturn rings mystery, it starts with a puzzle: Why don't young people donate more? Then we present a theory and a way of testing it. The mystery engages the members of our audience, causing them to wonder what happened and whether our theory was right.

The improvement here is driven by structure, not content. Let's face it, this is not a particularly interesting mystery. It would never make an episode of *Law & Order*. But our minds are extremely generous when it comes to mysteries—the *format* is inherently appealing.

SCORECARD

Checklist	Message 1	Message 2
Simple	-	-
Unexpected	-	✓
Concrete	-	-
Credible	✓	✓
Emotional	-	-
Story	-	-

PUNCH LINE: To hold people's interest, we can use the gap theory of curiosity to our advantage. A little bit of mystery goes a long way.

The news-teaser approach can be used with all sorts of ideas in all sorts of contexts. To make our communications more effective, we need to shift our thinking from "What information do I need to convey?" to "What questions do I want my audience to ask?"

Battling Overconfidence

The gap theory relies on our ability to point out things that people don't know. One complication is that people tend to think they know a lot. Research has shown that we are typically overconfident about how much we know.

In one study, researchers asked people to consider the serious parking problem faced by their university. Participants were given time to generate as many solutions as they could. The participants generated, in total, about 300 solutions, which were classified into seven major categories. One category suggested ways to reduce demand for parking (e.g., by raising parking fees), and another suggested ways to use parking space more efficiently (e.g., by creating spaces for "Compact Cars Only").

The average participant failed to identify more than 70 percent of the best solutions identified by an expert panel. This failure is understandable; we wouldn't expect any one person to be able to generate a database worth of solutions. However, when the individuals were asked to assess their own performance, they predicted that they had identified 75 percent. They thought they got the majority, but in reality they'd missed them.

If people believe they know everything, it's hard to make the gap theory work. Fortunately, there are strategies for combating overconfidence. For instance, Nora Ephron's journalism teacher prevented overconfidence by causing the students' schemas of journalism to fail. He made them commit to their preconceived ideas and then pulled the rug out from under them.

Making people commit to a prediction can help prevent overconfidence. Eric Mazur, a physics professor at Harvard, came up with a pedagogical innovation known as "concept testing." Every so often in his classes, Mazur will pose a conceptual question and then ask his students to vote publicly on the answer. The simple act of committing to an answer makes the students more engaged and more curious about the outcome.

Overconfident people are more likely to recognize a knowledge gap when they realize that others disagree with them. Nancy Lowry and David Johnson studied a teaching environment where fifth and sixth graders were assigned to interact on a topic. With one group, the discussion was led in a way that fostered a consensus. With the second group, the discussion was designed to produce disagreements about the right answer.

Students who achieved easy consensus were less interested in the topic, studied less, and were less likely to visit the library to get additional information. The most telling difference, though, was revealed when teachers showed a special film about the discussion topic—during recess! Only 18 percent of the consensus students missed recess to see the film, but 45 percent of the students from the disagreement group stayed for the film. The thirst to fill a knowledge gap—to find out who was right—can be more powerful than the thirst for slides and jungle gyms.

Gaps Start with Knowledge

If curiosity arises from knowledge gaps, we might assume that when we know more, we'll become less curious because there are fewer gaps in our knowledge. But Loewenstein argues that the opposite is true. He says that as we gain information we are more and more likely to focus on what we don't know. Someone who knows the state capitals of 17 of 50 states may be proud of her knowledge. But someone who knows 47 may be more likely to think of herself as *not knowing* 3 capitals.

Some topics naturally highlight gaps in our knowledge. Human-interest stories are fascinating because we know what it's like to be human—but we don't know what it's like to have certain dramatic experiences. How does it feel to win an Olympic medal? How does it feel to win the Lotto? How did it feel to be conjoined twins Chang and Eng Bunker (each of whom not only married but had ten children . . . which sparks several additional lines of questioning)?

Gossip is popular because we know a lot about some people but there's some information that we lack. We don't gossip about passing acquaintances. Celebrity gossip is particularly tantalizing. We have a sense of who Tiger Woods and Julia Roberts are, but we crave the missing pieces—their quirks, their romantic struggles, their secret vices.

Curiosity comes from gaps in our knowledge. But what if there's not much knowledge there to begin with? In the 1960s, an upstart television network, American Broadcasting Corporation, signed a contract to televise NCAA football games. College sports is a classic insiders' topic. With the exception of a fringe of die-hard sports junkies, most fans usually care only about their own schools' teams. But ABC could show only a few games each week in each region. For ABC's bet to pay off, it needed to make viewers care about games that didn't involve their home teams.

How do you go about making viewers in College Station, Texas, care about the Michigan vs. Ohio State matchup? A twenty-nine-year-old named Roone Arledge, whose previous responsibilities primarily involved assigning crews to cover baseball, boxing, and football games, wrote a memo suggesting ways to improve the coverage of college football games.

Arledge saw ample room for improvement. Sportscasters typically set up their cameras, focused on the field, and waited for something to happen in front of them. They ignored everything else—the fans, the color, the pageantry. "It was like looking out on the Grand Canyon through a peephole in a door," Arledge said.

One Saturday afternoon, after procrastinating all morning, he sat down to type out a proposal to his bosses:

> Heretofore, television has done a remarkable job of bringing the game to the viewer—now we are going to take the viewer to the game! . . .
>
> After our opening commercial billboards, instead of dissolving to the usual pan shots of the field we will have pre-shot film of the campus and the stadium so we can orient the viewer. He must know he is in Columbus, Ohio, where the town is football mad; or that he is part of a small but wildly enthusiastic crowd in Corvallis, Oregon. He must know what the surrounding country and campus look like, how many other people are watching this game with him, how the people dress at football games in this part of the country, and what the game means to the two schools involved.

The memo was three pages long. It discussed camera angles, impact shots, opening graphics. The heart of the memo, though, was a new way of engaging viewers who might not ordinarily care about a college game in Corvallis, Oregon. The trick, Arledge said, was to give people enough context about the game so that they'd start to care.

Other people at ABC were excited by what Arledge had written. Two days later, he was asked—at age twenty-nine, with a skimpy résumé—to produce a college-football game using the guidelines in his memo.

Arledge intuitively made use of Loewenstein's gap theory. How do you get people interested in a topic? You point out a gap in their knowledge. But what if they lack so much knowledge about, say, the Georgia Bulldogs, that they've got more of an abyss than a gap? In that case, you have to fill in enough knowledge to make the abyss into a gap. Arledge set the scene, showed the local fans, panned across the campus. He talked up the emotions, the rivalries, the histories. By the time the game started, some viewers had begun to care who won. Others were riveted.

Arledge's next assignment was to take over a series that was eventually renamed *Wide World of Sports*. The show introduced Americans to a variety of sports events they may never have seen before: the Tour de France, the Le Mans auto races, rodeo championships, ski races, and soccer matches. In covering these events, Arledge used the same philosophy he'd pioneered for the NCAA: Set the context and give people enough backstory that they start to care about the gaps in their knowledge. Who's going to falter during the grueling twenty-four-hour Le Mans? Will the teacher turned barrel racer win the championship? What the heck is a yellow card?

Arledge died in 2002. During his career, he became the head of ABC Sports and later ABC News. He founded the *Wide World of Sports, Monday Night Football, 20/20,* and *Nightline.* He won thirty-six Emmys. The tool kit he developed for NCAA football stood the test of time. The way to get people to care is to provide context. Today that seems obvious, because these techniques have become ubiquitous. But this avalanche of context started because a twenty-nine-year-old wrote a memo about how to make college football more interesting.

Many teachers use some version of the Arledge tool kit to prime their students' interest. Some label the strategy "advanced organizers." The idea is that to engage students in a new topic you should start by highlighting some things they already know. An earth-science teacher might ask her students to bring in pictures of an earthquake's devastation, as a way of leading up to a discussion of plate tectonics. Alternatively, the teacher can set the context, à la Arledge, so that students start to become interested. A chemistry teacher might lead into the periodic table of elements by discussing Mendeleyev and his long, passionate quest to organize the elements. In this way, the periodic table emerges from within the context of a sort of detective story.

Knowledge gaps create interest. But to prove that the knowledge gaps exist, it may be necessary to highlight some knowledge first. "Here's what you know. Now here's what you're missing." Alternatively, you can set context so people care what comes next. It's no accident that mystery novelists and crossword-puzzle writers give us clues. When we feel that we're close to the solution of a puzzle, curiosity takes over and propels us to the finish.

Treasure maps, as shown in the movies, are vague. They show a few key landmarks and a big X where the treasure is. Usually the adventurer knows just enough to find the first landmark, which becomes the first step in a long journey toward the treasure. If treasure maps were produced on MapQuest.com, with door-to-door directions, it would kill the adventure-movie genre. There is value in *sequencing* information—not dumping a stack of information on someone at once but dropping a clue, then another clue, then another. This method of communication resembles flirting more than lecturing.

Unexpected ideas, by opening a knowledge gap, tease and flirt. They mark a big red X on something that needs to be discovered but don't necessarily tell you how to get there. And, as we'll see, a red X of spectacular size can end up driving the actions of thousands of people for many years.

Walking on the Moon and Radios in Pockets

In the rubble of Tokyo after World War II, a young company, later named Sony, struggled to stay in business. It attracted a handful of smart scientists and engineers, but its first innovation, an electric rice cooker, was a failure. Initially, Sony survived by repairing shortwave radios.

Around this time, Masaru Ibuka, Sony's lead technologist, became intrigued by transistors, which had recently been invented by a team at Bell Laboratories. Ibuka craved a "substantial" project to motivate his team of fifty scientists and engineers, and he saw tremendous promise in transistors. But when he bid to license the technology from

Bell Labs, the Japanese Ministry of Trade and Industry denied the license. It was skeptical of the young company's ability to manage such a cutting-edge technology.

In 1953, Ibuka secured permission to license transistors. He had a vision for a radio that would be based on transistors. The advantage of a transistor radio was obvious to engineers; it would free radios from the big vacuum tubes that made them so bulky and unreliable. Bell Labs told Ibuka that it didn't think a "transistor radio" was possible. His engineers began to pursue the vision anyway.

Let's pause here for a moment to put ourselves in Ibuka's shoes. Your company has been struggling, and you've got a team of brilliant people whom you need to inspire. You have the potential to lead them in one hundred different directions—rice cookers or radios or telephones or whatever else R & D could dream up. But you're convinced that the idea of a transistor-based radio is the most promising path.

Your core message, then, is the dream of a transistor radio. How do you make this message unexpected? How do you engage the curiosity and interest of your team? The concept of a "transistor radio" is probably not enough, in and of itself, to motivate your team. It's focused more on technology than on value. A transistor radio—so what?

What about tapping into some of the classic managerial themes? Competition: "Sony will beat Bell Labs in making a transistor radio work." Quality: "Sony will be the world's most respected manufacturer of radios." Innovation: "Sony will create the most advanced radios in the world."

Here's the idea Ibuka proposed to his team: a "pocketable radio."

It's hard, in retrospect, to comprehend the hubris of that idea—how utterly unexpected, how preposterous, it must have seemed the first time a Sony engineer heard it. Radios were not things you put into your pocket; they were pieces of furniture. At the time, radio factories employed full-time cabinetmakers.

Furthermore, the idea that an upstart Japanese company would deliver such an innovation, when the brilliant minds at Bell Labs thought it impossible, was not credible. After all, the 1950s were a decade when "Made in Japan" was synonymous with shoddy workmanship.

But Sony engineers were talented and hungry. Ibuka's idea of a pocketable radio caught on internally and drove Sony through an incredible period of growth. By 1957, Sony had grown to 1,200 employees. In March 1957, just four years after Sony was grudgingly granted permission to tinker with transistors, the company released the TR-55, the world's first pocketable transistor radio. The TR-55 sold 1.5 million units and put Sony on the world map.

A "pocketable radio"—isn't this simply a brilliant product idea, rather than a brilliant "sticky idea"? No, it is both, and both elements are indispensable. There's no question that someone in the world would have invented a transistor radio, even if Ibuka had decided to build the world's fanciest rice cooker. Transistor radios were an inevitable technological progression. But the first transistor radios were nowhere near pocket-sized, and without Ibuka's unexpected idea his engineers might have stopped pursuing the technology long before it became small enough to be useful. Ibuka inspired years of effort because he came up with an unexpected idea that challenged hundreds of engineers to do their best work.

In May 1961, John F. Kennedy gave a speech to a special session of Congress. It was a time when the Cold War dominated global politics. The Cold War allowed for few ways to measure success—to record gains and losses—but, in one highly visible field, the United States was clearly lagging behind. That field was space.

Four years earlier, the United States—which had prided itself as the most technologically advanced nation—was stunned when the Soviet Union launched Sputnik, the first satellite. The United States eventually responded with its own satellite launches, but the Soviet Union maintained its lead, racking up first after first. In April 1961,

Soviet cosmonaut Yuri Gagarin became the first human in space. U.S. astronaut Alan Shepard followed a month later.

In Kennedy's address to Congress, he outlined a series of requests to help the United States maintain its leadership during the Cold War. He asked for funds to achieve a number of strategic goals: to establish the AID program for international development, to expand the NATO alliance, to build radio and television stations in Latin America and Southeast Asia, and to shore up civil defense.

But he ended the speech on a curious note. His final proposal had nothing to do with international aid or civil defense. It was this: "I believe that this nation should commit itself to achieving the goal, before this decade is out, of landing a man on the moon and returning him safely to the earth . . . if we make this judgment affirmatively, it will not be one man going to the moon, it will be an entire nation. For all of us must work to put him there."

Two unexpected ideas. Both create surprise. Radios are pieces of furniture, not something to slip into a pocket. Men don't walk on the moon. It's a long way up. The air is thin.

Both create insight. Rather than leading us along a plodding route from one incremental step to the next, the ideas give us a sudden, dramatic glimpse of how the world might unfold. And not just how but *why*.

Both create knowledge gaps. Loewenstein, the author of the gap theory, says it's important to remember that knowledge gaps are painful. "If people *like* curiosity, why do they work to resolve it?" he asks. "Why don't they put mystery novels down before the last chapter, or turn off the television before the final inning of a close ball game?"

Both of these unexpected ideas set up big knowledge gaps—but not so big that they seemed insurmountable. Kennedy didn't propose a "man on Mercury," and Ibuka didn't propose an "implantable radio." Each goal was audacious and provocative, but not paralyzing. Any engineer who heard the "man on the moon" speech must have begun brainstorming immediately: "Well, first we'd need to solve this problem, then we'd need to develop this technology, then . . ."

The vision of a pocketable radio sustained a company through a tricky period of growth and led it to become an internationally recognized player in technology. The vision of a man on the moon sustained tens of thousands of separate individuals, in dozens of organizations, for almost a decade. These are big, powerful, sticky ideas.

When we're skeptical about our ability to get people's attention, or our ability to keep people's attention, we should draw inspiration from Kennedy and Ibuka. And, on a smaller scale, from Nora Ephron's journalism teacher and Nordstrom's managers. Unexpectedness, in the service of core principles, can have surprising longevity.

CHAPTER 3

CONCRETE

One hot summer day a Fox was strolling through an orchard. He saw a bunch of Grapes ripening high on a grape vine. "Just the thing to quench my thirst," he said. Backing up a few paces, he took a run and jumped at the grapes, just missing. Turning around again, he ran faster and jumped again. Still a miss. Again and again he jumped, until at last he gave up out of exhaustion. Walking away with his nose in the air, he said: "I am sure they are sour." It is easy to despise what you can't get.

The fable above, "The Fox and the Grapes," was written by Aesop. According to Herodotus, he was a slave (though he was later freed). Aesop authored some of the stickiest stories in world history. We've all heard his greatest hits: "The Tortoise and the Hare," "The Boy Who Cried Wolf," "The Goose That Laid the Golden Eggs," "The Wolf in Sheep's Clothing," and many more. If any story told in this book is still circulating a few millennia from now, odds are it will be "The Fox and the Grapes."

Even English speakers who've never heard "The Fox and the Grapes" will recognize the phrase "sour grapes," which encapsulates the moral of the story. Aesop's lesson has traveled the world. In Hungary, people say *savanyu a szolo*—"sour grapes" in Hungarian. In China, they say, "Grapes are sour because you cannot reach them." In Sweden, a little local color was added; the Swedish expression *Surt sa räven om rönnbären* means "Sour, the fox said, about the rowanberries."

Clearly, Aesop was illustrating a universal human shortcoming. The fable would not have survived for more than 2,500 years if it didn't reflect some profound truth about human nature. But there are many profound truths that have not seeped into the day-to-day language and thinking of dozens of cultures. This truth is especially sticky because of the way it was *encoded*. The concrete images evoked by the fable—the grapes, the fox, the dismissive comment about sour grapes—allowed its message to persist. One suspects that the life span of Aesop's ideas would have been shorter if they'd been encoded as *Aesop's Helpful Suggestions*—"Don't be such a bitter jerk when you fail."

What the world needs is a lot more fables. On the Web, a satirical site features a "Business Buzzword Generator." Readers can produce their own business buzzwords by combining one word each from three columns, which yields phrases like "reciprocal cost-based re-engineering," "customer-oriented visionary paradigm," and "strategic logistical values." (All of these sound eerily plausible as buzzwords, by the way.) Teachers have their own buzzwords: metacognitive skills, intrinsic motivation, portfolio assessment, developmentally appropriate, thematic learning. And if you've ever talked to a doctor, we don't even have to provide examples. Our favorite from medicine: "idiopathic cardiomyopathy." "Cardiomyopathy" means something is wrong with your heart, and "idiopathic" means "we have no idea why yours isn't working."

Language is often abstract, but *life* is not abstract. Teachers teach students about battles and animals and books. Doctors repair prob-

lems with our stomachs, backs, and hearts. Companies create software, build planes, distribute newspapers; they build cars that are
cheaper, faster, or fancier than last year's. Even the most abstract business strategy must eventually show up in the tangible actions of
human beings. It's easier to understand those tangible actions than to
understand an abstract strategy statement—just as it's easier to understand a fox dissing some grapes than an abstract commentary about
the human psyche.

Abstraction makes it harder to understand an idea and to remember it. It also makes it harder to coordinate our activities with others,
who may interpret the abstraction in very different ways. Concreteness helps us avoid these problems. This is perhaps the most important lesson that Aesop can teach us.

The Nature Conservancy

For fifty years, The Nature Conservancy (TNC) has helped protect
environmentally precious areas in the world using the simplest possible method: It buys them. It buys land at market prices, making it off-
limits to environmentally damaging uses, such as development or
logging. This strategy has come to be known within TNC as "bucks
and acres." It had appeal to donors and benefactors, because the results of their gifts were so clear. A big gift bought a big piece of land.
A small gift bought a small piece of land. As one donor commented,
TNC produced "results you could walk around on."

In 2002, Mike Sweeney, the COO of TNC California, was facing
a big challenge. California is particularly important to TNC, because
it contains so many environmentally critical areas. California is one
of only five Mediterranean climate regions in the world. (The others
are the *fynbos* of South Africa, the *matorral* of Chile, the *kwongan* of
Australia, and, of course, the Mediterranean.) These Mediterranean
climate zones occupy only 2 percent of the world's landmass but host

more than 20 percent of its plant species. If you want to buy environmentally precious land, Mediterranean climates give you a lot of
bang for your buck.

In 2002, Sweeney and his staff had taken a map of California and
colored in the most environmentally sensitive areas, the areas worth
preserving. Astonishingly, 40 percent of the map was colored. This
was a non-starter: There weren't enough bucks out there to buy that
many acres.

Yet 9 percent of the state was classified as being in "critical danger." Nine percent of California was still far too much to contemplate
purchasing, but these regions were environmentally essential; TNC
couldn't simply give up on them.

TNC decided to implement some new approaches. "Bucks and
acres" couldn't succeed with this vast quantity of land. So instead of
owning the land outright, TNC would ensure that the critical areas
were *protected against damage*. The organization would pay land-
owners not to develop their land, buying what's known as a "conservation easement." It would work with local and state governments to
change policies and encourage conservation of private and public
land. It would focus on important marine areas, where there was no
land to buy.

These new strategies made sense—TNC could protect more areas
than it could reach through "bucks and acres." But they also had
drawbacks. First, they were much less concrete to donors. Donors
can't "walk around on" a favorable government regulation. Second,
they were also potentially demoralizing for employees—they made
progress less tangible. When TNC was focused on land deals,
Sweeney said, "it was easy to celebrate a deal closing, to tell everyone,
'John and Mary got this land,' and to pat them on the back." These
"milestone moments," so great for morale, were harder to find in the
new model. How could TNC make the new strategy more concrete?

What would you do in this situation? Is there a way to recapture the invaluable tangibility of the "bucks and acres" strategy in a context that was necessarily more ambiguous? You've got 40 percent (or at least 9 percent) of the state to protect, and you can't buy it. How do you explain yourself to donors and partners?

Chip has discussed this case with his students at Stanford, and in grappling with the need for concreteness some students respond by breaking up the impossibly large scale of the challenge — 40 percent of California! 9 percent in critical need! — by subdividing it into more tangible "subgoals." For example: "We will protect a 2 percent chunk of California every year for twenty years." Others try to invoke a unit of measurement that we can understand, such as the acre. Most people can visualize an acre. But the scale is too big: 2 percent of California is about two million acres. No one can picture two million acres.

The students are wisely trying to find a way to break up a big, abstract goal into smaller, more concrete subgoals. This is the right idea. But in this case the numbers are just too big. And "acreage" is not necessarily the best way to think. There are 1,500-acre plots of land that are more environmentally precious than other 90,000-acre plots. Thinking about "acreage per year" is akin to a museum curator thinking about "canvases per year," without regard to period, style, or painter.

Here's what TNC did: Instead of talking in terms of land area, it talked about a "landscape." A landscape is a contiguous plot of land with unique, environmentally precious features. The TNC set a goal of preserving fifty *landscapes* — of which twenty-five were an immediate priority — over a ten-year period. Five landscapes per year sounds more realistic than 2 million acres per year, and it's much more concrete.

To the east of Silicon Valley there is a set of brown hills that are the beginnings of a wilderness the size of Yosemite. The brown hills are an important watershed for the San Francisco Bay, but they are quickly being chipped away by Silicon Valley sprawl. Although the area is important ecologically, it is not like the redwoods or the coast, with beautiful visuals that engage people's imaginations. The hills are covered with grass interspersed with a few oak trees. Most of the year, the grass is brown. Sweeney admits that it's not very sexy. Even local groups in the Silicon Valley area that were interested in protecting open spaces weren't paying attention to the brown hills. But, says Sweeney, "We don't go after stuff because it's pretty. We go after it because it's an ecologically important part of creation."

TNC named the oak savanna the Mount Hamilton Wilderness (based on its highest peak, the site of a local observatory). Identifying the area as a coherent landscape and naming it put it on the map for local groups and policymakers. Before, Sweeney says, Silicon Valley groups wanted to protect important areas close to their homes, but they didn't know where to start. "If you say, 'There's a really important area to the east of Silicon Valley,' it's just not exciting, because it's not tangible. But when you say, 'The Mount Hamilton Wilderness,' their interest perks up."

The Packard Foundation, a Silicon Valley institution created by one of the founders of the Hewlett-Packard Company, provided a large grant to protect the Mount Hamilton Wilderness. Other environmental groups in the Bay Area started campaigning to preserve the area. Sweeney says, "We're always laughing now, because we see other people's documents and they're talking about the Mount Hamilton Wilderness. We say, 'You know we made that up.'"

People who live in cities tend to name and define their neighborhoods: "the Castro," "SoHo," "Lincoln Park," and so forth. These names come to define an area and its traits. Neighborhoods have personalities. The Nature Conservancy created the same effect with its landscapes. The Mount Hamilton Wilderness is not a set of acres; it's an eco-celebrity.

This is not a story about land; it's a story about abstraction. TNC avoided the trap of abstraction—saving 2 million acres per year—by converting abstract blobs on a map into tangible landscapes. TNC realized, wisely, that the context had grown more ambiguous, and the solutions had grown more ambiguous, but that their *messages* could not be allowed to grow more ambiguous. Concreteness is an indispensable component of sticky ideas.

Understanding Subtraction

What makes something "concrete"? If you can examine something with your senses, it's concrete. A V8 engine is concrete. "High-performance" is abstract. Most of the time, concreteness boils down to specific people doing specific things. In the "Unexpected" chapter, we talked about Nordstrom's world-class customer service. "World-class customer service" is abstract. A Nordie ironing a customer's shirt is concrete.

Concrete language helps people, especially novices, understand new concepts. Abstraction is the luxury of the expert. If you've got to teach an idea to a room full of people, and you aren't certain what they know, concreteness is the only safe language.

To see this, we can start by studying math classrooms in Asia. We know, from the news over the years, that East Asian children outperform American children in, well, just about everything (except the consumption of fatty foods). This is especially evident in math. The math skills of Americans fall behind those of Asians early—the gap is apparent in the first grade, and it widens throughout elementary school.

What are Asian schools doing differently? Our stereotype is that these schools operate with almost robotic efficiency: Hours are long and discipline is strict. We think of East Asian students as being less "creative" somehow; we like to think they outperform our students through rote mechanics and memorization. The truth, it turns out, is almost exactly the opposite.

In 1993, a group of researchers studied ten schools in Japan, ten in Taiwan, and twenty in the United States. In each school, they picked two different math teachers to observe, and they observed four lessons with each teacher. The researchers found that *all* the teachers used rote recall quite a bit; it was standard procedure in at least half the lessons observed in every country. But other techniques varied greatly among the three countries.

For instance, consider this question by a Japanese teacher: "You had 100 yen but then you bought a notebook for 70 yen. How much money do you still have?" Or this question, posed by a teacher in Taiwan: "Originally there are three kids playing ball. Two more came later, and then one more joined them. How many are playing now?" As she talked, she drew stick figures on the board and wrote down the equation $3 + 2 + 1$.

Notice that these teachers are explaining abstract mathematical concepts by emphasizing things that are concrete and familiar—buying school supplies and playing ball. Their explanations take advantage of preexisting schemas, a tactic we explored in the "Simple" chapter. Teachers take an existing schema—the dynamics of a six-person ball game—and overlay a new layer of abstraction.

The researchers called this style of questioning Computing in Context. It is pretty much the opposite of "rote recall." And, contrary to our stereotypes, it occurred about twice as much in Asia as it did in the United States (61 percent of lessons versus 31 percent).

In another case, a Japanese teacher placed on a desk 5 rows of 10 tiles each. Then she took away 3 rows of 10 tiles. She asked a student how many tiles were left, and he gave the correct answer: 20. The teacher then asked the students how they knew that this was a subtraction problem. This teacher provided her students with a visual image of subtraction. Students could build an abstract concept—"subtraction"—on a concrete foundation: 30 tiles being yanked away from an original set of 50. The researchers coded questions like this one as Conceptual Knowledge questions. This type of question was asked in 37 percent of lessons in Japan, 20 percent in Taiwan, but only 2 percent in the United States.

Using concreteness as a foundation for abstraction is not just good for mathematical instruction; it is a basic principle of understanding. Novices crave concreteness. Have you ever read an academic paper or a technical article or even a memo and found yourself so flummoxed by the fancy abstract language that you were crying out for *an example*?

Or maybe you've experienced the frustration of cooking from a recipe that was too abstract: "Cook until the mixture reaches a hearty consistency." Huh? Just tell me how many minutes to stir! Show me a picture of what it looks like! After we've cooked the dish a few times, then the phrase "hearty consistency" might start to make sense. We build a sensory image of what that phrase represents. But the first time it's as meaningless as 3 + 2 + 1 would be to a three-year-old.

This is how concreteness helps us understand—it helps us construct higher, more abstract insights on the building blocks of our existing knowledge and perceptions. Abstraction demands some concrete foundation. Trying to teach an abstract principle without concrete foundations is like trying to start a house by building a roof in the air.

Concrete Is Memorable

Concrete ideas are easier to remember. Take individual words, for instance. Experiments in human memory have shown that people are better at remembering concrete, easily visualized nouns ("bicycle" or "avocado") than abstract ones ("justice" or "personality").

Naturally sticky ideas are stuffed full of concrete words and images—think of the Kentucky Fried Rat or the Kidney Heist's ice-filled bathtub. The Kidney Heist legend would have been far less sticky if the man had woken up and found that someone had absconded with his self-esteem.

Yale researcher Eric Havelock studies tales that have been passed down by word of mouth, such as the *Iliad* and the *Odyssey*. He notes that these tales are characterized by lots of concrete actions, with few abstractions. Why? The ancient Greeks certainly had no problem with abstraction—this was the society that produced Plato and Aristotle, after all. Havelock believes that the stories evolved away from abstraction over time. When they were passed along from generation to generation, the more memorable concrete details survived and the abstractions evaporated.

Let's skip to the modern world and another timeless and beautiful domain of expression: accounting. Put yourself in the shoes of an accounting professor who has to introduce accounting principles to college students. To a new student, accounting can seem bewilderingly abstract—the income statement, the balance sheet, T-accounts, accounts receivable, treasury stock. No people or sensory data in sight.

As the teacher, how do you make accounting concepts vivid? Two professors from Georgia State University, Carol Springer and Faye Borthick, decided to try something radically different. In the fall of 2000, Springer and Borthick taught a semester of accounting using, as a centerpiece, a semester-long case study. The case study followed a new business launched by two imaginary college sophomores, Kris and Sandy, at LeGrande State University.

Kris and Sandy had an idea for a new product called Safe Night Out (SNO), a device targeted at parents with teenagers who were old enough to drive. Installed in the teenager's car, the device would record the route and speed of the car. For the first time, parents could confirm whether their car was being driven responsibly.

At this point you, as a student in introductory accounting, become part of the story. Kris and Sandy are your friends, and they've heard that you're taking an accounting class. They need your help. They ask, Is our business idea feasible? How many units would we have to sell in order to pay for our tuition? You are given guidance on how to track down the costs of the relevant materials (GPS receivers, storage hardware) and partnerships (how much it would cost to sell it on eBay).

The semester-long Kris and Sandy soap opera revealed the role that accounting plays in business life. Every accounting course defines the distinction between fixed and variable costs, but in the soap opera this distinction wasn't so much defined as *discovered*. Kris and Sandy have to pay some costs no matter what, such as the programming expense for developing the product. Those are fixed costs. Other costs are incurred only when products are made or sold—the cost of the materials or eBay's commission, for example. Those are variable costs. If your friends are pouring their tuition money into a start-up business, those distinctions matter.

The case study is an example of learning in context, similar to the teachers in the Asian math classrooms. But in the math classrooms a student might encounter 300 different examples over the course of a semester. In the accounting class, students had one example that was sufficiently rich to encompass a semester's worth of material.

As the semester progresses, you witness, from your hot seat as Kris and Sandy's accountant, the evolution of their business. A local court approaches Kris and Sandy wanting to use the SNO device for its parolees, but it wants to lease the device rather than buy it. How should Kris and Sandy respond? Later, the business begins to grow rapidly, but suddenly Kris and Sandy make a panicked call to you, having bounced a check. They've been selling more units than ever, yet there's no cash in the bank. How is that possible? (This problem is faced by many start-up businesses, and it introduces the difference between profitability and cash flow.) The answer becomes clear to you only after you've worked through a month of payment slips and eBay receipts.

So, did the students learn better? At first it was hard to say. The changes to the course made it hard to compare final exams directly with those of previous years. Some students seemed more enthusiastic about the new course, but others groused because the case study demanded a lot of time. Over time, however, the benefits of the concrete case study became increasingly obvious. After experiencing the case study, students with high GPAs were more likely to major in accounting. The concreteness actually made the most capable students *want* to become accountants.

But the case study also had positive effects for regular students. In the next accounting course—taken an average of two years later—the first section of the course built heavily on the concepts that students were supposed to have learned in introductory accounting. Students who had worked through the case study scored noticeably higher on this first exam. In fact, the difference in scores was particularly dramatic for students with a C average overall. Generally speaking, they scored twelve points higher. And remember, this is two years after the case study ended. Concreteness sticks.

The Velcro Theory of Memory

What is it about concreteness that makes ideas stick? The answer lies with the nature of our memories.

Many of us have a sense that remembering something is a bit like putting it in storage. To remember a story is to file it away in our cerebral filing cabinets. There's nothing wrong with that analogy. But the surprising thing is that there may be completely different filing cabinets for different kinds of memories.

You can actually test this idea for yourself. The following set of sentences will ask you to remember various ideas. Spend five or ten seconds lingering on each one—don't rush through them. As you move from one sentence to another, you'll notice that it *feels different* to remember different kinds of things.

- Remember the capital of Kansas.
- Remember the first line of "Hey Jude" (or some other song that you know well).
- Remember the *Mona Lisa*.

- Remember the house where you spent most of your childhood.
- Remember the definition of "truth."
- Remember the definition of "watermelon."

David Rubin, a cognitive psychologist at Duke University, uses this exercise to illustrate the nature of memory. Each command to remember seems to trigger a different mental activity. Remembering the capital of Kansas is an abstract exercise, unless you happen to live in Topeka. By contrast, when you think about "Hey Jude," you may hear Paul McCartney's voice and piano playing. (If the phrase "Hey Jude" drew a blank, please exchange this book for a Beatles album. You'll be happier.)

No doubt the *Mona Lisa* memory conjured a visual image of that famously enigmatic smile. Remembering your childhood home might have evoked a host of memories—smells, sounds, sights. You might even have felt yourself running through your home, or remembering where your parents used to sit.

The definition of "truth" may have been a bit harder to summon—you certainly have a sense of what "truth" means, but you probably had no preformulated definition to pluck out of memory, as with the *Mona Lisa*. You might have had to create a definition on the fly that seemed to fit with your sense of what "truth" means.

The definition of "watermelon" might also have involved some mental gyrations. The word "watermelon" immediately evoked sense memories—the striped green rind and red fruit, the sweet smell and taste, the heft of a whole watermelon. Then you might have felt your gears switch as you tried to encapsulate these sense memories into a definition.

Memory, then, is not like a single filing cabinet. It is more like Velcro. If you look at the two sides of Velcro material, you'll see that one is covered with thousands of tiny hooks and the other is covered with thousands of tiny loops. When you press the two sides together, a huge number of hooks get snagged inside the loops, and that's what causes Velcro to seal.

Your brain hosts a truly staggering number of loops. The more hooks an idea has, the better it will cling to memory. Your childhood home has a gazillion hooks in your brain. A new credit card number has one, if it's lucky.

Great teachers have a knack for multiplying the hooks in a particular idea. A teacher from Iowa named Jane Elliott once designed a message so powerful—tapping into so many different aspects of emotion and memory—that, twenty years later, her students still remember it vividly.

Brown Eyes, Blue Eyes

Martin Luther King, Jr., was assassinated on April 4, 1968. The next day, Jane Elliott, an elementary-school teacher in Iowa, found herself trying to explain his death to her classroom of third-graders. In the all-white town of Riceville, Iowa, students were familiar with King but could not understand who would want him dead, or why.

Elliott said, "I knew it was time to deal with this in a concrete way, because we'd *talked* about discrimination since the first day of school. But the shooting of Martin Luther King, one of our 'Heroes of the Month' two months earlier, couldn't be explained to little third-graders in Riceville, Iowa."

She came to class the next day with a plan: She aimed to make prejudice tangible to her students. At the start of class, she divided the students into two groups: brown-eyed kids and blue-eyed kids. She then made a shocking announcement: Brown-eyed kids were superior to blue-eyed kids—"They're the better people in this room." The groups were separated: Blue-eyed kids were forced to sit at the back of the classroom. Brown-eyed kids were told that they were smarter.

They were given extra time at recess. The blue-eyed kids had to wear special collars, so that everyone would know their eye color from a distance. The two groups were not allowed to mix at recess.

Elliott was shocked at how quickly the class was transformed. "I watched those kids turn into nasty, vicious, discriminating third-graders . . . it was ghastly," she said. "Friendships seemed to dissolve instantly, as brown-eyed kids taunted their blue-eyed former friends. One brown-eyed student asked Elliott how she could be the teacher "if you've got dem blue eyes."

At the start of class the following day, Elliott walked in and announced that she had been wrong. It was actually the *brown-eyed* children who were inferior. This reversal of fortune was embraced instantly. A shout of glee went up from the blue-eyed kids as they ran to place their collars on their lesser, brown-eyed counterparts.

On the day when they were in the inferior group, students described themselves as sad, bad, stupid, and mean. "When we were down," one boy said, his voice cracking, "it felt like everything bad was happening to us." When they were on top, the students felt happy, good, and smart.

Even their performance on academic tasks changed. One of the reading exercises was a phonics card pack that the kids were supposed to go through as quickly as possible. The first day, when the blue-eyed kids were on the bottom, it took them 5.5 minutes. On the second day, when they were on top, it took 2.5 minutes. "Why couldn't you go this fast yesterday?" Elliott asked. One blue-eyed girl said, "We had those collars on. . . ." Another student chimed in, "We couldn't stop thinking about those collars."

Elliott's simulation made prejudice concrete—brutally concrete. It also had an enduring impact on the students' lives. Studies conducted ten and twenty years later showed that Elliott's students were significantly less prejudiced than their peers who had not been through the exercise.

Students still remember the simulation vividly. A fifteen-year reunion of Elliott's students broadcast on the PBS series *Frontline* revealed how deeply it had moved them. Ray Hansen, remembering the way his understanding changed from one day to the next, said, "It was one of the most profound learning experiences I've ever had." Sue Ginder Rolland said, "Prejudice has to be worked out young or it will be with you all your life. Sometimes I catch myself [discriminating], stop myself, think back to the third grade, and remember what it was like to be put down."

Jane Elliott put hooks into the idea of prejudice. It would have been easy for her to treat the idea of prejudice the way other classroom ideas are treated—as an important but abstract bit of knowledge, like the capital of Kansas or the definition of "truth." She could have treated prejudice as something to be learned, like the story of a World War II battle. Instead, Elliott turned prejudice into an *experience*. Think of the "hooks" involved: The sight of a friend suddenly sneering at you. The feel of a collar around your neck. The despair at feeling inferior. The shock you get when you look at your own eyes in the mirror. This experience put so many hooks into the students' memories that, decades later, it could not be forgotten.

The Path to Abstraction: The Blueprint and the Machine

Jane Elliott's simulation of prejudice is compelling evidence of the power of concreteness. But if concreteness is so powerful, why do we slip so easily into abstraction?

The reason is simple: because the difference between an expert and a novice is the ability to think abstractly. New jurors are struck by lawyers' personalities and factual details and courtroom rituals. Meanwhile, judges weigh the current case against the abstract lessons of past cases and legal precedent. Biology students try to remember whether reptiles lay eggs or not. Biology teachers think in terms of the grand system of animal taxonomy.

Novices perceive concrete details as concrete details. Experts perceive concrete details as symbols of patterns and insights that they have learned through years of experience. And, because they are capable of *seeing* a higher level of insight, they naturally want to talk on a higher level. They want to talk about chess strategies, not about bishops moving diagonally.

And here is where our classic villain, the Curse of Knowledge, inserts itself. A researcher named Beth Bechky studied a manufacturing firm that designed and built the complicated machinery used to produce silicon chips. To build such machinery, the firm needed two sets of skills: engineers who could create brilliant designs, and skilled manufacturing people who could transform those designs into complex physical machines.

If the firm was to succeed, these two sets of people had to be able to communicate smoothly. But, not surprisingly, they spoke different languages. The engineers tended to think abstractly—they spent their day agonizing over drawings and blueprints. The manufacturing team, on the other hand, tended to think on a physical level—they spent their day building machines.

What's most revealing for the Curse of Knowledge is what happened when something went wrong on the manufacturing floor. The manufacturing folks would sometimes run into a problem—something didn't fit or perhaps wasn't receiving enough power. The manufacturers would bring the problem to the engineers, and the engineers would immediately get to work. Specifically, they'd get to work *fixing their drawings*.

For example, the manufacturing team might find a part that didn't fit on the machine. When the team showed the part to the engineers, they wanted to pull out the blueprints and move things around on the drawing. In other words, the engineers instinctively wanted to jump to a higher level of abstraction.

The engineers, Bechky found, made their drawings "increasingly elaborate" in the hope that the enhanced drawings would clarify the process for the manufacturers. Over time, the drawings became more abstract, which further hampered communication.

The engineers were behaving like American tourists who travel to foreign countries and try to make themselves understood by speaking English more slowly and loudly. They were suffering from the Curse of Knowledge. They had lost the ability to imagine what it was like to look at a technical drawing from the perspective of a nonexpert.

The manufacturing people were thinking, *Why don't you just come down to the factory floor and show me where the part should go?* And the engineering people were thinking, *What do I need to do to make the drawings better?*

The miscommunication has a quality that is familiar, no doubt, to many readers who don't work on silicon chip–making machinery. So how do you fix it? Should both parties learn greater empathy for the other and, in essence, meet in the middle? Actually, no. The solution is for the engineers to change their behavior. Why? As Bechky notes, the physical machine was the most effective and relevant domain of communication. *Everyone* understands the machines fluently. Therefore problems should be solved at the level of the machine.

It's easy to lose awareness that we're talking like an expert. We start to suffer from the Curse of Knowledge, like the tappers in the "tappers and listeners" game. It can feel unnatural to speak concretely about subject matter we've known intimately for years. But if we're willing to make the effort we'll see the rewards: Our audience will understand what we're saying and remember it.

The moral of this story is not to "dumb things down." The manufacturing people faced complex problems and they needed smart answers. Rather, the moral of the story is to find a "universal language," one that everyone speaks fluently. Inevitably, that universal language will be concrete.

Concrete Allows Coordination

In the last chapter, we closed with two unexpected slogans that were used to motivate and coordinate large groups of smart people. The slogans were challenges to build a "pocketable radio" and to "put a man on the moon within the decade." Notice that these slogans are also pleasingly concrete. It is doubtful that Japanese engineers were paralyzed with uncertainty about their mission, or that much time was spent at NASA quibbling about the meaning of "man," "moon," or "decade."

Concreteness makes targets transparent. Even experts need transparency. Consider a software start-up whose goal is to build "the next great search engine." Within the start-up are two programmers with nearly identical knowledge, working in neighboring cubes. To one "the next great search engine" means completeness, ensuring that the search engine returns everything on the Web that might be relevant, no matter how obscure. To the other it means speed, ensuring pretty good results very fast. Their efforts will not be fully aligned until the goal is made concrete.

When Boeing prepared to launch the design of the 727 passenger plane in the 1960s, its managers set a goal that was deliberately concrete: The 727 must seat 131 passengers, fly nonstop from Miami to New York City, and land on Runway 4-22 at La Guardia. (The 4-22 runway was chosen for its length—less than a mile, which was much too short for any of the existing passenger jets.) With a goal this concrete, Boeing effectively coordinated the actions of thousands of experts in various aspects of engineering or manufacturing. Imagine how much harder it would have been to build a 727 whose goal was to be "the best passenger plane in the world."

The Ferraris Go to Disney World in the R & D Lab

Stone Yamashita Partners, a small consulting firm in San Francisco, was founded by Robert Stone and Keith Yamashita, former Apple creatives. Stone Yamashita is a master of using concrete techniques to help organizations create change. "Almost everything we do is visceral and visual," Keith Yamashita says. The "product" of most consulting firms is often a PowerPoint presentation. At Stone Yamashita, it's much more likely to be a simulation, an event, or a creative installation.

Around 2002, Stone Yamashita was approached by Hewlett-Packard (HP). HP's top management team hoped to win a partnership with Disney, and they asked Stone Yamashita to help prepare a proposal that would highlight HP research, and show how it could help Disney run its theme parks.

HP, like many technology firms, generates great research in its laboratories, but that research isn't always translated into tangible physical products. Researchers get excited about pushing the boundaries of a technology, making products that are complex and sophisticated, while customers generally seek out products that are easy and reliable. The desires of researchers and customers don't always dovetail.

The "presentation" that Stone Yamashita designed was an exhibit that filled 6,000 square feet. Yamashita describes the gist: "We invented a fictitious family called the Ferraris, three generations of them, and built an exhibit about their life and their visit to Disney World."

Walking into the exhibit, you began in the Ferraris' living room, furnished with family photos. Each subsequent room followed the Ferraris through various scenes of their Disney World vacation. HP technology helped them buy tickets, sped their entry into the park, and scheduled their reservations for dinner. Another bit of technology helped them enjoy their favorite rides while minimizing waiting time. Back inside their hotel room at the end of the day, there was a final twist: A digital picture frame had automatically downloaded a picture of them as they rode a Disney World roller coaster.

Stone Yamashita, working with HP's engineers, turned a message about the benefits of collaboration—what could have been a Power-Point presentation—into a living, breathing simulation. Stone Yamashita put hooks into the idea of e-services. They took an abstract idea and made it concrete with an intense sensory experience.

Note that there were two different audiences for the exhibit. The first audience was Disney. Disney's execs were the "novices"—they needed to be shown, in tangible terms, what HP's technology could do for them. Then there were HP's employees, particularly the engineers. They were far from novices. Many engineers had been skeptical about the value of Yamashita's demos. Once the exhibit opened, however, it produced tremendous enthusiasm within HP. It was initially intended to stay up long enough to make the Disney pitch, but, because it was so popular, it remained for three or four months afterward. One observer said, "It became very viral in that others began to ask, 'Did you see that great thing that the labs team did? Did you know that we could do this? Did you know that they did it in only twenty-eight days?' "

Concreteness helped this team of experts coordinate. A diverse group of engineers, accustomed to contemplating difficult technology problems, suddenly came face-to-face with the Ferrari family. By grappling with one family's concrete needs—their tickets and reservations and photos—they did something remarkable: They took abstract ideas from their research labs and turned them into a family picture on a roller-coaster ride.

Concrete Brings Knowledge to Bear:
White Things

Grab a pencil and a piece of paper and find a way to time yourself (a watch, a spouse who likes to count, etc.). Here is a do-it-yourself test on concreteness. You'll do two brief fifteen-second exercises. When you've got your supplies ready, set your timer for fifteen seconds, then follow the instructions for Step 1 below.

STEP 1 INSTRUCTIONS:

Write down as many things that are white in color as you can think of.

STOP. Reset your timer for fifteen seconds. Turn the page for the instructions for Step 2.

STEP 2 INSTRUCTIONS:

Write down as many white things in your refrigerator as you can
think of.

Most people, remarkably, can list about as many white things
from their refrigerators as white anythings. This result is stunning because, well, our fridges don't include a particularly large part of the
universe. Even people who list more white anythings often feel that
the refrigerator test is "easier."

Why does this happen? Because concreteness is a way of mobiliz-
ing and focusing your brain. For another example of this phenomenon, consider these two statements: (1) Think of five silly things that
people have done in the world in the past ten years. (2) Think about
five silly things your child has done in the past ten years.

Sure, this is a neat brain trick. But what value does it have? Consider a situation where an entrepreneur used this neat brain trick to
earn a $4.5 million investment from a savvy and sophisticated group
of investors.

Kaplan and Go Computers

For an entrepreneur, having the chance to pitch a business idea to
local venture capitalists is a big deal, like a budding actor getting an
audition with an independent film director. But having a chance to
pitch an idea to Kleiner Perkins—the most prestigious firm in Silicon
Valley—is more like a private one-on-one audition with Steven Spiel-
berg. You could walk out a star, or you could walk out having blown
the biggest chance of your life.

And that's why twenty-nine-year-old Jerry Kaplan was nervous as he
stood in the Kleiner Perkins office in early 1987. His presentation
would start in about thirty minutes. Kaplan was a former researcher at
Stanford who had quit to work at Lotus in its early days. Lotus, with its
bestselling Lotus 1-2-3 spreadsheet, became a stock market darling.

Now Kaplan was ready for the next challenge. He had a vision for a smaller, more portable generation of personal computers.

He hung around outside the conference room as the previous entrepreneur finished his presentation. Watching the other entrepreneur, he felt underprepared. As he observed, his nervousness advanced toward panic. The other entrepreneur wore a dark pin-striped suit with a red power tie. Kaplan had on a sport jacket with an open-collared shirt. The other entrepreneur was projecting an impressive color graph onto the whiteboard. Kaplan was carrying a maroon portfolio with a blank pad of paper inside. This did not bode well.

Kaplan had thought that he was showing up for an informal "get to know you" session, but, standing there, he realized how naive he'd been. He had "no business plan, no slides, no charts, no financial projections, no prototypes." Worst of all, the überprepared entrepreneur in the boardroom was facing a skeptical audience that now peppered him with tough questions.

When Kaplan's turn arrived, one of the partners introduced him. Kaplan took a deep breath and started: "I believe that a new type of computer, more like a notebook than a typewriter, and operated by a pen rather than a keyboard, will serve the needs of professionals like ourselves when we are away from our desks. We will use them to take notes, send and receive messages through cellular telephone links; look up addresses, phone numbers, price lists, and inventories; do spreadsheet calculations; and fill out order forms."

He covered the required technology, highlighting the major unknown: whether a machine could reliably recognize handwriting and convert it into commands. Kaplan recounts what happened next:

> My audience seemed tense. I couldn't tell whether they were annoyed by my lack of preparation or merely concentrating on what I was saying. . . . Thinking I had already blown it, and therefore had little to lose, I decided to risk some theatrics.
>
> "If I were carrying a portable PC right now, you would sure as

hell know it. You probably didn't realize that I am holding a model of the future of computing right here in my hands."

I tossed my maroon leather case in the air. It sailed to the center of the table where it landed with a loud clap.

"Gentlemen, here is a model of next step in the computer revolution."

For a moment, I thought this final act of drama might get me thrown out of the room. They were sitting in stunned silence, staring at my plain leather folder—which lay motionless on the table—as though it were suddenly going to come to life. Brook Byers, the youthful-looking but long-time partner in the firm, slowly reached out and touched the portfolio as if it were some sort of talisman. He asked the first question.

"Just how much information could you store in something like this?"

John Doerr [another partner] answered before I could respond. "It doesn't matter. Memory chips are getting smaller and cheaper each year and the capacity will probably double for the same size and price annually."

Someone else chimed in. "But bear in mind, John, that unless you translate the handwriting efficiently, it's likely to take up a lot more room." The speaker was Vinod Khosla, the founding CEO of Sun Microsystems, who helped the partnership evaluate technology deals.

Kaplan said that from that point on he hardly had to speak, as partners and associates traded questions and insights that fleshed out his proposal. Periodically, he said, someone would reach out to touch or examine his portfolio. "It had been magically transformed from a stationery-store accessory into a symbol of the future of technology."

A few days later, Kaplan got a call from Kleiner Perkins. The partners had decided to back the idea. Their investment valued Kaplan's nonexistent company at $4.5 million.

What transformed this meeting from a grill session—with an anxious entrepreneur in the hot seat—to a brainstorming session? The maroon portfolio. The portfolio presented a challenge to the boardroom participants—a way of focusing their thoughts and bringing their existing knowledge to bear. It changed their attitude from reactive and critical to active and creative.

The presence of the portfolio made it easier for the venture capitalists to brainstorm, in the same way that focusing on "white things in our refrigerator" made it easier for us to brainstorm. When they saw the size of the portfolio, it sparked certain questions: How much memory could you fit in that thing? Which PC components will shrink in the next few years, and which won't? What new technology would have to be invented to make it feasible? This same process was sparked in Sony's Japanese engineering team by the concept of a "pocketable radio."

Concreteness creates a shared "turf" on which people can collaborate. Everybody in the room feels comfortable that they're tackling the same challenge. Even experts—even the Kleiner Perkins venture capitalists, the rock stars of the technology world—benefit from concrete talk that puts them on common ground.

CLINIC

Oral Rehydration Therapy Saves Children's Lives!

THE SITUATION: *Each year more than a million children in countries around the world die from dehydration caused by diarrhea. This problem can be prevented, at very low cost, by getting kids the right kind of fluids. How do you get people invested in this idea?*

MESSAGE 1: Here's an explanation from PSI, a nonprofit group that addresses health problems in developing countries:

Diarrhea is one of the leading killers of young children in developing countries, causing over 1.5 million child deaths annually. Diarrhea itself is not the cause of death, but rather dehydration, the loss of body fluid. Approximately three quarters of the body is composed of water, and if fluid loss exceeds ten percent of total body fluid, vital organs collapse, followed by death. If an episode is severe, as with cholera, death can occur within just eight hours.

To prevent life-threatening dehydration it is necessary to increase liquid intake in quantities sufficient to replenish the fluids and electrolytes lost with diarrhea. The best liquid for this purpose is a blend of electrolytes, sugar, and water, known as oral rehydration salts. ORS restores body fluid and electrolytes more rapidly than any other liquid, and does so even when the intestinal wall is compromised by disease.

COMMENTS ON MESSAGE 1: Quick: How solvable is this problem? Suppose you were a health official in a developing nation. What would you do tomorrow to start saving kids?

To be fair, this message appears on a Web page that describes what PSI has been doing to solve this problem. The text doesn't necessarily reflect how the organization might approach decision-makers to persuade them to act. The information is written in language that creates *credibility;* there is lots of scientific language and exposition. If the problem sounds too complex, however, that could deter people from trying to solve it.

MESSAGE 2: This message is from James Grant, who was the director of UNICEF for many years. Grant always traveled with a packet filled with one teaspoon of salt and eight teaspoons of sugar—the ingredi-ents for Oral Rehydration Therapy (ORT) when mixed with a liter of water. When he met with the prime ministers of developing countries, he would take out his packet of salt and sugar and say, "Do you know that this costs less than a cup of tea and it can save hundreds of thou-sands of children's lives in your country?"

COMMENTS ON MESSAGE 2: Quick: How solvable is this problem? What are you going to do tomorrow to start saving these children's lives? Grant's message brings you to the table, helps you bring your knowledge to bear. Maybe you're brainstorming ways of getting salt/sugar packets to schools. Maybe you're thinking about publicity campaigns to teach mothers the right ratio of salt and sugar.

Grant is clearly a master of making ideas stick. He brings out a *concrete* prop and starts with an attention-grabbing *unexpected* con-trast: This packet costs less than a cup of tea, but it can have a real impact. Prime ministers spend their time thinking about elaborate, complex social problems—building infrastructure, constructing hos-pitals, maintaining a healthy environment—and suddenly here's a bag of salt and sugar that can save hundreds of thousands of chil-dren.

Grant's message does sacrifice the statistics and the scientific de-scription that add *credibility* to the PSI message. But, as the director of UNICEF, he had enough credibility to keep people from questioning his facts. So Grant left the (uncontested) factual battle behind and fought the motivational battle. His bag of salt and sugar is the equiva-lent of Kaplan's maroon portfolio in the venture-capital presentation: It helps the members of the audience bring their expertise to the prob-lem. You can't see it and *not* start brainstorming about the possibilities.

SCORECARD

Checklist	Message 1	Message 2
Simple	-	✓
Unexpected	-	✓
Concrete	-	✓
Credible	✓	-
Emotional	✓	✓
Story	-	-

PUNCH LINE: This Clinic is one of our favorite before-and-after examples in the book, because it shows how powerful a concrete idea can be. The moral is to find some way to invite people to the table, to help them bring their knowledge to bear. Here, a prop works better than a scientific description.

Making Ideas Concrete

How do we move toward concrete ideas for our own messages? We might find our own decisions easier to make if they are guided by the needs of specific people: our readers, our students, our customers.

General Mills is one of the world's largest manufacturers of consumer products. Its brands include Pillsbury, Cheerios, Green Giant, Betty Crocker, Chex, and many others. One of the largest brands in the company, from a sales perspective, is Hamburger Helper. Melissa Studzinski, a twenty-eight-year-old from Michigan, joined General Mills in 2004 as Hamburger Helper's brand manager.

When she joined the team, Hamburger Helper had been in a decade-long slump. The CEO, frustrated by the decline, announced that his number one goal for 2005 was to fix and grow the Hamburger

Helper brand. Studzinski, the newest person on the team, was eager to tackle the challenge.

When she started the job, she was given three huge binders full of data and stats: sales and volume data, advertising-strategy briefs, product information, and market research on the brand's customers. The binders were difficult to pick up, let alone absorb into memory. She called them the "death binders."

A few months later, Studzinski's team decided to put the data aside and try something new. They made plans to send members of the Hamburger Helper team—marketing, advertising, and R & D staffers —out into the homes of Hamburger Helper customers. The idea was known informally as "Fingertips," because the General Mills employees needed to have a picture of the brand's customers at their fingertips.

A call went out for mothers (the predominant customers of Hamburger Helper) who were willing to let strangers come into their homes and gawk at them while they cooked. The team visited two to three dozen homes. Studzinski visited three homes, and the experience stuck with her. "I had read and I could recite all the data about our customers," she says. "I knew their demographics by heart. But it was a very different experience to walk into a customer's home and experience a little bit of her life. I'll never forget one woman, who had a toddler on her hip while she was mixing up dinner on the stove. We know that 'convenience' is an important attribute of our product, but it's a different thing to see the need for convenience firsthand."

Most of all, Studzinski learned that moms and their kids really valued predictability. Hamburger Helper had eleven different pasta shapes, but kids didn't care about different shapes. What they did care about was flavor, and moms just wanted to buy the same predictable flavor their kids wouldn't reject. But Hamburger Helper had more than thirty different flavors, and moms struggled to find their favorites among the massive grocery-store displays. Food and beverage companies constantly push to develop new flavors and packages, but Studzinski needed to resist this push. "Moms saw new flavors as risky," she says.

Using this concrete information about moms and kids, the team convinced a diverse collection of people across the organization—in groups ranging from supply chain and manufacturing to finance—to simplify the product line. According to Studzinski, the cost savings were "huge," yet moms were happier because it was easier to find their families' favorites on grocery stores shelves. The insight to simplify the product line—along with other key insights concerning pricing and advertising—sparked a turnaround for the brand. At the end of fiscal year 2005, Hamburger Helper's sales had increased 11 percent.

Studzinski says, "Now when I've got a decision to make about the brand, I think of the women I met. I wonder what they would do if they were in my shoes. And it's amazing how helpful it is to think that way."

The same philosophy is just as useful for ideas that are more transcendent. The Saddleback Church is a very successful church in a suburb of Irvine, California, that has grown to more than 50,000 members. Over the years, the church's leaders have created a detailed picture of the kind of person they're trying to reach. They call him "Saddleback Sam." Here's how Rick Warren, the minister of the Saddleback Church, describes him:

Saddleback Sam is the typical unchurched man who lives in our area. His age is late thirties or early forties. He has a college degree and may have an advanced degree. . . . He is married to Saddleback Samantha, and they have two kids, Steve and Sally.

Surveys show that Sam likes his job, he likes where he lives, and he thinks he's enjoying life more now than he was five years ago. He's self-satisfied, even smug, about his station in life. He's either a professional, a manager, or a successful entrepreneur.

. . . Another important characteristic of Sam is that he's skeptical of what he calls "organized" religion. He's likely to say, "I believe in Jesus. I just don't like organized religion."

The profile goes into much greater depth: Sam and Samantha's tastes in pop culture, their preferences about social events, and so on.

What does "Saddleback Sam" accomplish for church leaders? Sam forces them to view their decisions through a different lens. Say someone proposes a telemarketing campaign to local community members. It sounds as if it has great potential to reach new people. But the leaders know from their research that Sam hates telemarketers, so the idea is scratched.

And thinking about Saddleback Sam and Samantha isn't limited to church leaders. There are hundreds of small ministries at the Saddleback Church: grade school classes, Mother's Day Out programs, a men's basketball league. All are led by volunteer members who don't receive day-to-day direction from paid church staff. But these diverse programs work together because people throughout the church know whom they're trying to reach. "Most of our members would have no trouble describing Sam," Warren says.

By making Saddleback Sam and Samantha a living, breathing, concrete presence in the minds of the members of the Saddleback Church, the church has managed to reach 50,000 real Sams and Samanthas.

Of the six traits of stickiness that we review in this book, concreteness is perhaps the easiest to embrace. It may also be the most effective of the traits.

To be simple—to find our core message—is quite difficult. (It's certainly worth the effort, but let's not kid ourselves that it's easy.) Crafting our ideas in an unexpected way takes a fair amount of effort and applied creativity. But being concrete isn't hard, and it doesn't require a lot of effort. The barrier is simply forgetfulness—we forget that we're slipping into abstractspeak. We forget that other people don't know what we know. We're the engineers who keep flipping back to our drawings, not noticing that the assemblers just want us to follow them down to the factory floor.

CHAPTER 4

CREDIBLE

Over the course of a lifetime, one person in ten will develop an ulcer. Duodenal ulcers, the most common type, are almost never fatal, but they are extremely painful. For a long time, the cause of ulcers was a mystery. Conventional wisdom held that ulcers developed when surplus acid built up in the stomach, eating through the stomach wall. Such surplus acid could be caused, it was thought, by stress, spicy foods, or lots of alcohol. Ulcer treatments traditionally focused on mitigating the painful symptoms, since there was no clear way to "cure" an ulcer.

In the early 1980s, two medical researchers from Perth, Australia, made an astonishing discovery: Ulcers are caused by bacteria. The researchers, Barry Marshall and Robin Warren, identified a tiny spiral-shaped type of bacteria as the culprit. (It would later be named *Helicobacter pylori*, or *H. pylori*.) The significance of this discovery was enormous: If ulcers were caused by bacteria, they could be *cured*. In fact, they could be cured within a matter of days by a simple treatment with antibiotics.

The medical world, however, did not rejoice. There were no celebrations for Marshall and Warren, who had almost single-handedly improved the health prospects of several hundred million human beings. The reason for the lack of acclaim was simple: No one believed them.

There were several problems with the bacteria story. The first problem was common sense. The acid in the stomach is potent stuff—it can, obviously, eat through a thick steak, and it's (less obviously) strong enough to dissolve a nail. It was ludicrous to think that bacteria could survive in such an environment. It would be like stumbling across an igloo in the Sahara.

The second problem was the source. At the time of the discovery, Robin Warren was a staff pathologist at a hospital in Perth; Barry Marshall was a thirty-year-old internist in training, not even a doctor yet. The medical community expects important discoveries to come from Ph.D.s at research universities or professors at large, world-class medical centers. Internists do not cure diseases that affect 10 percent of the world's population.

The final problem was the location. A medical researcher in Perth is like a physicist from Mississippi. Science is science, but, thanks to basic human snobbery, we tend to think it will emerge from some places but not others.

Marshall and Warren could not even get their research paper accepted by a medical journal. When Marshall presented their findings at a professional conference, the scientists snickered. One of the researchers who heard one of his presentations commented that he "simply didn't have the demeanor of a scientist."

To be fair to the skeptics, they had a reasonable argument: Marshall and Warren's evidence was based on correlation, not causation. Almost all of the ulcer patients seemed to have H. pylori. Unfortunately, there were also people who had H. pylori but no ulcer. And, as for proving causation, the researchers couldn't very well dose a bunch of innocent people with bacteria to see whether they sprouted ulcers.

By 1984, Marshall's patience had run out. One morning he

skipped breakfast and asked his colleagues to meet him in the lab. While they watched in horror, he chugged a glass filled with about a billion *H. pylori*. "It tasted like swamp water," he said.

Within a few days, Marshall was experiencing pain, nausea, and vomiting—the classic symptoms of gastritis, the early stage of an ulcer. Using an endoscope, his colleagues found that his stomach lining, previously pink and healthy, was now red and inflamed. Like a magician, Marshall then cured himself with a course of antibiotics and bismuth (the active ingredient in Pepto-Bismol).

Even after this dramatic demonstration, the battle wasn't over. Other scientists quibbled with the demonstration. Marshall had cured himself before he developed a full-blown ulcer, they argued, so maybe he had just generated ulcer symptoms rather than a genuine ulcer. But Marshall's demonstration gave a second wind to supporters of the bacteria theory, and subsequent research amassed more and more evidence in its favor.

In 1994, ten years later, the National Institutes of Health finally endorsed the idea that antibiotics were the preferred treatment for ulcers. Marshall and Warren's research contributed to an important theme in modern medicine: that bacteria and viruses cause more diseases than we would think. It is now known that cervical cancer is caused by the contagious human papillomavirus, or HPV. Certain types of heart disease have been linked to cytomegalovirus, a common virus that infects about two thirds of the population.

In the fall of 2005, Marshall and Warren received the Nobel Prize in medicine for their work. These two men had a brilliant, Nobel-worthy, world-changing insight. So why did Marshall have to poison himself to get people to believe him?

Finding Credibility

Let's pose the question in the broadest possible terms: What makes people believe ideas? How's that for an ambitious question? Let's start with the obvious answers. We believe because our parents or our friends believe. We believe because we've had experiences that led us to our beliefs. We believe because of our religious faith. We believe because we trust authorities.

These are powerful forces—family, personal experience, faith. And, thankfully, we have no control over the way these forces affect people. We can't route our memos through people's mothers to add credibility. We can't construct a PowerPoint presentation that will nullify people's core beliefs.

If we're trying to persuade a skeptical audience to believe a new message, the reality is that we're fighting an uphill battle against a lifetime of personal learning and social relationships. It would seem that there's nothing much we can do to affect what people believe. But if we're skeptical about our ability to affect belief, we merely have to look at naturally sticky ideas, because some of them persuade us to believe some pretty incredible things.

Around 1999, an e-mail message spread over the Internet, forwarded from person to person, claiming that shipments of bananas from Costa Rica were infected with necrotizing fasciitis, otherwise known as flesh-eating bacteria. People were warned not to purchase bananas for the next three weeks, and urged to SEEK MEDICAL ATTENTION!!! if they contracted a rash after eating a banana. The e-mail also warned, "The skin infection from necrotizing fasciitis is very painful and eats two to three centimeters of flesh per hour. Amputation is likely, death is possible." It claimed that the Food and Drug Administration (FDA) was reluctant to issue a general warning because it feared a nationwide panic. (One would think that disappearing centimeters of flesh might be sufficient to cause a panic, even in the absence of the FDA's response.) This surprising message was attributed to the Manheim Research Institute.

This bizarre rumor spread at least in part because it had an air of authority. It was circulated by the *Manheim Research Institute!* And the *Food and Drug Administration* knew about the problem! The

Manheim Research Institute and the FDA are invoked as credibility-boosters. Their authority makes us think twice about what would otherwise be some pretty incredible statements: Necrotizing fasciitis consumes three centimeters of flesh per hour? If that's true, why isn't the story on the evening news?

Evidently, someone realized that the rumor's credibility could be improved. Later versions added, "This message has been verified by the Centers for Disease Control." If the rumor circulated long enough, no doubt it would eventually be "approved, by the Dalai Lama" and "heartily endorsed by the Security Council."

As the contaminated bananas show, authorities are a reliable source of credibility for our ideas. When we think of authorities who can add credibility, we tend to think of two kinds of people. The first kind is the expert—the kind of person whose wall is covered with framed credentials: Oliver Sachs for neuroscience, Alan Greenspan for economics, or Stephen Hawking for physics.

Celebrities and other aspirational figures make up the second class of "authorities." Why do we care that Michael Jordan likes McDonald's? Certainly he is not a certified nutritionist or a world-class gourmet. We care because we want to be like Mike, and if Mike likes McDonald's, so do we. If Oprah likes a book, it makes us more interested in that book. We trust the recommendations of people whom we want to be like.

If you have access to the endorsement of Stephen Hawking or Michael Jordan—renowned experts or celebrities—skip this part of the chapter. As for the rest of us, whom can we call on? Can we find external sources of credibility that don't involve celebrities or experts?

The answer, surprisingly, is yes. We can tap the credibility of anti-authorities. One antiauthority was a woman named Pam Laffin.

Pam Laffin, the Antiauthority

Pam Laffin was the star of a series of antismoking TV ads that were broadcast in the mid-1990s. Laffin is not a celebrity and she's not a health expert. She's a smoker.

At the time, Laffin was a twenty-nine-year-old mother of two. She had started smoking at age ten and had developed emphysema by age twenty-four. She'd suffered a failed lung transplant.

Greg Connolly, the director of tobacco control for the Massachusetts Department of Public Health (MDPH), was in charge of designing a public-service campaign against smoking. He became aware of Pam Laffin and asked her to share her story with the public. She agreed.

Connolly said, "What we've learned from previous campaigns is that telling stories using real people is the most compelling way." The MDPH filmed a series of thirty-second spots, broadcast during hip shows such as *Ally McBeal* and *Dawson's Creek*. The spots were brutal. They showed Laffin battling to live while slowly suffocating because of her failing lungs. The TV audience watched her enduring an invasive bronchoscopy—a procedure in which a tube with a camera at the end is inserted through the mouth and pushed into the lungs. The spots showed the nasty surgical scars on her back.

In another spot, featuring photos of Laffin as a child and as an adult, she talks about how her emphysema left her with a "fat face" and "a hump on my neck." She said, "I started smoking to look older and I'm sorry to say it worked."

The spots were difficult to watch, and contrasted jarringly with the light soap-opera fare of shows like *Dawson's Creek*. "We have no compunction at all about shocking smokers into waking up," Connolly said.

Laffin became a heroine of the antismoking movement. She was the subject of an MTV documentary. The Centers for Disease Control features her story in an antismoking Web campaign and a twenty-minute educational video titled *I Can't Breathe*.

She died in November 2000 at the age of thirty-one, three weeks before she was scheduled for a second lung transplant.

After hearing Laffin's story you're probably not surprised that she was an effective spokeswoman. There's no question that she knew from personal experience what she was talking about. She had a powerful tale to tell.

Another example of drawing credibility from antiauthorities comes from the Doe Fund in New York City, an organization that takes homeless men—the John Does of our society—and turns them into productive citizens through counseling, drug rehabilitation, and, most important, job training. A few years ago, some representatives from a grant organization—potential financial supporters— were going to visit the offices of the Doe Fund. The Doe Fund sent a driver, Dennis, to pick them up and drive them to the home office.

Dennis had been homeless before he turned to the Doe Fund for help. During the forty-five-minute car trip, Dennis shared his story with the grant representatives. One commented, "We weren't just sitting around listening to a bunch of directors telling us how effective their services are; Dennis was the best ambassador that the Doe Fund could provide—he was living proof." The Doe Fund also uses this principle internally. Every homeless man who enters the program is matched with a mentor who, two years before, was in the same situation.

It's worth reminding ourselves that it wasn't *obvious* that Laffin or Dennis would be effective authorities. Thirty years ago, an antismoking campaign like Laffin's would probably not have happened. Instead, the Surgeon General would have given us a stern lecture on the dangers of smoking. Or Burt Reynolds would have extolled the virtues of a smoke-free life.

A citizen of the modern world, constantly inundated with messages, learns to develop skepticism about the *sources* of those messages. Who's behind these messages? Should I trust them? What do they have to gain if I believe them?

A commercial claiming that a new shampoo makes your hair bouncier has less credibility than hearing your best friend rave about how a new shampoo made her own hair bouncier. Well, duh. The company wants to sell you shampoo. Your friend doesn't, so she gets more trust points. The takeaway is that it can be the *honesty and trustworthiness* of our sources, not their *status*, that allows them to act as authorities. Sometimes antiauthorities are even better than authorities.

The Power of Details

We don't always have an external authority who can vouch for our message; most of the time our messages have to vouch for themselves. They must have "internal credibility." Of course, internal credibility frequently depends on what topic we're discussing: A credible math proof looks different from a credible movie review. But, surprisingly, there are some general principles for establishing internal credibility. To see these principles in action, we can again turn to urban legends.

The Boyfriend's Death is a famous urban legend that begins with a couple heading out on a date in the boyfriend's car. The car runs out of gas under a tree on a deserted road. The girl suspects that the guy is faking in order to make out with her, but soon she realizes they're really stuck. The boyfriend decides to walk to the nearest house for help, and the girl stays behind. He has been gone for a long time—it feels like hours—and the girl is frightened by a creepy scratching coming from the roof of the car, possibly the scrapings of a low-hanging tree branch. After several hours of anxious waiting, the girl gets out of the car to discover—cue the horror music!—her boyfriend, murdered and hanging from the tree above the car. His toes scrape the roof as he swings in the wind.

When people pass this legend along, they always add particular details. It's always set in a specific location, which varies when it is told in different parts of the country: "It happened right off Farm Road 121"; "It happened right on top of that bluff over Lake Travis." An expert on folk legends, Jan Brunvand, says that legends "acquire a good deal of their credibility and effect from their localized details."

A person's knowledge of details is often a good proxy for her expertise. Think of how a history buff can quickly establish her credibility by telling an interesting Civil War anecdote. But concrete details don't just lend credibility to the *authorities* who provide them; they lend credibility to the idea itself. The Civil War anecdote, with lots of interesting details, is credible in *anyone's* telling. By making a claim tangible and concrete, details make it seem more real, more believable.

Jurors and the Darth Vader Toothbrush

In 1986, Jonathan Shedler and Melvin Manis, researchers at the University of Michigan, created an experiment to simulate a trial. Subjects were asked to play the role of jurors and were given the transcript of a (fictitious) trial to read. The jurors were asked to assess the fitness of a mother, Mrs. Johnson, and to decide whether her seven-year-old son should remain in her care.

The transcript was constructed to be closely balanced: There were eight arguments against Mrs. Johnson and eight arguments for Mrs. Johnson. All the jurors heard the same arguments. The only difference was the *level of detail* in those arguments. In one experimental group, all the arguments that supported Mrs. Johnson had some vivid detail, whereas the arguments against her had no extra details; they were pallid by comparison. The other group heard the opposite combination.

As an example, one argument in Mrs. Johnson's favor said: "Mrs. Johnson sees to it that her child washes and brushes his teeth before bedtime." In the vivid form, the argument added a detail: "He uses a *Star Wars* toothbrush that looks like Darth Vader."

An argument against Mrs. Johnson was: "The child went to school with a badly scraped arm which Mrs. Johnson had not cleaned or attended to. The school nurse had to clean the scrape." The vivid form added the detail that, as the nurse was cleaning the scrape, she spilled Mercurochrome on herself, staining her uniform red.

The researchers carefully tested the arguments with and without vivid details to ensure that they had the same perceived importance—the details were designed to be irrelevant to the judgment of Mrs. Johnson's worthiness. It mattered that Mrs. Johnson didn't attend to the scraped arm; it didn't matter that the nurse's uniform got stained in the process.

But even though the details shouldn't have mattered, they did. Jurors who heard the favorable arguments with vivid details judged Mrs. Johnson to be a more suitable parent (5.8 out of 10) than did jurors who heard the unfavorable arguments with vivid details (4.3 out of 10). The details had a big impact.

We can take comfort, perhaps, in the fact that the swing wasn't more dramatic. (If the mother's fitness had dropped from eight to two, we might have had to worry a bit about our justice system.) But the jurors did make different judgments based on *irrelevant* vivid details. So why did the details make a difference? They boosted the credibility of the argument. If I can mentally see the Darth Vader toothbrush, it's easier for me to picture the boy diligently brushing his teeth in the bathroom, which in turn reinforces the notion that Mrs. Johnson is a good mother.

What we should learn from urban legends and the Mrs. Johnson trial is that vivid details boost credibility. But what should also be added is that we need to make use of truthful, core details. We need to identify details that are as compelling and human as the "Darth Vader toothbrush" but more meaningful—details that symbolize and support our core idea.

In 2004, two Stanford Business School professors held a workshop with arts organizations in Washington, D.C. One exercise was designed to make the arts leaders focus on the enduring principles of their organizations, the principles they would not compromise under any circumstances. One organization at the workshop was the Liz Lerman Dance Exchange (LLDE), "a company of dance artists that creates, performs, teaches, and engages people in making art." At the workshop, the leaders from the LLDE maintained that one of their core values was "diversity."

"Come on," scoffed one of the professors, suspecting an exaggeration. "Everyone claims that they value diversity, but you're a dance company. You're probably filled with a bunch of twenty-five-year-old dancers, all of them tall and thin. Some of them are probably people of color, but is that diversity?" Other people in the audience, unfamiliar with the LLDE, nodded at this skeptical response.

Peter DiMuro, the artistic director of the LLDE, responded with an example. "As a matter of fact," he said, "the longest-term member of our company is a seventy-three-year-old man named Thomas Dwyer. He came to the LLDE after a full career working for the U.S. government when he retired in 1988, and had no previous dance experience. He has now been with the LLDE for seventeen years."

This detail— seventy-three-year-old Thomas Dwyer—silenced the skepticism in the room. The professors experienced a rare moment of speechlessness.

And there was a good reason that DiMuro could respond quickly with a vivid example. The reason is that diversity *truly is* a core value at the LLDE. It's part of the LLDE's organizational DNA.

In 2002, Liz Lerman won a MacArthur "genius grant" for her work creating modern dance involving communities throughout the United States. In a dance project called Hallelujah/U.S.A., Lerman visited communities across the country and asked residents what made them thankful. Then she choreographed dances around those themes of praise. The final performances featured members of the local community: teenage female Hmong dancers in Minneapolis, Border collie owners in Virginia, and a group of six card-playing ladies from Burlington, Vermont, who'd missed only two of their weekly card games in forty years.

Now, a brief aside to the eye-rolling skeptics out there, to whom a modern dance performance sounds as appealing as being buried alive: Whether or not you'd like to spend your weekends watching the gyrations of Border collie owners, you've got to admit that the LLDE is diverse. It's real diversity, not workspeak diversity.

The example of Thomas Dwyer—the seventy-three-year-old former government employee—is a vivid, concrete symbol of a core organization value. It's a symbol both to supporters and to the dancers themselves. No one wants to participate in a "dance project" and be the only balding, middle-aged guy on a stage full of Twiggys. The LLDE's claim that diversity was a core value gained credibility from the details of Dwyer's example, rather than from an external source.

Beyond War

The use of vivid details is one way to create internal credibility—to weave sources of credibility into the idea itself. Another way is to use statistics. Since grade school, we've been taught to support our arguments with statistical evidence. But statistics tend to be eye-glazing. How can we use them while still managing to engage our audience?

Geoff Ainscow and other leaders of the Beyond War movement in the 1980s were determined to find a way to address the following paradox: When we see a child running with scissors, we wince. We shout at her to stop. Yet when we read newspaper articles about nuclear weapons—which have the power to destroy millions of children—it provokes, at best, only a moment of dismay.

Beyond War was started by a group of citizens who were alarmed by the arms race between the United States and the Soviet Union. At this point, the combined Soviet and American nuclear arsenals were sufficient to destroy the world multiple times. The Beyond War participants went door-to-door in their neighborhoods, hoping to galvanize a public outcry against the arms race. They struggled with the problem of how to make credible their belief that the arms race was out of control. How do you make clear to people the staggering destructive capability of the world's nuclear stockpile? It's so intangible, so invisible. And yet telling stories, or providing details, seems inadequate: Grappling with the nuclear arms race *requires* us to grapple with the scale of it. Scale relies on numbers.

Beyond War would arrange "house parties," in which a host family invited a group of friends and neighbors over, along with a Beyond War representative to speak to them. Ainscow recounts a simple demonstration that the group used in its presentations. He always carried a metal bucket to the gatherings. At the appropriate point in the presentation, he'd take a BB out of his pocket and drop it into the empty bucket. The BB made a loud clatter as it ricocheted and settled. Ainscow would say, "This is the Hiroshima bomb." He then spent a few minutes describing the devastation of the Hiroshima bomb—the miles of flattened buildings, the tens of thousands killed immediately, the larger number of people with burns or other long-term health problems.

Next, he'd drop ten BBs into the bucket. The clatter was louder and more chaotic. "This is the firepower of the missiles on *one* U.S. or Soviet nuclear submarine," he'd say.

Finally, he asked the attendees to close their eyes. He'd say, "This is the world's current arsenal of nuclear weapons." Then he poured 5,000 BBs into the bucket (one for every nuclear warhead in the world). The noise was startling, even terrifying. "The roar of the BBs went on and on," said Ainscow. "Afterward there was always dead silence."

This approach is an ingenious way to convey a statistic. Let's unpack it a bit. First, Beyond War had a core belief: "The public needs to wake up and do something about the arms race." Second, the group's members determined what was unexpected about the message: Everyone knew that the world's nuclear arsenal had grown since World War II, but no one realized the *scale* of the growth. Third, they had a statistic to make their belief credible—i.e., that the world had 5,000 nuclear warheads when a single one was enough to decimate a city. But the problem was that the number 5,000 means very little to people. The trick was to make this large number meaningful.

The final twist was the demonstration—the bucket and the BBs, which added a sensory dimension to an otherwise abstract concept. Furthermore, the demonstration was carefully chosen—BBs are weapons, and the sound of the BBs hitting the bucket was fittingly threatening.

Notice something that may be counterintuitive: The statistic didn't stick. It couldn't possibly stick. No one who saw the demonstration would remember, a week later, that there were 5,000 nuclear warheads in the world.

What did stick was the sudden, visceral awareness of a huge danger—the massive scale-up from World War II's limited atomic weaponry to the present worldwide arsenal. It was irrelevant whether there were 4,135 nuclear warheads or 9,437. The point was to hit people in the gut with the realization that *this was a problem that was out of control*.

This is the most important thing to remember about using statistics effectively. Statistics are rarely meaningful in and of themselves. Statistics will, and should, almost always be used to illustrate a *relationship*. It's more important for people to remember the relationship than the number.

The Human-Scale Principle

Another way to bring statistics to life is to contextualize them in terms that are more human, more everyday. As a scientific example, contrast the following two statements:

1. Scientists recently computed an important physical constraint to an extraordinary accuracy. To put the accuracy in perspective, imagine throwing a rock from the sun to the

earth and hitting the target within one third of a mile of dead center.

2. Scientists recently computed an important physical constraint to an extraordinary accuracy. To put the accuracy in perspective, imagine throwing a rock from New York to Los Angeles and hitting the target within two thirds of an inch of dead center.

Which statement seems more accurate?

As you may have guessed, the accuracy levels in both questions are exactly the same, but when different groups evaluated the two statements, 58 percent of respondents ranked the statistic about the sun to the earth as "very impressive." That jumped to 83 percent for the statistic about New York to Los Angeles. We have no human experience, no intuition, about the distance between the sun and the earth. The distance from New York to Los Angeles is much more tangible. (Though, frankly, it's still far from tangible. The problem is that if you make the distance more tangible—like a football field—then the accuracy becomes intangible. "Throwing a rock the distance of a football field to an accuracy of 3.4 microns" doesn't help.)

Stephen Covey, in his book *The 8th Habit*, describes a poll of 23,000 employees drawn from a number of companies and industries. He reports the poll's findings:

- Only 37 percent said they have a clear understanding of what their organization is trying to achieve and why.
- Only one in five was enthusiastic about their team's and their organization's goals.
- Only one in five said they had a clear "line of sight" between their tasks and their team's and organization's goals.
- Only 15 percent felt that their organization fully enables them to execute key goals.
- Only 20 percent fully trusted the organization they work for.

Pretty sobering stuff. It's also pretty abstract. You probably walk away from these stats thinking something like "There's a lot of dissatisfaction and confusion in most companies."

Then Covey superimposes a very human metaphor over the statistics. He says, "If, say, a soccer team had these same scores, only 4 of the 11 players on the field would know which goal is theirs. Only 2 of the 11 would care. Only 2 of the 11 would know what position they play and know exactly what they are supposed to do. And all but 2 players would, in some way, be competing against their own team members rather than the opponent."

The soccer analogy generates a human context for the statistics. It creates a sense of drama and a sense of movement. We can't help but imagine the actions of the two players trying to score a goal, being opposed at every stage by the rest of their team.

Why does the analogy work? It relies on our schema of soccer teams and the fact that this schema is somehow cleaner, more well-defined, than our schemas of organizations. It's more vivid to think of a lack of cooperation on a soccer team—where teamwork is paramount—than in a corporation. And this is exactly Covey's point: Corporations *should* operate like teams, but they don't. Humanizing the statistics gives the argument greater wallop.

As another example of the human-scale principle, take a mundane situation: figuring out whether a particular technological upgrade is worth the money. One example comes from Cisco, when it had to decide whether to add a wireless network for its employees. The cost of maintaining a wireless network was estimated at $500 per year per employee. That price sounds hefty—on the order of adding dental or vision insurance for all employees. But it's not a *benefit*, it's an *investment*. So how do you compute the value of an investment? You've got to decide whether you can get $501 worth of additional value from each employee each year after adding the network.

One Cisco employee figured out a better way to think about the investment: "If you believe you can increase an employee's productivity by one to two minutes a day, you've paid back the cost of wireless." On this scale, the investment is much easier to assess. Our intuition *works* at this scale. We can easily simulate scenarios where employees can save a few minutes from wireless access—for instance, sending someone a request for a forgotten document during a critical meeting.

Statistics aren't inherently helpful; it's the scale and context that make them so. Not many people have an intuition about whether wireless networking can generate $500 worth of marginal value per employee per year. The right scale changes everything. We saw that Concreteness allows people to bring their knowledge to bear—remember HP's simulation of a family at Disney World? Similarly, the human-scale principle allows us to bring our intuition to bear in assessing whether the content of a message is credible.

Statistics are a good source of internal credibility when they are used to illustrate relationships. In the introduction of this book, we discussed the example of the CSPI's campaign against saturated-fat-loaded movie popcorn. The relevant statistic was that a medium-sized bag of popcorn had 37 grams of saturated fat. So what? Is that good or bad?

Art Silverman, of the CSPI, cleverly placed the popcorn's saturated-fat content in a relevant context for comparison. He said that one bag of popcorn was equivalent to a whole day's worth of unhealthy eating. Silverman knew that most people would be appalled by this finding.

What if Silverman had been a sleazebag? He could have picked a food item that was notoriously unhealthy but relatively low in saturated fat, such as lollipops. "One bag of popcorn has the fat equivalent of 712,000 lollipops!" (Or an infinite number of lollipops, since they're fat-free.) This statistic is sleazy because it draws its power from sleight of hand involving different senses of unhealthy food. A sleazy movie-theater executive, to retaliate, might have changed the domain of comparison from saturated fat to some positive attribute of corn: "A bag of popcorn has as much Vitamin J as 71 pounds of broccoli!" (We made this up.)

These possibilities are examples of why writing about statistics filled us with anxiety. Particularly in the realm of politics, tinkering with statistics provides lucrative employment for untold numbers of issue advocates. Ethically challenged people with lots of analytical smarts can, with enough contortions, make almost any case from a given set of statistics.

Of course, let's also remember that it's easier to lie without statistics than with them. Data enforces boundaries. Unless people are unethical enough to make up data, the reality of the data constrains them. That's a good thing, but it still leaves a lot of wiggle room.

So what about the rest of us, who aren't spinmeisters? What do we do? We will still be tempted to put the best possible spin on our statistics. All of us do it. "I scored sixteen points for the church basketball team tonight!" (Not mentioned: twenty-two missed shots and the loss of the game.) "I'm five feet six." (Not mentioned: The three-inch heels.) "Revenue was up 10 percent this year, so I think I deserve a bonus." (Not mentioned: Profits tanked.)

When it comes to statistics, our best advice is to use them as input, not output. Use them to make up your mind on an issue. Don't make up your mind and then go looking for the numbers to support yourself—that's asking for temptation and trouble. But if we use statistics to help us make up our minds, we'll be in a great position to share the pivotal numbers with others, as did Geoff Ainscow and the Beyond War supporters.

CLINIC

Dealing with Shark Attack Hysteria

THE SITUATION: *Every few years the media go frothy over shark attacks. Shark attacks, however, remain extremely rare and do not vary much from one year to the next. So why do they consume so much media and public attention? The answer is that shark attacks spawn terrifying, dream-haunting stories like the following, from* The Oprah Winfrey Show:

> OPRAH: Bethany Hamilton loved to ride the waves. Surfing daily since she was 8 years old, Bethany was such a phenom, people said she had salt water running through her veins. At the young age of 13, Bethany was a rising star on the surfing circuit and had become a local celebrity, but what happened next landed Bethany in headlines around the world.
>
> It was early morning. Bethany was in the ocean lying on her board with her arm dangling in the water. Suddenly, a deadly fifteen-foot tiger shark seized her arm. Violently, he jerked and yanked it until her arm was ripped right off of her small body. Seconds later the shark and her entire arm were gone, and Bethany was left alone on her board surrounded by bloody water.

Imagine that you are forced to combat these vivid stories. Maybe you're the publicity director of the Save the Sharks Foundation, or maybe you're trying to convince your junior high school daughter that it's okay to go to the beach. How do you do it? You've got the truth on your side—attacks are very rare—but that's no guarantee that people will believe you. So what source of credibility do you tap to get people to believe you?

MESSAGE 1: We based this message on statistics published by the Florida Museum of Natural History:

You're more likely to drown on a beach in an area protected by a lifeguard than you are to be attacked by a shark, much less killed by one. In the United States in 2000, twelve people died in lifeguard-protected areas. There were no fatalities from sharks. (In a typical year there are only 0.4 fatalities.)

COMMENTS ON MESSAGE 1: This is okay but not great. This message taps internal credibility—the credibility of hard statistics. We have two comments: First, drowning does not seem like the right comparison to make, because many people may think drowning is a common cause of death. "Drowning is more common than shark attacks" does not feel particularly unexpected. (And maybe we're too skeptical, but the presence of the college-student lifeguard never struck us as an ironclad guarantee of safety.) Second, the statistical comparison—12 deaths versus 0.4—is good, but it isn't particularly vivid or meaningful on a human scale. It's unlikely that anyone would remember these numbers a week later.

MESSAGE 2: This message is also based on statistics published by the Florida Museum of Natural History:

Which of these animals is more likely to kill you?

A SHARK   A DEER

ANSWER: The deer is more likely to kill you. In fact, it's *300 times* more likely to kill you (via a collision with your car).

COMMENTS ON MESSAGE 2: We like the unexpected idea that Bambi is more dangerous than the evil shark, followed by the doubly unexpected statistic that Bambi is *wildly more dangerous* (*300 times more deadly!*). It's absurd to the point of being funny, and humor is a nice antidote to the fear generated by shark-attack stories. In a sense, we're fighting emotional associations with emotional associations (see the next chapter).

This message taps internal credibility with the statistic, but it also taps into the audience as a source of credibility. People in the audience know how much they fear deer when they're driving around—i.e., not much. Few of us are afraid to go out in the evening on account of lurking deer. We know that we don't fear deer, so why should we fear sharks? (This is more effective than comparing shark attacks with drowning—after all, most of us have at least a mild fear of drowning.)

SCORECARD

Checklist	Message 1	Message 2
Simple	✓	✓
Unexpected	-	✓
Concrete	✓	✓
Credible	✓	✓ ✓
Emotional	-	✓
Story	-	-

PUNCH LINE: When we use statistics, the less we rely on the actual numbers the better. The numbers inform us about the underlying relationship, but there are better ways to *illustrate* the underlying relationship than the numbers themselves. Juxtaposing the deer and the shark is similar to Ainscow's use of BBs in a bucket.

The Sinatra Test and Safexpress

We've seen that we can make our ideas more credible, on their own merits, by using compelling details or by using statistics. A third way to develop internal credibility is to use a particular type of example, an example that passes what we call the Sinatra Test.

In Frank Sinatra's classic "New York, New York," he sings about starting a new life in New York City, and the chorus declares, "If I can make it there, I'll make it anywhere." An example passes the Sinatra Test when *one example alone* is enough to establish credibility in a given domain. For instance, if you've got the security contract for Fort Knox, you're in the running for *any* security contract (even if you have no other clients). If you catered a White House function, you can compete for any catering contract. It's the Sinatra Test: If you can make it there, you can make it anywhere.

Safexpress, a family-owned business based in India, used the Sinatra Test to its advantage. Safexpress competes in the shipping business, where competition is fierce. And, while the competition led to low prices, there was a catch: Most shipping firms would not guarantee safe, on-time deliveries. With some firms, you couldn't be guaranteed that deliveries would be made, ever.

To distinguish itself from the competition, Safexpress assured its customers of safe, on-time delivery. International companies operating in India—companies accustomed to the reliability of FedEx—embraced Safexpress immediately. But Safexpress struggled to attract business from Indian companies that weren't accustomed to paying higher rates. Rubal Jain, a member of the founding family of Safexpress, was determined to make inroads with Indian companies.

To do so, Jain set his sights on winning the account of a major Bollywood studio. When Jain proposed that Safexpress distribute the studio's films, the reaction was "Are you kidding?"

The skepticism was predictable and plausible: Piracy is a major concern in India, as it is in the rest of the world, so distribution is mission-critical. If films end up "misplaced" en route, bootlegged versions show up a few weeks later on street corners. This risk wasn't one that the movie studio could take.

Fortunately, Jain had a powerful credential ready. Safexpress had handled the release of the fifth *Harry Potter* book—every *Potter* book in every bookstore in India had been delivered there by Safexpress, an insanely complicated delivery: All the books had to arrive in stores by 8 A.M. on the morning of the release. Not too early, or the bookstore owners might try to sell them early and the secret would be blown; and not too late, or the bookstore owners would be irate at lost sales. Also, the *Potter* books needed the same piracy protections as the studio's films—there could be no leaks.

And Jain had a second story. He knew from an earlier conversation that the Bollywood studio executive had a brother who had recently taken his high school board exams. After telling the *Harry Potter* story, Jain mentioned, "By the way, we also safely delivered the examination papers for your brother's boards and carried the return answer sheets." Safexpress handles the distribution of all the central examinations for high school and university admissions.

Two months later, the deal was signed.

Both of Jain's stories passed the Sinatra Test. Jain could have used statistics instead of stories— "98.84 percent of our deliveries arrive on time." Or he could have drawn on an external source of credibility, such as a testimonial from the CEO of a multinational company: "We've used Safexpress for all our deliveries in India and we've found them to be an excellent service provider." Both of these are good credibility-boosters. But there is something *extraordinary* about being the company that carries completed board exams and the latest *Harry Potter* book. Their power comes from their concreteness rather than from numbers or authority. These stories make you think, "If Safexpress can make it there, they can make it anywhere."

Edible Fabrics

For an example that unites all three of the "internal credibility" sources—details, statistics, and the Sinatra Test—we can turn to Bill McDonough, an environmentalist known for helping companies improve both the environment and the bottom line.

Most executives tend to be skeptical and suspicious when approached by an environmentalist, even a "business-friendly" environmentalist like McDonough. To overcome such skepticism—to prove that there can be perfect consistency between business goals and environmental goals—McDonough tells a story that passes the Sinatra Test.

The story goes as follows. In 1993, McDonough and a chemist, Michael Braungart, were hired by the Swiss textile manufacturer Rohner Textil, which produces the fabrics for Steelcase chairs. Their mission was one that most people in the textile industry considered impossible: Create a manufacturing process without using toxic chemicals.

The textile industry routinely deals with hazardous chemicals. Most dye colors contain toxic elements. In fact, the trimmings from Rohner Textil's factory—the excess cloth not used on the chairs—contained so many questionable chemicals that the Swiss government classified them as hazardous waste. Furthermore, the trimmings couldn't be buried or burned in Switzerland—to comply with government regulations, they had to be exported—shipped to a country with laxer regulations, such as Spain. (Note the vivid, concrete detail.) McDonough said, "If your trimmings are declared hazardous waste but you can sell what's in the middle, you don't need to be a rocket scientist to know you're selling hazardous waste."

To tackle this problem—eliminating toxic chemicals from the furniture-manufacturing process—McDonough needed to find a willing partner in the chemical industry. He had to provide Rohner Textil with a source for clean chemicals that would fit the company's production needs. So he and Braungart started approaching executives in the chemical industry. They said, "We'd like to see all products in the future be as safe as pediatric pharmaceuticals. We'd like our babies to be able to suck on them and get health and not sickness."

They asked chemical factories to open their books and talk about how the chemicals were manufactured. McDonough told the companies, "Don't tell us 'it's proprietary and legal.' If we don't know what it is, we're not using it." Sixty chemical companies turned them down. Finally, the chairman of one firm, Ciba-Geigy, said okay.

McDonough and Braungart studied 8,000 chemicals commonly used in the textile industry. They measured each chemical against a set of safety criteria. Of the chemicals they tested, 7,962 failed. They were left with 38 chemicals—but those 38 were "safe enough to eat," according to McDonough. (Note the concrete detail—"safe enough to eat"—plus a statistic that establishes a relationship—a tiny number of good chemicals out of a larger number of toxic chemicals.)

Amazingly, using just those 38 chemicals, they were able to create a complete line of fabrics, containing every color but black. The fabric they chose was made from natural materials—wool and a plant fiber called ramie. When the production process went online, inspectors from the Swiss government came to check the water flowing out of the plant to make sure chemical emissions were within legal limits. "At first, the inspectors thought their equipment had broken," McDonough says. The instruments were detecting nothing in the water. Then the inspectors tested the water flowing into the factory, which was Swiss drinking water, and found that the equipment was fine. McDonough says, "The fabrics during the production process were further filtering the water."

McDonough's new process wasn't just safer, it was cheaper. Manufacturing costs shrank 20 percent. The savings came, in part, from the reduced hassle and expense of dealing with toxic chemicals. Workers no longer had to wear protective clothing. And the scraps—instead of being shipped off to Spain for burial—were converted into felt, which was sold to Swiss farmers and gardeners for crop insulation.

This story is remarkable. Think about all the memorable elements: The impossible mission. The elimination of all but 38 of 8,000 chemicals. The factory's water turned so clean that Swiss inspectors thought their instruments were broken. The scraps were transformed from hazardous waste into crop insulation. The idea that this fabric was "safe enough to eat." And the happy business result— workers made safer and costs down 20 percent.

If McDonough approaches any business, in any industry, with a suggestion for a more environment-friendly process, this story will give him enormous credibility. It easily clears the bar set by the Sinatra Test.

So far we've talked about creating credibility by drawing on external sources—authorities and antiauthorities. And we've talked about creating credibility by drawing on sources inside the message itself— by using details and statistics and examples that pass the Sinatra Test. But there's one remaining source of credibility that we haven't discussed. And it may be the most powerful source of all.

Where's the Beef?

One of the most brilliant television ad campaigns of all time was launched by Wendy's in 1984. The first commercial opens on three elderly women standing together at a counter. On the counter there's a hamburger on a plate, and they're gawking at it, because it's huge— about a foot in diameter.

"It certainly is a big bun," says the woman on the left.

"A *very* big bun," echoes the one in the center.

"A big, *fluffy* bun," says the first.

"A *very* big fluffy . . ."

There's a pause as the woman in the middle lifts the top half of the bun and reveals a meager, overcooked beef patty and a single pickle. The patty is dwarfed by the bun.

For the first time, we hear from the woman on the right, played by eighty-year-old Clara Peller. She squints through her glasses and says, cantankerously, "Where's the beef?"

The announcer says, "Some hamburger places give you a *lot* less beef on a fluffy bun. . . ."

Peller: "Where's the beef?"

Announcer: "The Wendy's Single has more beef than the Whopper or the Big Mac. At Wendy's you get more beef and less bun."

Peller: "Hey! Where's the beef?" She peers over the counter. "I don't think there's anybody back there."

There's a lot to love about these commercials. They're funny and well produced. Clara Peller became a minor celebrity. More remarkably, the ads highlighted a true advantage of Wendy's hamburgers: They really did have more beef. The ads were a refreshing departure from the standard advertiser tool kit that attempts to paint powerful but irrelevant emotions on consumer goods—for instance, associating a mother's love of her children with a particular brand of fabric softener. Wendy's did something more admirable: It highlighted a genuine advantage of its product and presented it in an enjoyable way.

The ads had a big impact. According to polls taken by Wendy's, the number of customers who believed that Wendy's Single was larger than the Whopper or the Big Mac increased by 47 percent in the two months after the commercial aired. During the first full year after the ads ran, Wendy's revenues rose 31 percent.

The claim Wendy's had made was that its burgers had more beef. This information was probably not something most people would have given much thought to before. Certainly it was not common sense at the time. So how did Wendy's make this claim credible?

Notice that something different is going on here. This message doesn't draw on external credibility—Wendy's didn't invite Larry Bird to weigh in on burger sizes. (Nor did it use an antiauthority, like an obese burger-eating giant.) It doesn't draw on internal credibility, either, quoting a statistic like "11 percent more beef!" Instead, the commercials developed a brand-new source of credibility: the audience. Wendy's outsourced its credibility to its customers.

The spots implicitly challenged customers to verify Wendy's claims: *See for yourself—look at our burgers versus McDonald's burgers. You'll notice the size difference!* To use scientific language, Wendy's made a falsifiable claim. Any customer with a ruler and a scale could have verified the claim's truth value. (Though Wendy's advantage was sufficiently substantial that just eyeballing the difference was enough.)

This challenge—asking customers to test a claim for themselves—is a "testable credential." Testable credentials can provide an enormous credibility boost, since they essentially allow your audience members to "try before they buy."

Testable Credentials

Testable credentials have a colorful history in urban legends. In the 1990s, Snapple struggled to shake rumors that it supported the Ku Klux Klan. Rumormongers thought they had a few pieces of "evidence" on their side: "Look on any bottle of Snapple—there's a picture of a slave ship on the front!" Doubters were also encouraged to look for the strange symbol showing a *K* inside a circle—allegedly, evidence of the Klan's ownership.

Sure enough, Snapple's labels *did* feature a picture of a ship and a *K* in a circle. They just had nothing to do with the Klan. The ship was from an engraving of the Boston Tea Party. The circled *K* is a symbol for "kosher." But some uninformed people saw these symbols and bought into the rumors.

Notice that the Snapple rumor provides a kind of bait-and-switch version of "Where's the Beef?" Wendy's says, "See for yourself—our burgers have more beef." The Rumormongers say, "See for yourself—there's a circled *K*. Therefore Snapple supports the Ku Klux Klan." The validity of the see-for-yourself claim causes some people to leap, illogically, to the rumormongers' conclusion. This is how testable credentials can backfire—the "see for yourself" step can be valid, while the resulting conclusion can be entirely invalid.

Testable credentials are useful in many domains. For example, take the question "Are you better off now than you were four years ago?" Ronald Reagan famously posed this question to the audience during his 1980 presidential debate with Jimmy Carter. Reagan could have focused on statistics—the high inflation rate, the loss of jobs, the rising interest rates. But instead of selling his case he deferred to his audience.

Another example of testable credentials comes from Jim Thompson, the founder of the Positive Coaching Alliance (PCA). The mission of the PCA is to emphasize that youth sports should not be about winning at all costs; it should be about learning life lessons.

The PCA holds positive-coaching seminars for youth sports coaches. At the seminars, trainers use the analogy of an "Emotional Tank" to get coaches to think about the right ratio of praise, support, and critical feedback. "The Emotional Tank is like the gas tank of an automobile. If your car's tank is empty, you can't drive very far. If your Emotional Tank is empty, you are not going to be able to perform at your best."

After the Emotional Tank analogy is introduced, the trainers begin an exercise. First, they ask the coaches to imagine that the person next to them has just flubbed a key play in the game. The coaches are challenged to say something to the person to *drain* his Emotional Tank. Since clever put-downs are a staple of many sports interactions, this exercise is embraced with noticeable enthusiasm. Thompson says, "The room fills with laughter as coaches get into the exercise, sometimes with great creativity."

Then the coaches are asked to imagine that someone else has made the same mistake, but now they're in charge of *filling* that person's Emotional Tank instead of draining it. This generates a more muted response. Thompson says, "The room often gets very quiet, and you finally hear a feeble, 'Nice try!' "

Observing their own behavior, the coaches learn the lesson—how they found it easier to criticize than to support, to think of ten clever insults rather than a single consolation. Thompson found a way to transform his point into a testable credential, something the coaches could experience for themselves.

CLINIC

Our Intuition Is Flawed, but Who Wants to Believe That?

THE SITUATION: *People often trust their intuition, but our intuition is flawed by identifiable biases. Still, most people feel pretty good about their intuition, and it's hard to convince them otherwise. This is the uphill battle faced by psychologists who study decision-making. Pretend that you're the editor of an introductory psychology textbook, and you're looking at two competing ways of explaining the concept of "availability bias."*

• • • •

MESSAGE 1: Get ready to make a few predictions. Which of the following events kill more people: Homicide or suicide? Floods or tuberculosis? Tornadoes or asthma? Take a second to think about your answers.

You might have thought that homicide, floods, and tornadoes are more common. People generally do. But in the United States there are 50 percent more deaths from suicide than from homicide, nine times more deaths from tuberculosis than from floods, and eighty times more deaths from asthma than from tornadoes.

So why do people predict badly? Because of the availability bias. The *availability bias* is a natural tendency that causes us, when estimating the probability of a particular event, to judge the event's probability by its availability in our memory. We intuitively think that events are more likely when they are easier to remember. But often the things we remember are not an accurate summary of the world.

We may remember things better because they evoke more emotion, not because they are more frequent. We may remember things better because the media spend more time covering them (perhaps because they provide more vivid images), not because they are more common. The availability bias may lead our intuition astray, prompting us to treat unusual things as common and unlikely things as probable.

COMMENTS ON MESSAGE 1: This passage uses a simple but effective testable credential: Which problem do *you* think kills more people? With any luck, readers will botch at least one of the predictions, thus illustrating for themselves the reality of the availability bias.

• • • •

MESSAGE 2: Here's an alternative passage illustrating the availability bias that is more typical of introductory textbooks:

The *availability bias* is a natural tendency that causes us, when estimating the probability of a particular event, to judge the event's probability by its availability in our memory. We intuitively think that events are more likely when they're easier to remember. But often the things we remember are not an accurate summary of the world. For example, in a study by decision researchers at the University of Oregon, experimental participants thought that 20 percent more people died in homicides than in suicides, when the truth is that there are 50 percent more deaths from suicides. Subjects thought that more people were killed by floods than tuberculosis, but nine times more people are killed by tuberculosis. Subjects believed that approximately as many people were killed by tornadoes as by asthma, but there are eighty times more deaths from asthma.

People remember things better because they evoke more emotion, not because they are more frequent. People remember things better because the media spend more time covering them (perhaps because they provide more vivid images), not because they are more common. The availability bias may lead our intuition astray, prompting us to treat unusual things as common and unlikely things as probable.

COMMENTS ON MESSAGE 2: This is less involving. You could imagine a student reading the second paragraph—which gives away the punch line that asthma kills eighty times more people than tornadoes—and thinking, Wow, *those research participants were dumb.* It's much more powerful to experience the effect for yourself.

SCORECARD

Checklist	Message 1	Message 2
Simple	✓	✓
Unexpected	✓	-
Concrete	✓	✓
Credible	✓✓	✓
Emotional	-	-
Story	-	-

PUNCH LINE: Using testable credentials allows people to try out an idea for themselves.

Rookie Orientation

Let's shift to a different sports domain: the National Basketball Association. Imagine that it's your job to educate incoming NBA rookies about the danger of AIDS. NBA players are young men—rookies are often under twenty-one. And they are sudden celebrities, with all the attention that goes with this new fame. They've heard about AIDS their entire lives, so the risk is not that they're unaware of AIDS; the risk is that the circumstances of their lives prompt them to drop their guard for a night.

How do you make the threat of AIDS credible and immediate? Think through the possible sources of credibility. You could draw on external credibility—a celebrity/expert like Magic Johnson, or an antiauthority, such as an athlete in the terminal stages of AIDS. You could use statistics on a human scale (perhaps the odds of contracting AIDS from a single encounter with a stranger). You could use vivid details—an athlete could recount how his normal safe-sex vigilance was eroded by a particularly wild night of partying. Any of these could be quite effective. But what if you wanted to move the source of credibility inward, inside the heads of the players? The NBA came up with an ingenious way to do just that.

A few weeks before the NBA season begins, all the rookie players are required to meet in Tarrytown, New York, for a mandatory orientation session. They're essentially locked in a hotel for six days: no pagers, no cell phones. The rookies are taught about life in the big leagues—everything from how to deal with the media to how to make sensible investments with their new riches.

One year, despite the secrecy surrounding the orientation, a group of female fans staked out the location. On the first night of the orientation, they were hanging out in the hotel bar and restaurant, dressed to be noticed. The players were pleased by the attention. There was a lot of flirting, and the players made plans to meet up with some of the women later in the orientation.

The next morning, the rookies dutifully showed up for their session. They were surprised to see the female fans in front of the room. The women introduced themselves again, one by one. "Hi, I'm Sheila and I'm HIV positive." "Hi, I'm Donna and I'm HIV positive."

Suddenly the talk about AIDS clicked for the rookies. They saw how life could get out of control, how a single night could cause a lifetime of regret.

Contrast the NBA's approach with the NFL's approach. At the NFL's orientation one year, league personnel had every rookie put a condom on a banana. No doubt eye-rolling was epidemic. Later, two women—former football groupies—talked about how they would try to seduce players, hoping to get pregnant. The women's session was powerful—it was a well-designed message. But what's more likely to stick with someone: hearing about someone who fooled someone else, or being fooled yourself?

How do we get people to believe our ideas? We've got to find a source of credibility to draw on. Sometimes the wellsprings are dry, as Barry Marshall discovered in his quest to cure the ulcer. Drawing on external credibility didn't work—the endorsement of his supervisors and his institution in Perth didn't seem to be enough. Drawing on internal credibility didn't work—his careful marshaling of data and detail still didn't help him clear the bar. In the end, what he did was draw on the audience's credibility—he essentially "modeled" a testable credential by gulping a glass of bacteria. The implicit challenge was: See for yourself—if you drink this gunk, you'll get an ulcer, just like I did.

It's not always obvious which wellspring of credibility we should draw from. What Marshall showed so brilliantly was perseverance—knowing when it was time to draw on a different well. In this chapter we've seen that the most obvious sources of credibility—external validation and statistics—aren't always the best. A few vivid details might be more persuasive than a barrage of statistics. An antiauthority might work better than an authority. A single story that passes the Sinatra Test might overcome a mountain of skepticism. It's inspirational to know that a medical genius like Marshall had to climb over the same hurdles with his idea as we'll have to climb with ours—and to see that he eventually prevailed, to the benefit of us all.

CHAPTER 5

EMOTIONAL

Mother Teresa once said, "If I look at the mass, I will never act. If I look at the one, I will." In 2004, some researchers at Carnegie Mellon University decided to see whether most people act like Mother Teresa.

The researchers wanted to see how people responded to an opportunity to make a charitable contribution to an abstract cause versus a charitable contribution to a single person. They offered participants five dollars to complete a survey about their usage of various technology products. (The survey was irrelevant; the point was to ensure that the participants would have some cash on hand to consider donating to charity.)

When people finished the survey, they received their payment in five one-dollar bills. They also received, unexpectedly, an envelope and a charity-request letter giving them an opportunity to donate some of their money to Save the Children, a charity that focuses on the well-being of children worldwide.

The researchers tested two versions of the request letter. The first version featured statistics about the magnitude of the problems facing children in Africa, such as the following:

- Food shortages in Malawi are affecting more than 3 million children.
- In Zambia, severe rainfall deficits have resulted in a 42 percent drop in maize production from 2000. As a result, an estimated 3 million Zambians face hunger.
- Four million Angolans—one third of the population—have been forced to flee their homes.
- More than 11 million people in Ethiopia need immediate food assistance.

The other version of the letter gave information about a single young girl:

- Any money that you donate will go to Rokia, a seven-year-old girl from Mali, Africa. Rokia is desperately poor and faces the threat of severe hunger or even starvation. Her life will be changed for the better as a result of your financial gift. With your support, and the support of other caring sponsors, Save the Children will work with Rokia's family and other members of the community to help feed and educate her and provide basic medical care and hygiene education.

The researchers gave participants one of the two different letters, then left them alone. They chose how much money, if any, to put back into the envelope, then they sealed the envelope and handed it back to a researcher.

On average, the people who read the statistics contributed $1.14. The people who read about Rokia contributed $2.38—more than twice as much. It seems that most people have something in common with Mother Teresa: When it comes to our hearts, one individual trumps the masses.

The researchers believed that the smaller donations for the statistical letter could be a result of what they called the "drop in the bucket effect." If people felt overwhelmed by the scale of the problem, their small donations might have seemed meaningless. But here's where things get even more interesting. The researchers decided to give a third group of people *both* sets of information—the statistics and the story about Rokia. The researchers wondered whether people who got all the information would give more, on average, than the $2.38 that had been given by the Rokia group. Perhaps the combination of statistics and stories—the power of individual need coupled with the statistical scale of the problem— would inspire a whole new level of giving.

Nope. The people who received both letters gave $1.43, almost a dollar less than the people who got the Rokia story alone. Somehow the statistics—evidence of massive human suffering in Africa— actually made people less charitable. What was going on?

The researchers theorized that thinking about statistics shifts people into a more analytical frame of mind. When people think analytically, they're less likely to think emotionally. And the researchers believed it was people's emotional response to Rokia's plight that led them to act.

To prove this argument, they ran a second study. In this study they primed some people to think in an analytical way by asking questions such as, "If an object travels at five feet per minute, then by your calculations how many feet will it travel in 360 seconds?" Other people were primed to think in terms of feelings: "Please write down one word to describe how you feel when you hear the word 'baby.'"

Then both groups were given the Rokia letter. And, confirming the researchers' theory, the analytically primed people gave less. When people were primed to *feel* before they read about Rokia, they gave $2.34, about the same as before. But when they were primed to *calculate* before they read about Rokia, they gave $1.26.

These results are shocking. The mere *act of calculation* reduced people's charity. Once we put on our analytical hat, we react to emotional appeals differently. We hinder our ability to feel.

I n the last chapter, we discussed how to convince people that our ideas are credible, how to make them believe. Belief counts for a lot, but belief isn't enough. For people to take action, they have to *care*.

Everyone believes there is tremendous human suffering in Africa; there's no doubt about the facts. But belief does not necessarily make people care enough to act. Everyone believes that eating lots of fatty food leads to health problems; there's no doubt about the facts. But the belief does not make people care enough to act.

Charities have long since figured out the Mother Teresa effect— they know that donors respond better to individuals than to abstract causes. You don't give to "African poverty," you sponsor a specific child. (In fact, the idea of sponsoring a child as a charitable hook dates back to the 1950s, when a young Christian minister encouraged Americans to sponsor needy Korean orphans.) The concept works with animals, too. At Farm Sanctuary, a nonprofit organization that fights to reduce cruel treatment of farm animals, donors can "adopt a chicken" ($10 per month), a goat ($25), or a cow ($50).

No one wants to donate to the General Administrative Fund of a charity. It's easy to understand, intellectually, why general funds would be needed—someone's got to buy the staples—but it's hard to generate a lot of passion for office supplies.

Charities have learned how to arouse sympathy and compassion in donors—and thank goodness they're good at it, because their skills ease a lot of suffering. But "making people care" isn't something that only charities need to do. Managers have to make people care enough to work long and hard on complex tasks. Teachers have to make students care about literature. Activists have to make people care about city council initiatives.

This chapter tackles the emotional component of stickiness, but it's not about pushing people's emotional buttons, like some kind of movie tearjerker. Rather, the goal of making messages "emotional" is to make people care. Feelings inspire people to act.

As an example, most teenagers believe that cigarette smoking is dangerous. There's no credibility problem with that message. Yet teenagers still take up smoking. So how do you transform their belief into action? You have to make them care. And, in 1998, someone finally figured out how to do that.

The Truth

The commercial starts with a shot of a city street in New York City. The footage is video, not film — it's a bit dark, a bit unprofessional. It feels like a documentary, not a commercial. A caption flashes at the bottom of the screen: "Outside the headquarters of a major tobacco company."

An eighteen-wheeler pulls up in front of the building, and a group of teenagers jump out. The teens begin to unload long white sacks marked "Body Bag." They stack the bags on top of one another near the edge of the building. As the commercial progresses, the pile of body bags gets bigger and bigger. By the end of the ad, there are hundreds of bags in the pile. One of the teens shouts at the building through a megaphone, "Do you know how many people tobacco kills every day?" The daily death toll is revealed to be 1,800 — the number of body bags the teens have piled up in front of the tobacco headquarters.

This ad is part of a series of ads called the Truth campaign. The campaign was launched by the American Legacy Foundation, which was formed in November 1998 after forty-six state attorneys-general settled a lawsuit against major U.S. tobacco companies.

You can't watch the Truth ads without getting angry at tobacco companies. After the ads began airing, Philip Morris invoked a special Big Tobacco "anti-vilification" clause to have the spots yanked from the air. The tobacco companies inserted this clause in the settlements of a number of antitobacco lawsuits; it gives them some veto power over how the settlement money can be spent on antismoking advertising. "We felt that [the Truth ads] are not consistent with the focus and mission of the American Legacy Foundation," said Carolyn Levy, Philip Morris's senior vice president for youth-smoking prevention, in reference to the censorship effort.

One translation of this complaint: The ads were working.

Meanwhile, another series of antismoking ads started to run. As part of the tobacco settlement, Philip Morris agreed to air its own series of antismoking ads. The Philip Morris tagline was "Think. Don't Smoke."

Two campaigns were launched, almost simultaneously, with two different approaches. This juxtaposition set up an exciting, head-to-head horse race in the marketplace of ideas. In fact, in June 2002, an article in the *American Journal of Public Health* surveyed 10,692 teenagers to compare the Truth campaign with "Think. Don't Smoke."

It turns out that some horses run better than others. When kids were asked to recall any antitobacco advertising they had seen, the Truth campaign was remembered spontaneously by 22 percent of them; the Think campaign by 3 percent. What's particularly striking about this statistic is that when the kids were *prompted* with information from the campaigns, more than 70 percent of them remembered seeing *both*. In other words, teens had seen both ads on TV, but one stuck better than the other. Something about the Truth campaign was spontaneously memorable.

Memory is important, but it's only the first step. What about action? When the survey asked kids whether they were likely to smoke a cigarette during the next year, those who were exposed to the Truth campaign were 66 percent less likely to smoke. Those who were exposed to "Think. Don't Smoke" were 36 percent *more* likely to smoke! Tobacco execs must have taken the news quite hard.

It wasn't just surveys that registered the difference. A study measured teen smoking in Florida, where the Truth campaign had its debut, versus the rest of the country. After two years of the campaign, smoking among high school students dropped by 18 percent and among middle school students by 40 percent. (About half of this decline may have been associated with a rise in cigarette taxes during the time of the study.)

What happened here? It's the Save the Children example revisited. What is the "Think. Don't Smoke" campaign about? Er, thinking. It's the Analytical Hat. Remember what happened with contributions to Rokia when donors were asked to think analytically before donating?

What's the Truth campaign about? It's about tapping into anti-authority resentment, the classic teenage emotion. Once, teens smoked to rebel against The Man. Thanks to the ingenious framing of the Truth campaign—which paints a picture of a duplicitous Big Tobacco—teens now rebel against The Man by *not* smoking.

The Truth campaign isn't about rational decision-making; it's about rebellion. And it made a lot of teens care enough to do something. In this case, that something was nothing.

Semantic Stretch and the Power of Association

So far we've been talking about what you might expect from a chapter on emotion—complex, fundamental human emotions like empathy (Rokia) and anger (the Truth). But the main question of this chapter is even more basic: How do we make people care about our messages? The good news is that to make people care about our ideas we don't have to produce emotion from an absence of emotion. In fact, many ideas use a sort of piggybacking strategy, associating themselves with emotions that already exist.

Consider the following sentence from a movie review: "*Rashomon* can be seen as a cinematic extension of Einstein's theory of relativity." *Rashomon* is a classic 1950 film by the Japanese director Akira

Kurosawa. In the film, four different characters describe the same event—a murder and rape—from their own perspectives. The movie is told in a series of flashbacks, as each of the characters recounts his or her version of events. But the characters' tales are self-serving and contradictory, and at the end of the movie the viewer is still uncertain about what actually happened. The movie questions the existence of absolute truth—or, at least, our ability to uncover it.

So the movie reviewer, in the quote above, was comparing *Rashomon*'s "relative truth" to Einstein's theory of relativity. But Einstein's theory of relativity wasn't designed to say that "everything is relative." In fact, its actual meaning was essentially the opposite. The theory was designed to explain how the laws of physics are *identical in every frame of reference*. From Einstein's view, things don't look unpredictable; they look surprisingly orderly.

Why did the reviewer link *Rashomon* with relativity? This reference doesn't look like an appeal to Einstein's authority; it claims that *Rashomon* is the cinematic "equivalent" of Einstein's theory. Instead, the analogy seems intended to create a sense of awe—when we watch *Rashomon*, it implies, we will be in the presence of something profound.

The theory of relativity is borrowed, as an association, because it lends an aura of emotional resonance—profundity, awe—to the movie. The movie review above is just one example among thousands. "Relativity" becomes, in a sense, a color on the idea palette. When you want to conjure up awe, you dab your brush into "relativity." Other scientific terms—the "uncertainty principle," "chaos theory," the "quantum leap" of quantum mechanics—are also colors on this palette.

In 1929, Einstein protested, "Philosophers play with the word, like a child with a doll. . . . It does not mean that everything in life is relative." To Einstein's chagrin, the number of people trying to tap into the resonance of "relativity" began to exceed the number of people who were trying to understand relativity.

When associations to certain terms are drawn repeatedly—sometimes with precision, sometimes with crudeness—the effect is to dilute the power of the terms and their underlying concepts. When everyone paints with lime green, lime green no longer stands out.

Research conducted at Stanford and Yale shows that this process—exploiting terms and concepts for their emotional associations—is a common characteristic of communication. People tend to overuse any idea or concept that delivers an emotional kick. The research labeled this overuse "semantic stretch."

Let's look at a nonscientific example: the word "unique." "Unique" used to mean one of a kind. "Unique" was special.

The researchers used a database to examine every newspaper article in each of the top fifty newspapers in the United States over a twenty-year period. During this time, the percentage of articles in which something was described as "unique" increased by 73 percent. So either there's a lot more unique stuff in the world today or the "uniqueness bar" has been lowered.

Perhaps some skeptics, contemplating robot vacuum cleaners or Paris Hilton, would protest, "Hey, there *is* a lot more unique stuff in the world these days." But at the same time that the word "unique" was rising in popularity, the word "unusual" was falling. In 1985, articles were more than twice as likely to use the word "unusual" as the word "unique." By 2005, the two words were about equally likely to be used.

Unique things should be a subset of unusual things—unique (i.e., one of a kind) is about as unusual as you can get. So if there really were more unique things today, we should see more "unusual" things as well. The fact that unusual things are getting less common makes the rise in unique things look like a case of semantic stretch. What we used to call "unusual" we now stretch and call "unique."

So where's the emotion in "relativity" and in "unique"? Here's the punch line: The most basic way to make people care is to form an association between something they don't yet care about and something they do care about. We all naturally practice the tactic of association. What "relativity" and "unique" teach us is that in using associations we can overuse colors. Over time, associations get overused and become diluted in value; people end up saying things like "This is really, truly unique."

The superlatives of one generation—groovy, awesome, cool, phat—fade over time because they've been associated with too many things. When you hear your father call something "cool," coolness loses its punch. When your finance professor starts using the word "dude," you must eliminate the word from your vocabulary. Using associations, then, is an arms race of sorts. The other guy builds a missile, so you have to build two. If he's "unique," you've got to be "super-unique."

This emotional-association arms race creates problems for people who are trying to make others care. In fact, as we'll see, the arms race essentially bankrupted the term "sportsmanship."

Fighting Semantic Stretch: The Case of "Sportsmanship"

In the last chapter, we discussed the coaching seminars held by Jim Thompson, the founder of the Positive Coaching Alliance (PCA). Since 1988, when he founded the PCA, Thompson has struggled with an important problem. How do you clean up the bad behavior often associated with youth sports? In grappling with this problem, Thompson had to confront the issue of semantic stretch.

The tennis player John McEnroe was once the poster child of poor sportsmanship, with his racket-throwing and bratty arguments with officials. But today McEnroe's behavior wouldn't raise an eyebrow at many youth sports games. Bad behavior is now common not only among athletes but also among parents and other spectators. According to the National Alliance for Youth Sports, nearly 15 percent of youth sports games involved a confrontation between parents or coaches and officials, up from 5 percent a few years ago.

Sportsmanship was once a powerful idea in athletics, but Thompson felt that it had become a weak term. "Sportsmanship trophies are seen as consolation prizes for losers," he says. One woman told Thompson that her high school basketball coach said that if his players ever won a sportsmanship trophy, they'd have to run laps. Thompson adds, "Sportsmanship seems like it is mostly about not doing something bad: 'Don't yell at officials. Don't break the rules.' But it's not enough to simply refuse to do bad things. We need to expect much more of participants in youth sports. Unfortunately, 'Be a good sport!' is not the rallying cry that we need to transform youth sports."

Everyone enjoys hearing about real examples of good sportsmanship. Thompson uses the example of Lance Armstrong, who reacted unexpectedly when one of his chief opponents, Jan Ullrich, crashed during the Tour de France. Instead of taking advantage of this lucky break to increase his lead, Armstrong slowed down and waited for Ullrich to remount. He later said that he rode better when he was competing with a great athlete like Ullrich. *That's* sportsmanship.

Thompson knew that people still admired the underlying ideals of sportsmanship. Parents *did* want their kids to learn respect and manners from athletics. Coaches *did* want to be mentors, not just victorious taskmasters. Kids *did* want their teams to be respected by others. All three groups sometimes slipped up and acted like jerks. But Thompson saw that the need and the desire for sportsmanship remained, even though the term "sportsmanship" had lost its ability to motivate good behavior.

"Sportsmanship" had been stretched too far. Like "relativity," it had migrated far afield from its original meaning. It used to refer to the kind of behavior that Lance Armstrong showed Jan Ullrich. But over time the term was stretched to include unimpressive, nonchivalrous behavior, like losing without whining too much or making it through an entire game without assaulting a referee.

Thompson and the PCA needed a different way of encouraging people, not just to avoid bad behavior but to embrace good behavior.

They called it Honoring the Game. People care about sports, they care about the Game. It's a way of making the point that the Game and its integrity are *larger* than the individual participants. "Honoring the Game" is a kind of sports patriotism. It implies that you *owe your sport* basic respect. Armstrong wasn't being a "good sport"; he was Honoring the Game. And Honoring the Game also works for people other than players. It reminds anyone that sports is a civic institution. It's unseemly to mess with an institution. It's dishonorable.

Is there any proof that Honoring the Game works? Consider the data gathered by a basketball league in Dallas, Texas: "In the 2002 basketball season, on average there was a technical foul called every fifteen games. Since that time, we've conducted six Double-Goal Coach workshops. In the 2004 basketball season, there was a technical foul called every fifty-two games." A baseball league in Northern California found that after Positive Coaching training, there was a dramatic reduction (90 percent!) in the number of people who were ejected from games for bad behavior. Team morale improved so much that the number of players enrolling in the league increased by 20 percent. The only complaint was that they were running out of fields.

Thompson doesn't want to change just the culture of youth sports. He wants to change the culture of all sports: "I have a fantasy. I'm watching the World Series and a manager comes rushing onto the field to berate an umpire who made a call he disagrees with. On national TV, Bob Costas says, 'That's really too bad to see the manager dishonoring the game of baseball that way.'" (As a side note, notice how wonderfully concrete this vision is.)

Youth sports hasn't been purged of discourtesy, but Thompson is making a tangible difference in the places he's reached. And, with Honoring the Game, he has managed to sidestep semantic stretch and peg an idea that makes people care.

The lesson for the rest of us is that if we want to make people care, we've got to tap into the things they care about. When everybody taps into the same thing, an arms race emerges. To avoid it, we've either got to shift onto new turf, as Thompson did, or find associations that are distinctive for our ideas.

Appealing to Self-Interest

We're searching for ways to make people care about our ideas—to make them care about the African child Rokia, about smoking, about charity, about sportsmanship. We make people care by appealing to the things that matter to them.

And what matters to people? So far, we've dealt with associations, but there's a more direct answer. In fact, it might be the most obvious answer of all. What matters to people? People matter to themselves. It will come as no surprise that one reliable way of making people care is by invoking self-interest.

In 1925, John Caples was assigned to write a headline for an advertisement promoting the correspondence music course offered by the U.S. School of Music. Caples had no advertising experience, but he was a natural. He sat at his typewriter and pecked out the most famous headline in print-advertising history: "They Laughed When I Sat Down at the Piano . . . But When I Started to Play!"

This is a classic underdog story in fifteen words. People *laughed at him!* And he *shut them up* through his playing! (The headline is enthralling enough that it makes us overlook commonsense reactions like, Um, why would anyone laugh at someone sitting down at a piano? When was the last time *you* laughed at someone who sat down at a piano?)

The headline was so successful at selling correspondence courses that it's still being ripped off by copywriters decades later. Sixty years later, the following knockoff headline increased sales by 26 percent over the previous year: "My Husband Laughed When I Ordered Our Carpet Through the Mail. But When I Saved 50% . . ." (Our publisher rejected the following subtitle for this book: "They Laughed

When We Wrote This Book. But When They Woke Up in an Ice-Filled Bathtub . . .")

Caples helped establish mail-order advertising, the forerunner of the modern infomercial. In mail-order advertising, unlike most other forms of advertising, advertisers know *exactly* how well an ad works. Say there's an ad for a "stock-picking guide" in a newspaper or a magazine. If you want to order the stock-picking guide, you send off a check to the address listed in the ad. But each version of an ad lists a slightly different address, so when your order shows up at a particular address the marketer knows precisely which ad generated the sale.

Contrast mail-order ads with a classic consumer product like Crest. Why does someone buy a tube of Crest? Is it because of the new TV ads? Or was it the discount price at retail? Or the fancy new package design? Or the fact that Mom always used Crest? Or that it was the only brand in stock that day? Marketers have surprisingly little ability to tell.

Because mail-order advertising is so transparent, it's essentially a laboratory for assessing motivational appeals. What makes people care? Ask a direct-mail copywriter. And John Caples is often cited as the greatest copywriter of all time. He says, "First and foremost, try to get self-interest into every headline you write. Make your headline suggest to readers that here is something they want. This rule is so fundamental that it would seem obvious. Yet the rule is violated every day by scores of writers."

Caples's ads get self-interest into their headlines by promising huge benefits for trivial costs:

- You Can Laugh at Money Worries if You Follow This Simple Plan
- Give Me 5 Days and I'll Give You a Magnetic Personality . . . Let Me Prove It—Free
- The Secret of How to Be Taller

- How You Can Improve Your Memory in One Evening
- Retire at 55

Caples says companies often emphasize features when they should be emphasizing benefits. "The most frequent reason for unsuccessful advertising is advertisers who are so full of their own accomplishments (the world's best seed!) that they forget to tell us why *we* should buy (the world's best lawn!)." An old advertising maxim says you've got to spell out *the benefit of the benefit*. In other words, people don't buy quarter-inch drill bits. They buy quarter-inch holes so they can hang their children's pictures.

We get uncomfortable looking at Caples's handiwork: Many of his ads are shady. Deceptive. The manufacturers of the Magnetic Personality Kit may enjoy a conscience-free existence, but most of us aspire to a working relationship with the truth.

So what's the nonadvertising, nonschlocky takeaway from the Caples techniques? The first lesson is not to overlook self-interest. Jerry Weissman, a former TV producer and screenwriter who now coaches CEOs in how to deliver speeches, says that you shouldn't dance around the appeal to self-interest. He says that the WIIFY— "what's in it for you," pronounced *whiff-y*—should be a central aspect of every speech.

Weissman notes that some people resist spelling out the message. "But my audiences aren't stupid," he quotes the resisters. "They might even feel insulted if I spell it out for them!" For an audience that may be distracted, though, spelling it out has value: "Even if it takes them just a few seconds to connect the dots between the feature you describe and the implied benefit, by the time they catch up, you will have moved on to your next point, and they probably won't have time to absorb the benefit . . . or the next point."

Teachers are all too familiar with the student refrain "How are we ever going to *use* this?" In other words, what's in it for me? If the

WIIFY was that algebra made students better at video games, would any teacher hesitate to say so? Does any teacher doubt that students would pay more attention?

If you've got self-interest on your side, don't bury it. Don't talk around it. Even subtle tweaks can make a difference. It's important, Caples says, to keep the self in self-interest: "Don't say, 'People will enjoy a sense of security when they use Goodyear Tires.' Say, '*You* enjoy a sense of security when you use Goodyear Tires.'"

Of course, there are less obnoxious, less overt ways to appeal to self-interest than those promoted by mail-order ads. To explore this, we'll start with a rather odd study conducted in Tempe, Arizona.

Cable TV in Tempe

In 1982, psychologists conducted a study on persuasion with a group of homeowners in Tempe, Arizona. The homeowners were visited by student volunteers who asked them to fill out surveys for a class project.

At the time, cable TV was just starting to appear—it was still unfamiliar to most people. The research study was designed to compare the success of two different approaches to educating the homeowners about the potential benefits of cable TV.

One group of homeowners was presented with some information about why cable might be worthwhile:

CATV will provide a broader entertainment and informational service to its subscribers. Used properly, a person can plan in advance to enjoy events offered. Instead of spending money on the babysitter and gas, and putting up with the hassles of going out, more time can be spent at home with family, alone, or with friends.

The second group of homeowners was asked to imagine themselves in a detailed scenario:

Take a moment and imagine how CATV will provide you with a broader entertainment and informational service. When you use it properly, you will be able to plan in advance which of the events offered you wish to enjoy. Take a moment and think of how, instead of spending money on the babysitter and gas, and then having to put up with the hassles of going out, you will be able to spend your time at home, with your family, alone, or with your friends.

Some readers have said that at first they didn't see any difference between the two appeals. The difference *is* subtle. But go back and count up the number of times the word "you" appears in each appeal.

In a sense, the study was a more elaborate version of Caples's advice to avoid talking about abstract benefits ("People will enjoy a sense of security when they use Goodyear Tires") and focus on personal benefits ("*You* enjoy a sense of security when you use Goodyear Tires"). The Arizona study, though, took it a step further. It asked people to *visualize* the feeling of security they would get by using Goodyear tires.

The homeowners filled out a questionnaire for the students and said goodbye. They thought they were finished with the research project, but the researchers still had another stage to complete. A month after the survey was conducted, cable TV arrived in Tempe. The local cable company approached the homeowners for subscriptions. The university researchers managed to get subscriber data from the cable company. They then analyzed which homeowners had subscribed and which hadn't.

The homeowners who got information about cable subscribed at a rate of 20 percent, which was about the same as the rest of the neighborhood. But the homeowners who *imagined themselves* subscribing to cable subscribed at a rate of 47 percent. The research paper, when it was published, was subtitled "Does Imagining Make It So?" The answer was yes.

Compared with a typical mail-order ad, the "imagine cable television" appeal is a much more subtle appeal to self-interest. Note that the benefits offered were not fantastic in a Caples-esque way. The gist was that you could avoid the hassle of leaving home (!) by ordering cable. Indeed, just hearing about the benefits, in the abstract, wasn't enough to lure additional subscribers. It was only when people put themselves in the starring role—*I can see myself watching a good movie at home with my hubby, and I can get up and check on the kids in the next room whenever I like . . . and think of all that babysitting money I'd save!*—that their interest grew.

This finding suggests that it may be the tangibility, rather than the magnitude, of the benefits that makes people care. You don't have to promise riches and sex appeal and magnetic personalities. It may be enough to promise reasonable benefits that *people can easily imagine themselves enjoying*.

Imagine that Save the Children incorporated this idea into its pitches for sponsorship. Right now the pitch is "You can sponsor Rokia, a little girl in Mali, for $30 per month"—a pitch that is already successful. But what if the pitch was expanded? "Imagine yourself as the sponsor of Rokia, a little girl in Mali. You've got a picture of her on your desk at work, next to your kids' pictures. During the past year you've traded letters with her three times, and you know from the letters that she loves to read and frequently gets annoyed by her little brother. She is excited that next year she'll get to play on the soccer team." That's powerful. (And it's not crass.)

Maslow

Self-interest isn't the whole story, of course—especially if we define "self-interest" narrowly, as we often do, in terms of wealth and security. If it were the whole story, no one would ever serve in the armed forces. There are things people care about that would never appear in a Caples ad.

In 1954, a psychologist named Abraham Maslow surveyed the research in psychology about what motivates people. He boiled down volumes of existing research to a list of needs and desires that people try to fulfill:

- Transcendence: help others realize their potential
- Self-actualization: realize our own potential, self-fulfillment, peak experiences
- Aesthetic: symmetry, order, beauty, balance
- Learning: know, understand, mentally connect
- Esteem: achieve, be competent, gain approval, independence, status
- Belonging: love, family, friends, affection
- Security: protection, safety, stability
- Physical: hunger, thirst, bodily comfort

You may remember this list as Maslow's Pyramid, or Maslow's Hierarchy of Needs. Maslow's list of needs was incredibly insightful, but he was wrong to describe it as a "hierarchy." Maslow saw the hierarchy as a ladder—to be climbed rung by rung from the bottom up. You couldn't fill your longing for Esteem until you satisfied your longing for Security. You couldn't fill your Aesthetic needs until your Physical needs were taken care of. (In Maslow's world, there were no starving artists.)

Subsequent research suggests that the hierarchical aspect of Maslow's theory is bogus—people pursue all of these needs pretty much simultaneously. There's no question that most starving men would rather eat than transcend, but there's an awful lot of overlap in the middle.

When people talk about "self-interest," they're typically invoking the Physical, Security, and Esteem layers. Sometimes Belonging gets acknowledged if the speaker is touchy-feely. Not many marketers or managers venture far beyond these categories. Even appeals that seem to fall under the Aesthetic category are often really Esteem-related, but in disguise (e.g., a luxury-auto ad).

There could be a very good reason that people focus on those particular categories. Maybe those are the ones that truly matter. The rest of them—Self-actualization, Transcendence, and so on—do seem a bit academic. Recent research has explored this question, helping to shed light on which of Maslow's categories made people care.

Imagine that a company offers its employees a $1,000 bonus if they meet certain performance targets. There are three different ways of presenting the bonus to the employees:

1. Think of what that $1,000 means: a down payment on a new car or that new home improvement you've been wanting to make.
2. Think of the increased security of having that $1,000 in your bank account for a rainy day.
3. Think of what the $1,000 means: the company recognizes how important you are to its overall performance. It doesn't spend money for nothing.

When people are asked which positioning would appeal to them personally, most of them say No. 3. It's good for the self-esteem—and, as for No. 1 and No. 2, isn't it kind of obvious that $1,000 can be spent or saved? Most of us have no trouble at all visualizing ourselves spending $1,000. (It's a bit less common to find people who like to visualize themselves saving.)

Here's the twist, though: When people are asked which is the best positioning for *other people* (not them), they rank No. 1 most fulfilling, followed by No. 2. That is, *we* are motivated by self-esteem, but *others* are motivated by down payments. This single insight explains almost everything about the way incentives are structured in most large organizations.

Or consider another version of the same task. Let's say you're trying to persuade someone to take a new job in a department that's crucial to the company's success. Here are three possible pitches for the new job:

1. Think about how much security this job provides. It's so important that the company will always need someone in this job.
2. Think about the visibility provided by this job. Because the job is so important, a lot of people will be watching your performance.
3. Think about how rewarding it will be to work in such a central job. It offers a unique opportunity to learn how the company really works.

The chasm between ourselves and others opens again. Most people say No. 3—an appeal to Learning—would be most motivating for them. Those same people predict that others would be most motivated by No. 1 (Security) and No. 2 (Esteem).

In other words, a lot of us think everyone else is living in Maslow's basement—we may have a penthouse apartment, but everyone else is living below. The result of spending too much time in Maslow's basement is that we may overlook lots of opportunities to motivate people. It's not that the "bottom floors"—or the more tangible, physical needs, to avoid the hierarchy metaphor—aren't motivational. Of course they are. We all like to get bonuses and to have job security and to feel like we fit in. But to focus on these needs exclusively robs us of the chance to tap more profound motivations.

A great example of using these more profound motivations involves a retired member of the U.S. Army—not a battlefield commander but a guy who ran a mess hall.

Dining in Iraq

Army food is just about what you'd expect: bland, overcooked, and prepared in massive quantities. The dishes are not garnished with sprigs of parsley. The mess halls are essentially calorie factories, giving the troops the fuel they need to do their jobs. An old Army proverb says, "An Army travels on its stomach."

The Pegasus chow hall, just outside the Baghdad airport, has developed a different reputation. At Pegasus, the prime rib is perfectly prepared. The fruit platter is a beautiful assortment of watermelon, kiwi fruit, and grapes. There are legends of soldiers driving to Pegasus from the Green Zone (the well-protected Americanized area of Baghdad), along one of the most treacherous roads in Iraq, just to eat a meal.

Floyd Lee, the man in charge of Pegasus, was retired from his twenty-five-year career as a Marine Corps and Army cook when the Iraq war began. He came out of retirement to take the job. "The good Lord gave me a second chance to feed soldiers," he said. "I've waited for this job all my life, and here I am in Baghdad."

Lee is well aware that being a soldier is relentlessly difficult. The soldiers often work eighteen-hour days, seven days a week. The threat of danger in Iraq is constant. Lee wants Pegasus to provide a respite from the turmoil. He's clear about his leadership mission: "As I see it, I am not just in charge of food service; I am in charge of morale."

Think about that: *I am in charge of morale.* In terms of Maslow's hierarchy, Lee is going for Transcendence.

This vision manifests itself in hundreds of small actions taken by Lee's staff on a daily basis. At Pegasus, the white walls of the typical mess hall are covered with sports banners. There are gold treatments on the windows, and green tablecloths with tassels. The harsh fluorescent lights have been replaced by ceiling fans with soft bulbs. The servers wear tall white chef's hats.

The remarkable thing about Pegasus's reputation for great food is that Pegasus works with exactly the same raw materials that everyone else does. Pegasus serves the same twenty-one-day Army menu as other dining halls. Its food comes from the same suppliers. It's the attitude that makes the difference. A chef sorts through the daily fruit shipment, culling the bad grapes, selecting the best parts of the watermelon and kiwi, to prepare the perfect fruit tray. At night, the dessert table features five kinds of pie and three kinds of cake. The Sunday prime rib is marinated for two full days. A cook from New Orleans orders spices that are mailed to Iraq to enhance the entrées. A dessert chef describes her strawberry cake as "sexual and sensual"—two adjectives never before applied to Army food.

Lee realizes that serving food is a job, but improving morale is a mission. Improving morale involves creativity and experimentation and mastery. Serving food involves a ladle.

One of the soldiers who commute to Pegasus for Sunday dinner said, "The time you are in here, you forget you're in Iraq." Lee is tapping into Maslow's forgotten categories—the Aesthetic, Learning, and Transcendence needs. In redefining the mission of his mess hall, he has inspired his co-workers to create an oasis in the desert.

The Popcorn Popper and Political Science

Even John Caples, the mail-order copywriter, admits that there are powerful motivations outside narrow self-interest. He tells a story about a marketer who was promoting a new educational film on fire safety that was intended to help firemen. This marketer had been taught that there are three basic consumer appeals: sex, greed, and fear.

The marketer's instinct was that greed would work best in this situation. He came up with a couple of ideas for free giveaways that would persuade firemen to check out the film. He began calling local units to figure out which giveaway would have the most appeal. When he called, he would describe the new film and ask, "Would you like to see the film for possible purchase for your educational programs?" The universal answer was an enthusiastic "Yes!"

The second question tested two versions of his greed appeal: "Would your firefighters prefer a large electric popcorn popper or an excellent set of chef's carving knives as a thank-you for reviewing the film?"

The first two calls yielded definitive answers to this question: "Do you think we'd use a fire safety program because of some #*$@%! popcorn popper?!"

The marketer stopped asking about the free gifts.

So, sometimes self-interest helps people care, and sometimes it backfires. What are we to make of this?

The mystery deepens if we consider politics. The conventional wisdom is that voters are paragons of self-interest. If there's a proposal on the table to raise the marginal tax rate on the highest incomes, we expect rich people to vote against it and everyone else to vote for it.

Actually, this conventional wisdom is wrong. There's not much evidence that public opinion can be predicted by narrow self-interest. In 1998, Donald Kinder, a professor of political science at the University of Michigan, wrote an influential survey of thirty years of research on this topic. He summarizes the effects of self-interest on political views as "trifling." Trifling! Kinder writes:

> When faced with affirmative action, white and black Americans come to their views without calculating personal harms or benefits. The unemployed do not line up behind policies designed to alleviate economic distress. The medically needy are no more likely to favor government health insurance than the fully insured. Parents of children in public schools are not more likely to support government aid to education than other citizens. Americans who are likely to be drafted are not more likely to oppose military intervention or escalating conflicts that are under way. Women employed outside the home do not differ from homemakers in

their support of policies intended to benefit women at work. On such diverse matters as racial busing for the purpose of school de-segregation, anti-drinking ordinances, mandatory college exami-nations, housing policy, bilingual education, compliance with laws, satisfaction with the resolution of legal disputes, gun control and more, self-interest turns out to be quite unimportant.

These findings are bracingly counterintuitive. If people aren't supporting their own self-interest, whose interests are they support-ing?

The answer is nuanced. First, self-interest does seem to matter, quite a bit, when the effects of a public policy are significant, tangi-ble, and immediate. For example, in California in 1978, a ballot ini-tiative called Proposition 13 called for a sharp reduction in property taxes in exchange for equally sharp reductions in public services such as schools, libraries, and police and fire departments. On this issue, homeowners—tired of the huge tax increases that accompany rising property values—voted for Proposition 13. Librarians and firefighters, among others, voted against it. Second, self-interest shapes what we pay attention to, even if it doesn't dictate our stance. For example, on Proposition 13 homeowners and public employees were more likely to have a well-formed opinion on the initiative—even if their opinion was inconsistent with their personal self-interest.

But self-interest isn't the whole story. Principles—equality, indi-vidualism, ideals about government, human rights, and the like—may matter to us even when they violate our immediate self-interest. We may dislike hearing the views of some fringe political group but support its right to speak because we treasure free speech.

And perhaps the most important part of the story is this: "Group interest" is often a better predictor of political opinions than self-interest. Kinder says that in forming opinions people seem to ask not "What's in it for me?" but, rather, "What's in it for my group?" Our group affiliation may be based on race, class, religion, gender, region, political party, industry, or countless other dimensions of difference.

A related idea comes from James March, a professor at Stanford University, who proposes that we use two basic models to make decisions. The first model involves calculating consequences. We weigh our alternatives, assessing the value of each one, and we choose the alternative that yields us the most value. This model is the standard view of decision-making in economics classes: People are self-interested and rational. The rational agent asks, Which sofa will provide me with the greatest comfort and the best aesthetics for the price? Which political candidate will best serve my economic and social interests? The second model is quite different. It assumes that people make decisions based on identity. They ask themselves three questions: Who am I? What kind of situation is this? And what do people like me do in this kind of situation?

Notice that in the second model people aren't analyzing the consequences or outcomes for themselves. There are no calculations, only norms and principles. Which sofa would someone like me— a Southeastern accountant—be more likely to buy? Which political candidate should a Hollywood Buddhist get behind? It's almost as if people consulted an ideal self-image: *What would someone like me do?*

This second model of decision-making helps shed light on why the firefighters got angry about the popcorn popper. Bear in mind that the popcorn popper wasn't a bribe. If the marketer had said, "Order this film for your firehouse and I'll give you a popcorn popper for your family," clearly most people would reject the offer on ethical grounds. On the contrary, the offer was innocuous: *We will give you a popcorn popper to thank you for the trouble you're taking to review the film. You can have the popper regardless of your decision on the film.* There's nothing unethical about accepting this offer.

And we can go further than that: From a self-interested, value-maximizing point of view, it is simply stupid to turn down this offer. If you make Decision A, you end up with a popcorn popper. If you make Decision B, you end up with no popcorn popper. Everything else is the same. So unless popcorn destroys value in your world, you'd better make Decision A.

But from the perspective of the identity model of decision-making, turning down the popper makes perfect sense. The thought process would be more like this: "I'm a firefighter. You're offering me a popcorn popper to get me to view a film on safety. But firefighters aren't the kind of people who need little gifts to motivate us to learn about safety. We risk our lives, going into burning buildings to save people. Shame on you for implying that I need a popcorn popper!"

There are ways to unite these two decision models. What if the marketer had offered to donate fifty dollars to a school's fire-safety program in exchange for the firemen's viewing the film? It's less clear that this offer would have violated the firefighters' sense of identity.

Self-interest is important. There's no question that we can make people care by appealing to it. But it makes for a limited palette. Always structuring our ideas around self-interest is like always painting with one color. It's stifling for us and uninspiring for others.

Floyd Lee, the manager of the Pegasus dining hall, has it right. He could have generated motivation through a strict self-interest appeal: perhaps by offering to let his employees off ten minutes early every night if they worked hard, or by giving them the first choice of the steaks. Instead, he helped create a kind of Pegasus identity: *A Pegasus chef is in charge of morale, not food.* You can imagine hundreds of decisions being made by staffers in the tent who think to themselves, *What should a Pegasus person do in this situation?*

CLINIC

The Need for Algebra and Maslow's Basement

THE SITUATION: *Every algebra teacher in recorded history has had to deal with two student questions: "Why do I need to know this? When will I ever use this?" This Clinic examines three attempts to answer these questions.*

MESSAGE 1: In a 1993 conference on "Algebra for All," the following points were made in response to the question "Why study algebra?"

- Algebra provides methods for moving from the specific to the general. It involves discovering the patterns among items in a set and developing the language needed to think about and communicate it to others.
- Algebra provides procedures for manipulating symbols to allow for understanding of the world around us.
- Algebra provides a vehicle for understanding our world through mathematical models.
- Algebra is the science of variables. It enables us to deal with large bodies of data by identifying variables (quantities which change in value) and by imposing or finding structures within the data.
- Algebra is the basic set of ideas and techniques for describing and reasoning about relations between variable quantities.

COMMENTS ON MESSAGE 1: This message illustrates the problems posed by the Curse of Knowledge. Presumably, this conference was filled with a group of algebra experts and they came up with an answer that seemed plausible to other experts. But let's get real: Will any restless student jump on the algebra bandwagon after being told that it "provides procedures for manipulating symbols to allow for understanding of the world"? As a *definition* of algebra, the bullets above seem quite logical. But as *reasons* for studying algebra, they don't work. We need a message that makes students care about algebra.

. . .

MESSAGE 2: We made up the following response. It was inspired by several examples that we saw floating around the Internet:

Here's what I tell my students about why they need to learn algebra:

- You need it to get your high school diploma.
- Every future math and science class you take will require a knowledge of algebra.
- To get admitted to a good college, you'll need a good record in math.
- And even if you don't ever plan to attend college, the reasoning skills you learn in algebra will help you buy a home, create a budget, etc.

My brother is a sales rep for a high-tech firm . . . he always had trouble with math in school but now realizes the hard work he put into the course has improved his analytical skills and has made him a better presenter to his clients.

COMMENTS ON MESSAGE 2: This teacher avoids the Curse of Knowledge by speaking practically, but he stays close to Maslow's Basement. Why study algebra? The first reason: You have to do it because you have to do it. The second: You have to do it so that you can do more of it. The primary appeal is to Esteem—the desire to be competent, to gain approval and status. The most effective part is the part about the author's brother, who later realized that his struggles with math paid off. The brother story is an Esteem appeal that builds in an almost Caples-esque victory story. ("They laughed when I botched the equation, but when I won the account . . .")

• • •

MESSAGE 3: This is a response from a high school algebra teacher, Dean Sherman, to an Internet discussion of this topic among high school teachers:

My grade 9 students have difficulty appreciating the usefulness of the Standard Form of the equation of a line, prompting them to ask, "When are we ever going to need this?"

This question used to really bother me, and I would look, as a result, for justification for everything I taught. Now I say, "Never. You will never use this."

I then go on to remind them that people don't lift weights so that they will be prepared should, one day, [someone] knock them over on the street and lay a barbell across their chests. You lift weights so that you can knock over a defensive lineman, or carry your groceries or lift your grandchildren without being sore the next day. You do math exercises so that you can improve your ability to think logically, so that you can be a better lawyer, doctor, architect, prison warden or parent.

MATH IS MENTAL WEIGHT TRAINING. It is a means to an end (for most people), not an end in itself.

COMMENTS ON MESSAGE 3: This is a great response. Note the elements we've seen before in the book: The surprise opening to grab attention ("Never. You will never use this"). Also, the use of analogy is brilliant—he taps our existing schema of weight lifting to change our model of "learning algebra" (i.e., it's not that in the future you're going to have a daily need to find the slope of a line; it's that you're making your brain more muscular).

He is also moving up Maslow's hierarchy. The appeal here is to higher levels like Learning and Self-actualization. The idea is that learning algebra makes you realize more of your potential.

SCORECARD

Checklist	Msg. 1	Msg. 2	Msg. 3
Simple	-	-	✓
Unexpected	-	-	✓
Concrete	-	✓	✓
Credible	-	-	-
Emotional	-	✓	✓ ✓
Story	-	✓	-

PUNCH LINE: "Math is mental weight training" reminds us that, even in the most mundane situations, there's an opportunity to move out of Maslow's basement and into the higher levels of motivation.

Don't Mess with Texas

Dan Syrek is the nation's leading researcher on litter. He has worked with sixteen states—from New York to Alaska—on antilitter initiatives. He often begins his projects by selecting random stretches of road—from interstates to farm roads—and walking the roads personally, a clicker in each hand, manually counting litter.

In the 1980s, Syrek and his Sacramento-based organization, the Institute for Applied Research, were hired by the state of Texas. Texas had a serious litter problem. The state was spending $25 million per year on cleanup, and the costs were rising 15 percent per year. The state's attempts to encourage better behavior—"Please Don't Litter" signs, lots of roadside trash cans marked "Pitch In"—weren't working. Texas hired Syrek to help craft a new strategy.

The standard antilitter message is emotional, but it tends to focus on a limited set of emotions. There are appeals to guilt and shame, as in a spot that shows a Native American shedding a tear over litter. There are also appeals to our feelings for cuddly wildlife, such as the campaign starring a cartoon owl who says, "Give a Hoot—Don't Pollute."

Syrek knew that this type of messaging wouldn't solve Texas's problem. In his view, those kinds of ads are just "preaching to the choir." What Texas needed to do was reach people who weren't inclined to shed tears over roadside trash. The profile of the typical litterer in Texas was an eighteen- to thirty-five-year-old, pickup-driving male who liked sports and country music. He didn't like authority and he wasn't motivated by emotional associations with cuddly owls. One member of the Texas Department of Transportation said, "Saying 'please' to these guys falls on deaf ears."

"We found that people who throw the stuff are real slobs," Syrek says. "You had to explain to them that what they were doing was littering." Syrek kept with him a photo of a macho-looking man in a pickup truck. "This is our target market," he said. "We call him Bubba."

Designing an antilitter campaign based on self-interest wasn't likely to work with this group. After all, what do the Bubbas really have to gain by not littering? Throwing things away properly takes effort, for which there are no obvious rewards. The situation doesn't lend itself to a greed or sex-based appeal, à la Caples. It might be possible to design a fear-based approach—highlighting hefty fines or other punishments—but the Bubbas' antiauthority streak would likely render it useless (or even cause it to backfire).

Syrek knew that the best way to change Bubba's behavior was to convince him that *people like him* did not litter. Based on his research, the Texas Department of Transportation approved a campaign built around the slogan "Don't Mess with Texas."

One of the earliest TV commercials featured two Dallas Cowboy players who were famous in Texas: defensive end Ed "Too-Tall" Jones and defensive tackle Randy White. In the spot, they're picking up trash on the side of a highway:

> Too-Tall Jones steps toward the camera and says, "You see the guy who threw this out the window . . . you tell him I got a message for him."
>
> Randy White steps forward with a beer can and says, "I got a message for him too . . ."
>
> An off-camera voice asks, "What's that?"
>
> White crushes the can with his fist and says threateningly, "Well, I kinda need to see him to deliver it."
>
> Too-Tall Jones adds, "Don't mess with Texas."

This commercial is a far cry from cute owls and weepy Native Americans.

Another ad features Houston Astros pitcher Mike Scott, famous for his split-fingered fastball. Scott says that throwing stuff away is "the Texas thing to do." He demonstrates his "split-fingered trashball," hurling some litter into a roadside can, which explodes with a pillar of fire. Subtle stuff.

The campaign featured athletes and musicians, most of whom probably weren't household names outside Texas but were all well-known to Texans as *Texans:* Houston Oiler quarterback Warren Moon, boxer George Foreman, blues guitarist Stevie Ray Vaughan, and country artist Jerry Jeff Walker. Willie Nelson contributed an ad with the line "Mamas, tell all your babies, 'Don't mess with Texas.'"

But isn't this just a garden-variety celebrity endorsement? No, it's more subtle than that. Certainly, the spots are not driven by pure celebrity—Barbra Streisand wouldn't pack much of a punch with Bubba. And even macho celebrities wouldn't have worked the same way. Schwarzenegger is macho but does nothing to evoke Texanness.

What if the campaign used the same celebrities but adopted a more conventional PSA-type approach? "I'm pro boxer George Foreman. It's uncool to litter." That, too, would be unlikely to work: Foreman would be stepping into the authority role that Bubba hates.

The message of the campaign was *Texans don't litter*. Notice that the celebrities are valuable only insofar as they can quickly establish the schema of "Texas"—or, more specifically, of "ideal, masculine Texans." Even people who dislike Willie Nelson's music can appreciate his quality of Texan-ness.

The campaign was an instant success. Within a few months of the launch, an astonishing 73 percent of Texans polled could recall the message and identify it as an antilitter message. Within one year, litter had declined 29 percent.

The Department of Transportation originally planned to accompany the "Don't Mess with Texas" campaign with a separate $1 million program to enforce litter laws more vigorously. This was a fear tactic: If you litter, you're more likely to get caught and prosecuted. But the effect of "Don't Mess with Texas" was so strong and immediate that the enforcement program was abandoned. By offering Bubba a compelling message about identity, the campaign made appeals to fear unnecessary.

During the first five years of the campaign, visible roadside litter in Texas decreased 72 percent and the number of cans along Texas roads dropped 81 percent. In 1988, Syrek found that Texas had less than half the trash he found along the roads of other states that had run antilitter programs for comparable periods.

"Don't Mess with Texas," as a phrase, is a great slogan. But we shouldn't confuse the slogan with the idea. The idea was that Syrek could make Bubba care about litter by showing him that real Texans didn't litter. The idea was that Bubba would respond to an identity appeal better than he would to a rational self-interest appeal. Even if a second-rate copywriter had been hired, and the slogan had been "Don't Disrespect Texas," the campaign would still have decreased cans on Texas highways.

The Music of Duo Piano

So far we've looked at three strategies for making people care: using associations (or avoiding associations, as the case may be), appealing to self-interest, and appealing to identity. All three strategies can be effective, but we've got to watch out for our old nemesis, the Curse of Knowledge, which can interfere with our ability to implement them.

In 2002, Chip helped a group of professors lead a seminar for nonprofit arts leaders in Miami and Ft. Lauderdale, Florida. One of the exercises was intended to help the leaders articulate and refine the core mission of their organization. The questions put to the attendees were difficult ones: Why does your organization exist? Can other organizations do what you do—and if so, what is it you do that is unique?

One question asked participants to define the purpose of their organization in a way that would motivate other people to care about it. Volunteers must care enough to contribute their time, donors must care enough to donate their money, and employees must care enough to stick by the organization (even when they get lucrative job offers from other, for-profit organizations). One of the organizations attending the seminar was the Murray Dranoff Duo Piano Foundation. When it was their turn, Chip asked the representatives to read their emotion-evoking purpose statement:

Duo Piano group: We exist to protect, preserve, and promote the music of duo piano.

CHIP: Why is it important to protect the music of duo piano?

DUO PIANO GROUP: Well, not much duo piano music is being performed anymore. We want to keep it from dying out.

One attendee admitted later that when he first heard the phrase "duo piano" he immediately thought of the "dueling pianos" that you find in touristy bars, with people drunkenly singing along to "Piano Man." Some people in the room thought that perhaps the death of duo piano music should not be prevented but hastened.

The conversation went around in circles for a few minutes without much progress in making the people in the room care about duo piano as an art form. Finally, one of the other participants chimed in: I don't want to be rude, but why would the world be a less rich place if duo piano music disappeared completely?

DUO PIANO GROUP: (Clearly taken aback). Wow . . .

The piano is this magnificent instrument. It was created to put the entire range and tonal quality of the whole orchestra under the control of one performer. There is no other instrument that has the same breadth and range.

And when you put two of these magnificent instruments in the same room, and the performers can respond to each other and build on each other, it's like having the sound of the orchestra but the intimacy of chamber music.

At that point, surprise brows went up around the room and there was an audible murmur of approval. This phrase — "the sound of the orchestra but the intimacy of chamber music" — was profound and evocative. Suddenly the people in the room *understood*, for the first time, why the Murray Dranoff team was, and should be, committed to the duo piano.

Why did it take ten minutes for the Murray Dranoff group to

come up with a message that made other people care? You'd think that a group devoted to the duo piano would be in the best position of anyone on earth to explain the value of the music.

The reality is that they *did* in fact know better than anyone on earth why the duo piano was worth preserving. But the Curse of Knowledge prevented them from expressing it well. The mission to "preserve duo piano music" was effective and meaningful inside Murray Dranoff, but outside the organization it was opaque. Several attendees later commented that they had sympathized with the question "Why would the world be a less rich place if duo piano music disappeared completely?" What's so special about the duo piano? Who cares?

If you come to work every day for years, focused on duo piano issues, it's easy to forget that a lot of the world has never heard of the duo piano. It's easy to forget that you're the tapper and the world is the listener. The duo piano group was rescued from the Curse of Knowledge by a roomful of people relentlessly asking them, "Why?" By asking "Why?" three times, the duo piano group moved from talking about *what* they were doing to *why* they were doing it. They moved from a set of associations that had no power (except to someone who already knew duo piano music) to a set of deeper, more concrete associations that connected emotionally with outsiders.

This tactic of the "Three Whys" can be useful in bypassing the Curse of Knowledge. (Toyota actually has a "Five Whys" process for getting to the bottom of problems on its production line. Feel free to use as many "Whys" as you like.) Asking "Why?" helps to remind us of the core values, the core principles, that underlie our ideas.

A few years back, a group of hospital administrators asked the design firm IDEO to help improve the hospital's workflow. The team at IDEO knew that they would probably face a lot of internal resistance to their recommendations. The first step in motivating the hospital staff to change was to get them to realize that there was a problem and get them to care about it.

IDEO created a video, shot from the perspective of a patient who goes to the emergency room for a leg fracture. In the video, we see what the patient sees. We *are* the patient. We come in through the door to the ER—we hunt around for check-in instructions and interact with the admissions people, who are speaking in a foreign medical tongue. Eventually, we are laid on a gurney and wheeled through the hospital. We see long stretches of the hospital ceiling. We hear disembodied voices, because we can't see the person addressing us. Every now and then, someone pokes his or her head into our field of view. Frequently, there are long pauses where we just sit idle, staring at the ceiling, unsure what's coming next.

Jane Fulton Suri, a psychologist at IDEO, said that when the hospital staff was shown the video it had an immediate impact. "The first reaction was always something like 'Oh, I never *realized* . . .'" Suri says she likes the word *realized*. Before the hospital workers saw the video, the problem wasn't quite *real*. Afterward, she said, "There's an immediate motivation to fix things. It's no longer just some problem on a problem list."

IDEO also created role-playing exercises, putting the staffers in the patients' shoes. The exercises included such tasks as, "Imagine that you are French and you are trying to locate your father in the hospital, but you don't speak any English." IDEO has become known for this type of simulation—simulations that drive employees to empathize with their customers. Time seems to erode empathy in some contexts, and IDEO's simulations manage to restore the natural empathy that we have for others. "The world of business tends to emphasize the pattern over the particular," Suri said. "The intellectual aspects of the pattern prevent people from caring."

· · ·

This realization—that empathy emerges from the particular rather than the pattern—brings us back full circle to the Mother Teresa quote at the beginning of the chapter: "If I look at the mass, I will never act. If I look at the one, I will."

How can we make people care about our ideas? We get them to take off their Analytical Hats. We create empathy for specific individuals. We show how our ideas are associated with things that people already care about. We appeal to their self-interest, but we also appeal to their identities—not only to the people they are right now but also to the people they would like to be

And, while we should always think about "what's in it" for our audience, we should remember to stay clear of Maslow's Basement. "What's in it" for our audience might be aesthetic motivation or the desire for transcendence rather than a $250 bonus. Floyd Lee said, "As I see it, I am not just in charge of food service; I am in charge of morale." Who wouldn't want a leader like Floyd Lee?

CHAPTER 6

STORIES

The nurse was working in the neonatal intensive-care unit, where newborns with serious health problems are treated and monitored. She'd been watching one baby in particular for several hours, and she didn't like what she was seeing. His color, a key indicator of potential problems, had been fluctuating—wavering between a healthy shade of pink and a duller, more troublesome hue.

Suddenly, within a matter of seconds, the baby turned a deep blue-black. The nurse's stomach fell. Others in the ICU yelled for an X-ray technician and a doctor.

The gathering medical team was operating on the assumption that the baby's lung had collapsed, a common problem for babies on ventilators. The team prepared for the typical response to a collapsed lung, which involves piercing the chest and inserting a tube to suck the air from around the collapsed lung, allowing it to reinflate.

But the nurse thought it was a heart problem. As soon as she saw the baby's color—that awful blue-black—she suspected a pneumopericardium, a condition in which air fills the sac surrounding the heart, pressing inward and preventing the heart from beating. The nurse was terrified, because the last time she witnessed a pneumopericardium the baby died before the problem could even be diagnosed.

The nurse tried to stop the frantic preparations to treat the lung. "It's the heart!" she said. But in response the other medical personnel pointed to the heart monitor, which showed that the baby's heart was fine; his heart rate was bouncing along steadily, at the normal new-born rate of 130 beats per minute. The nurse, still insistent, pushed their hands away and screamed for quiet as she lowered a stethoscope to check for a heartbeat.

There was no sound—the heart was *not* beating.

She started doing compressions on the baby's chest. The chief neonatologist burst into the room and the nurse slapped a syringe in his hand. "It's a pneumopericardium," she said. "Stick the heart."

The X-ray technician, who was finally receiving results from his scan, confirmed the nurse's diagnosis. The neonatologist guided the syringe into the heart and slowly released the air that had been strangling the baby's heart. The baby's life was saved. His color slowly returned to normal.

Later, the group realized why the heart monitor misled them. It is designed to measure electrical activity, not actual heartbeats. The baby's heart nerves were firing—telling the heart to beat at the appropriate rate—but the air in the sac around the heart prevented the heart from actually beating. Only when the nurse used the stethoscope—so she could hear whether the heart was pumping correctly—did it become clear that his heart had stopped.

This story was collected by Gary Klein, a psychologist who studies how people make decisions in high-pressure, high-stakes environments. He spends time with firefighters, air-traffic controllers, power-plant operators, and intensive-care workers. The story about the baby appears in a chapter called "The Power of Stories," in Klein's book *Sources of Power*.

Klein says that, in the environments he studies, stories are told and retold because they contain wisdom. Stories are effective teaching tools. They show how context can mislead people to make the wrong decisions. Stories illustrate causal relationships that people hadn't recognized before and highlight unexpected, resourceful ways in which people have solved problems.

Medically, the story related above teaches important lessons. It instructs people in how to spot and treat the specific condition pneumopericardium. More broadly, it warns medical personnel about relying too much on machines. The heart monitor was functioning perfectly well, but it couldn't substitute for the insight of a human being with a simple stethoscope.

These medical lessons are not particularly useful to people who don't work in health care. But the story is *inspiring* to everyone. It's a story about a woman who stuck to her guns, despite implicit pressure to conform to the group's opinion. It's an underdog story—in the hierarchical hospital environment, it was the *nurse* who told the *chief neonatologist* the right diagnosis. A life hinged on her willingness to step out of her "proper place."

The story's power, then, is twofold: It provides simulation (knowledge about how to act) and inspiration (motivation to act). Note that both benefits, simulation and inspiration, are geared to generating *action*. In the last few chapters, we've seen that a *credible* idea makes people believe. An *emotional* idea makes people care. And in this chapter we'll see that the right stories make people act.

Shop Talk in the Xerox Lunchroom

Photocopiers are perhaps the most complex machines that most of us will ever use. What other everyday machine combines optical, mechanical, chemical, and electrical technologies? It's a wonder copiers work at all. And often they don't. When there's a problem—and it's not one that a cubicle-dweller can fix by opening and shutting the paper tray a few times—it takes a very sophisticated repair person to troubleshoot the situation.

Researcher Julian Orr spent a lot of time among Xerox copier repairmen and found that they spent a lot of time swapping stories.
Take the story below, which was told by a Xerox copier salesperson
over a game of cribbage at lunch. (We've provided some explanatory
comments in brackets.) The salesperson starts with a reference to a
recent mechanical change made by copier designers in an attempt to
prevent an ordinary power surge from frying multiple components:

> The new XER board configuration won't cook the board if you
> had an arcing dicorotron. Instead, it now trips the 24-Volt inter-
> lock on the Low Voltage Power Supply, and the machine will
> crash. But when it comes back up it'll give you an E053 error.
> [This is a misleading error code that refers to an area of the ma-
> chine that is unrelated to the real problem.]
>
> That's exactly what I had down there, at the end of the hall,
> and Weber and I ran for four hours trying to chase that thing.
> All it was was a bad dicorotron. We finally got it running long
> enough so that we got an E053 with an F066 and the minute we
> checked the dicorotrons we had one that was totally dead. . . .
> [Orr reports that there was a long pause for cribbage.] Yeah that
> was a fun one.

These cribbage-playing guys in the lunchroom are simply talking
shop, as we all do. A misleading E053 error may not constitute
drama in your world, but no doubt we all have our equivalents.

Why do people talk shop? Part of the reason is simply Humanity
101—we want to talk to other people about the things that we have in
common. Xerox repairmen work with photocopiers, so they talk
about them. But that's not the only factor at play here. For example,
the storyteller above could have shared the general arc of the story
without the details: "I had a real bear of a problem today—it took me
four hours to get to the bottom of it. I'm glad that one's over." Or he

could have leapt straight to the punch line: "After hours of hassle, I traced the problem back to a measly burned-out dicorotron. How was *your* morning?"

Instead, he tells a story that's much more interesting to his lunch partners. It has built-in drama—a misleading code leads two men on a wild goose chase until they uncover, through lots of work and thought, that the problem is simpler than they initially thought. Why is this story format more interesting? Because it allows his lunch partners to play along. He's giving them enough information so that they can mentally test out how they would have handled the situation. The people in the room who weren't aware of the misleading E053 code have now had their "E053 schema" fixed. Before, there was only one way to respond to an E053 code. Now, repairmen know to be aware of the "misleading E053" scenario.

In other words, this story is part entertainment and part instruction. Shop talk conveys important clues about how to respond to the world. It teaches nurses not to have blind faith in heart monitors. It teaches copy repairmen to beware of the misleading E053 code.

But the stories above aren't simply transferring nuggets of information. The Xerox story is *not* functionally equivalent to an e-mail sent around the company that contains the line "Watch out for false E053 codes related to burned-out dicorotrons." Something more profound is happening here. It will take a bit of unpacking to reveal the additional value that these stories bring.

The Un-passive Audience

Stories are strongly associated with entertainment—movies and books and TV shows and magazines. When children say "Tell me a story," they're begging for entertainment, not instruction.

Being the "audience" for a story seems like a passive role— audiences who get their stories from television are called "couch potatoes," after all. But "passive" may be overstating the case. When we read books, we have the sensation of being drawn into the author's world. When friends tell us stories, we instinctively empathize. When we watch movies, we identify with the protagonists.

But what if stories involve us in less intuitive, more dramatic ways? One team of researchers has produced some exciting evidence suggesting that the line between a story's "audience" and a story's "protagonist" may be a bit blurry.

Three psychologists interested in how people come to understand stories created a few for their study participants to read on a computer. They divided the participants into two groups. The first group read a story in which a critical object was *associated* with the main character in the story—for instance, "John *put on* his sweatshirt before he went jogging." The second group read a story in which the same critical object was *separated* from the main character: "John *took off* his sweatshirt before jogging."

Two sentences later, the story threw in a reference to the sweatshirt, and the computer was able to track how long it took people to read that sentence. Something strange happened: The people who thought John had taken off his sweatshirt before the jog *took more time to read the sentence* than the people who thought John had it on.

This result is subtle but fascinating. It implies that we create a kind of geographic simulation of the stories we hear. It's one thing to say "Reading stories makes us see pictures in our head." We'd all find that statement intuitive. It's quite another thing to say that when John left his sweatshirt behind, he left it back at the house in a more remote place in our heads. For that to be true, we cannot simply *visualize* the story on a movie screen in our heads; we must somehow *simulate* it, complete with some analogue (however loose) to the spatial relationships described in the story. These studies suggest that there's no such thing as a passive audience. When we hear a story, our minds move from room to room. When we hear a story, we simulate it. But what good is simulation?

A group of UCLA students were asked to think about a current problem in their lives, one that was "stressing them out" but was potentially solvable in the future, such as a problem with schoolwork or with a relationship.

The students were told that the goal of the experiment was to help them deal with the problem effectively, and they got some brief instructions on problem-solving: "It is important to think about the problem, learn more about it, think about what you can do, take steps to deal with it. . . . Resolving it could reduce your stress, make you feel pleased with how you dealt with it, and help you grow from the experience." After receiving these instructions, this "control group" was sent home and asked to report back to the lab a week later.

A second group of students, the "event-simulation" group, were kept in the lab. They were asked to mentally simulate how the problem had unfolded:

> We would like you to visualize how this problem arose. Visualize the beginning of the problem, going over in detail the first incident. . . . Go over the incidents as they occurred step by step. Visualize the actions you took. Remember what you said, what you did. Visualize the environment, who was around, where you were.

The event-simulation participants had to retrace, step by step, the events that led to their problem. Presumably, reviewing the chain of causation might help the students think about how to fix the problem, like programmers engaged in systematic debugging.

A third group, the "outcome-simulation" group, was asked to mentally simulate a positive outcome emerging from the problem:

> Picture this problem beginning to resolve, you are coming out of the stressful situation. . . . Picture the relief you feel. Visualize the satisfaction you would feel at having dealt with the problem. Picture the confidence you feel in yourself, knowing that you have dealt successfully with the problem.

The outcome-simulators kept their focus on the desired future outcome: What will it be like once this problem is behind me?

After this initial exercise, both of the simulation groups were sent home. Both groups were asked to spend five minutes every day repeating their simulations, and to report back to the lab a week later.

Now it's play-at-home time: Make a quick prediction about which group of students fared best in coping with their problems. (Hint: It's not the control group.)

Here's the answer: The event-simulation group—the people who simulated how the events unfolded—did better on almost every dimension. Simulating past events is much more helpful than simulating future outcomes. In fact, the gap between the groups opened up immediately after the first session in the lab. By the first night, the event-simulation people were already experiencing a positive mood boost compared with the other two groups.

When the groups returned a week later, the event simulators' advantage had grown wider. They were more likely to have taken specific action to solve their problems. They were more likely to have sought advice and support from others. They were more likely to report that they had learned something and grown.

You may find these results a bit counterintuitive, because the pop-psychology literature is full of gurus urging you to visualize success. It turns out that a positive mental attitude isn't quite enough to get the job done. Maybe financial gurus shouldn't be telling us to imagine that we're filthy rich; instead, they should be telling us to replay the steps that led to our being poor.

Why does mental simulation work? It works because we can't imagine events or sequences without evoking the same modules of the brain that are evoked in real physical activity. Brain scans show that when people *imagine* a flashing light, they activate the visual area of the brain; when they *imagine* someone tapping on their skin, they activate tactile areas of the brain. The activity of mental simulation is not limited to the insides of our heads. People who imagine words that start with *b* or *p* can't resist subtle lip movements, and people who imagine looking at the Eiffel Tower can't resist moving their eyes upward. Mental simulation can even alter visceral physical responses: When people drink water but imagine that it's lemon juice, they salivate more. Even more surprisingly, when people drink lemon juice but imagine that it's water, they salivate less.

Mental simulations help us manage emotions. There is a standard treatment for phobias of various kinds—spiders, public speaking, airplane travel, and others. Patients are introduced to a relaxation procedure that inhibits anxiety, and then asked to visualize exposure to the thing they fear. The first visualizations start at the periphery of the fear. For example, someone who's afraid of air travel might start by thinking about the drive to the airport. The therapist leads the patient through a series of visualizations that get closer and closer to the heart of the fear ("Now the airplanes' engines are revving up on the runway, sounding louder and louder . . ."). Each time the visualizations create anxiety, the person pauses for a moment and uses the relaxation technique to restore equilibrium.

Notice that these visualizations focus on the events themselves—the process, rather than the outcomes. No one has ever been cured of a phobia by imagining how happy they'll be when it's gone.

Mental simulation helps with problem-solving. Even in mundane planning situations, mentally simulating an event helps us think of things that we might otherwise have neglected. Imagining a trip to the grocery store reminds us that we could drop off the dry cleaning at the store in the same shopping center. Mental simulations help us anticipate appropriate responses to future situations. Picturing a potential argument with our boss, imagining what she will say, may lead us to have the right words available when the time comes (and avoid saying the wrong words). Research has suggested that mental rehearsal can prevent people from relapsing into bad habits such as smoking, excessive drinking, or overeating. A man trying to kick a drinking problem will be better off if he mentally rehearses how he will handle Super Bowl Sunday: How should he respond when someone gets up for beers?

Perhaps most surprisingly, mental simulation can also build skills. A review of thirty-five studies featuring 3,214 participants showed that mental practice alone — sitting quietly, without moving, and picturing yourself performing a task successfully from start to finish — improves performance significantly. The results were borne out over a large number of tasks: Mental simulation helped people weld better and throw darts better. Trombonists improved their playing, and competitive figure skaters improved their skating. Not surprisingly, mental practice is more effective when a task involves more mental activity (e.g., trombone playing) as opposed to physical activity (e.g., balancing), but the magnitude of gains from mental practice is large on average: Overall, mental practice alone produced about *two thirds of the benefits of actual physical practice*.

The takeaway is simple: Mental simulation is not as good as actually doing something, but it's the next best thing. And, to circle back to the world of sticky ideas, what we're suggesting is that the right kind of story is, effectively, a simulation. Stories are like flight simulators for the brain. Hearing the nurse's heart-monitor story isn't like being there, but it's the next best thing.

Or think about the Xerox E053 code story. Why is hearing this story better than a warning about "misleading E053 indicators" in the training manual? It's better for precisely the reason that flight simulators are better for pilots than stacks of instructional flash cards. The more that training simulates the actions we must take in the world, the more effective it will be.

A story is powerful because it provides the context missing from abstract prose. It's back to the Velcro theory of memory, the idea that the more hooks we put into our ideas, the better they'll stick. The E053 story builds in emotions—the frustration of failing to find the problem and being misled by the machine's code. It builds in historical background—the idea that the recent change in the "XER board configuration" led to this new error. At the end, it delivers a kind of meta-level moral: You shouldn't have complete faith in the error code. This "code skepticism" is something the repairmen can apply to every future job they undertake.

It's easy for a doctor to treat appendicitis once it's been diagnosed, but the problem is learning to distinguish an inflamed appendix from an upset stomach or food poisoning or an ulcer. Or think about beginning algebra students, who can solve complex equations but grind to a halt when they're presented with a simple word problem that involves exactly the same math. Problem X doesn't always identify itself as Problem X.

This is the role that stories play—putting knowledge into a framework that is more lifelike, more true to our day-to-day existence. More like a flight simulator. Being the audience for a story isn't so passive, after all. Inside, we're getting ready to act.

Dealing with Problem Students

THE SITUATION: *Professors have to deal with the occasional nuisance in class—an angry, aggressive, or challenging student. Many professors are caught by surprise and aren't sure how to deal with the situation. In this Clinic we'll compare two different messages that were intended to share strategies for coping with these students.*

• • •

MESSAGE 1: The first message was produced by Indiana University as a resource for instructors.

- Remain calm. Slow down and regularize your breathing. Don't become defensive.
- Don't ignore them. Attempt to diffuse their anger. Arrange to meet them during a break or after class. During the meeting, acknowledge the student's emotions and listen. Talk in a professional and courteous manner.

COMMENTS ON MESSAGE 1: Notice that there's nothing unexpected here—nothing that is uncommon sense. (And if dealing with difficult students is common sense, then why do we need to publish tips for dealing with them?) Most of the advice—"Remain calm"; "Don't become defensive"; "Attempt to diffuse their anger"—is both too abstract and too obvious to stick. (Few teachers believe that you should *freak out* in response to a problem student.)

MESSAGE 2: The second message was posted, informally, to a newsgroup by a professor named Alyson Buckman, who wanted to share her experience with other teachers in the group:

I had a student . . . who talked loudly and often in the back of the class, generally when I was speaking. I could hear his comments at the front of the room, and so could everyone else. He also disagreed with me on every point I made, no matter what it was. Students began very quickly to complain about his behavior in their journals and suggest methods, generally designed to humiliate, of dealing with him.

I tried several things from the beginning, but finally called he and his confidante in class up to the front at the end of class one day and scheduled appointments with me in my office. I made sure I had witnesses to these appointments as well—one of the perks of being in a shared office space. The confidante, I believe, had been trapped into that role—the other student just utilized his body as a means to disruption.

When I met with the bully, he came in with sunglasses on and a totally defiant behavior. I started with "Why don't you tell me what's going on in the back of the room . . ." and he responded, "I disagree with you." I attempted to talk about this and met with silence.

It was not until I told him that other students were complaining and suggesting treatments for the situation that he listened. His body language totally changed as did his manner. I didn't have a problem with him from then on. My basic understanding of this little teaching lesson was that students who display contempt for the teacher might very well be brought into check by other students. After all, he thought he was showing off for them and found that they didn't want to hear or see it.

COMMENTS ON MESSAGE 2: This story allows us to simulate the process of dealing with a problem student. We follow along with Buckman as she works her way through the problem. Notice that many of the bulleted points from the first message are shown, rather than told, in the story. The professor attempts to "diffuse" the student's anger. She arranges "to talk with the student in a more private setting." She stays calm throughout.

The solution—in essence, using peer pressure to get the student under control—is both concrete and unexpected. It's uncommon sense. We might have expected a problem student not to care about what his peers thought. We empathize with Buckman, which makes us care about the outcome. It's easier to care about a person than a list of bulleted instructions.

SCORECARD

Checklist	Message 1	Message 2
Simple	-	-
Unexpected	-	✓
Concrete	✓	✓
Credible	-	-
Emotional	-	✓
Story	-	✓

PUNCH LINE: A few stories like Professor Buckman's—flight simulators for reining in problem students—would be much more interesting and effective in training professors than the list of bullet points in Message 1. This solution is not intuitive; nine out of ten training departments would create Message 1. We must fight the temptation to skip directly to the "tips" and leave out the story.

Stories as Inspiration: The Tale of Jared

In the late 1990s, the fast-food giant Subway launched a campaign to tout the healthiness of a new line of sandwiches. The campaign was based on a statistic: Seven subs under six grams of fat. As far as statistics go, that's pretty good—a spoonful of alliteration helps the medicine go down. But "7 Under 6" didn't stick like Subway's next campaign, which focused on the remarkable story of a college student named Jared Fogle.

Jared had a serious weight problem. By his junior year in college, he had ballooned to 425 pounds. He wore size XXXXXXL shirts, the largest size available in big-and-tall clothing stores. His pants had a 60-inch waist.

Jared's father, a general practitioner in Indianapolis, had been warning his son about his weight for years without much success. Then, one day in December, Jared's roommate, a premed major, noticed that Jared's ankles were swollen. He correctly diagnosed edema, a condition in which the body retains fluid because the blood can't transport enough liquid; it often leads to diabetes, heart problems, and even early heart attacks. Jared's father told him that, given his weight and general health, he might not live past thirty-five.

By the spring break following his December hospital visit, Jared had decided to slim down. Motivated by the "7 Under 6" campaign, he had his first turkey club. He liked the sandwich, and eventually he developed his own, all-Subway diet: a foot-long veggie sub for lunch and a six-inch turkey sub for dinner.

After three months of the "Subway diet," as he called it, he stepped on the scale. It read 330 pounds. He had dropped almost 100 pounds in three months by eating at Subway. He stuck with the diet for several more months, sometimes losing as much as a pound a day. As soon as his health permitted, he began walking as much as he could—not taking the bus to classes and even walking up stairs rather than taking the department-store escalator.

The story of how Jared's inspiring weight-loss became a national phenomenon begins with an article that appeared in the *Indiana Daily Student* in April 1999. It was written by Ryan Coleman, a former dormmate of Jared's. Coleman saw Jared after he had lost weight and almost didn't recognize him. He wrote movingly about what it was like for Jared to be obese:

> When Fogle registered for a class, he didn't base his choice on professor or class time like most students. He based which classes to register on whether he could fit into the classroom seats.
>
> When most folks worried whether they could find a parking spot close to campus, Fogle worried whether he could find a parking spot without a car already parked nearby — he needed the extra room in order to open the driver's side door so he could get out.

The article ended with this quote from Jared: "Subway helped save my life and start over. I can't ever repay that." This may have been the first time that a fast-food chain was credited with transforming someone's life in a profoundly positive way.

Then a reporter at *Men's Health* magazine, who was writing an article called "Crazy Diets That Work," happened to see the *Indiana Daily* article about Jared, and he included a blurb about a "subway sandwich diet." The article didn't mention Jared's name or even where he had bought the sandwiches; it simply referred generically to "subway sandwiches."

The key link in the chain was a Subway franchise owner named Bob Ocwieja, who spotted the article and thought it had potential. He took time out of his schedule to track down the creative director at Subway's Chicago ad agency, a man named Richard Coad, and suggested that he check out the article. Coad says, "I kind of laughed at first, but we followed up on it."

Jared is the hero of the weight-loss story, but Ocwieja and Coad are the heroes of our idea story. Ocwieja is a hero for spotting potential in a story, and Coad is a hero for spending the resources to follow up on it.

Coad and Barry Krause, the president of the advertising agency called Hal Riney, sent an intern to Bloomington, Indiana, with vague instructions to find the mystery sandwich-diet guy—and also to find out whose sandwiches he had been eating. It could easily have turned out that Jared had been dining at Flo's Sub Shop.

The intern wasn't exactly sure what he was supposed to do. His tentative plan was to show up in Bloomington, look through the Yellow Pages, and start dropping by the town's sub shops. Fortunately for the intern, the operation never became that complex. The first sub shop the intern visited was a Subway franchise close to campus. He launched into his description of the mystery eater, and about one sentence into the description the counter worker said, "Oh, that's Jared. He comes here every day."

The intern returned victorious. Jared was real, and he'd shed pounds by eating at Subway. The agency thought, *We've got a great story on our hands*.

And that's when the Jared story hit another hurdle. Ad agency president Krause called Subway's marketing director to unveil the tale of Jared, but the marketing director wasn't impressed. He had just started his job at Subway, having previously worked for another fast-food company. "I've seen that before," he said. "Fast foods can't do healthy." The marketing director preferred to launch a campaign focused on the taste of Subway's sandwiches.

To satisfy Krause, though, the director ran the Jared campaign idea by Subway's lawyers. The lawyers, predictably, said a Jared campaign couldn't be done. It would appear to be making a medical claim that might create a liability, blah blah blah. The only way to avoid any liability was to run disclaimers like "We don't recommend this diet. See your doctor first."

The idea seemed dead. But Krause and Coad weren't ready to

give up. Subway, like many franchise-based firms, runs ad campaigns at two levels: national and regional. While the national Subway office had vetoed Jared, some regional Subway franchisees expressed interest in the story and were willing to run the ads using regional advertising money.

Then came another hurdle: Franchisees didn't usually pay to make the actual commercials; they just paid to run the commercials in their regions. The commercials were generally funded by the national office. So who would pay for the Jared commercials?

Krause decided to make the spots for free. He said, "For the first and only time in my career, I gave the go-ahead to shoot an ad that we weren't going to be paid for."

The ad first ran on January 1, 2000—just in time for the annual epidemic of diet-related New Year's resolutions. It showed Jared in front of his home. "This is Jared," the announcer said. "He used to weigh 425 pounds"—we see a photo of Jared in his old 60-inch-waist pants—"but today he weighs 180 thanks to what he calls the Subway diet." The announcer describes Jared's meal plan, then concludes, "That, combined with a lot of walking, worked for Jared. We're not saying this is for everyone. You should check with your doctor before starting any diet program. But it worked for Jared."

The next day, Krause said, the phones started ringing in the morning and didn't let up. USA Today called, ABC and Fox News called. On the third day, Oprah called. "I've talked to a lot of marketers over the years who wanted to get media attention" Krause said. "No one ever got anywhere by lavishing calls on Oprah. The only time I've succeeded in my career with Oprah was with Jared, and Oprah called us."

A few days later, Subway's national office called Krause, asking if the ad could be aired nationally. In 1999, Subway's sales were flat. In 2000, sales jumped 18 percent, and they jumped another 16 percent in 2001. At the time, other (much smaller) sandwich chains such as Schlotzsky's and Quiznos were growing at about 7 percent per year.

. . . .

The Jared story has a morsel of simulation value. It makes it relatively easy to imagine what it would be like to embrace the Subway diet—the lunch order, the dinner order, the walking in between.
But this story is not so much a flight simulator as it is a pep talk. This
huge guy lost 245 pounds on a diet that he invented! Wow! The story
provides a good kick in the pants for anyone who's been struggling to
lose that last 10 pounds.

Like the nurse story that opened the chapter, this story, too, has
emotional resonance. Even skinny people who aren't interested in di-
eting will be inspired by Jared's tale. He fought big odds and prevailed through perseverance. And this is the second major payoff that
stories provide: inspiration. Inspiration drives action, as does simulation.

By the way, note how much better this campaign functions than
the "7 Under 6" campaign. Both campaigns are mining the same
turf—they both highlight the availability of nutritious, low-fat sandwiches. They both hold out the promise of weight loss. But one campaign was a modest success and one was a sensation.

What we have argued in this book—and we hope we've made you
a believer by now—is that *you could have predicted in advance* that
Jared would be the winner in these two campaigns.

Note how well the Jared story does on the SUCCESs checklist:

- It's simple: Eat subs and lose weight. (It may be oversimpli-
  fied, frankly, since the meatball sub with extra mayo won't
  help you lose weight.)
- It's unexpected: A guy lost a ton of weight by eating *fast food*!
  This story violates our schema of fast food, a schema that's
  more consistent with the picture of a fat Jared than a skinny
  Jared.
- It's concrete: Think of the oversized pants, the massive loss

of girth, the diet composed of particular sandwiches. It's much more like an Aesop fable than an abstraction.

- It's credible: It has the same kind of antiauthority truthfulness that we saw with the Pam Laffin antismoking campaign. *The guy who wore 60-inch pants is giving us diet advice!*

- It's emotional: We care more about an individual, Jared, than about a mass. And it taps into profound areas of Maslow's hierarchy—it's about a guy who reached his potential with the help of a sub shop.

- It's a story: Our protagonist overcomes big odds to triumph. It inspires the rest of us to do the same.

By contrast, let's size up "7 Under 6" on the checklist. It's simple, but notice that it has a much less compelling core message. Its core message is "We've got a variety of low-fat sandwiches," versus Jared's "Eat Subway, lose weight, change your life." The first message sells drill bits; the second tells you how to hang your kid's picture.

"7 Under 6" is *far* less unexpected. Jared's story packs a wallop because it violates the powerful schema that fast food is fatty. If "7 Under 6" is attacking the same schema, it makes the point much more tangentially.

"7 Under 6" isn't concrete. Numbers aren't concrete. It's credible only because it hasn't set the bar very high—not many of us will be floored to hear that a sandwich has less than 6 grams of fat, so we don't need much convincing. It's not emotional, and it's not a story.

Any reader of this book could have analyzed these two multimillion-dollar national ad campaigns and chosen the right one, just by laying them side by side on the SUCCESs checklist. (Note, though, that nonreaders might not be so savvy. The national advertising director, who had a lifetime of experience in trying to make ideas stick, wanted to walk away from the Jared story.)

Another compelling aspect of the Jared tale is how many people had to work hard to make it a reality. Look at how many unlikely

events had to take place in order for Jared to hit TV: The Subway
store manager had to be proactive enough to bring the magazine article to the creative director's attention. (Would your frontline people do this?) The creative director had to be savvy enough to invest
resources in what could have been a fruitless errand. (Was this really
an errand with a good return on investment?) The president of the
ad agency had to make the spot *for free* because he knew he was onto
something big. (Free!) The national Subway marketing team had to
swallow its pride and realize that it had made a mistake by not em-
bracing Jared earlier.

These are not trivial actions. This behavior is not routine. How
many great ideas have been extinguished because someone in the middle—a link between the source of the idea and its eventual outlet—
dropped the ball? In the normal world, a franchise owner would have
been amused by the Jared tale. He would have tacked it up on the bulletin board, on the wall of the hallway leading to the bathroom, as a
source of amusement for his employees. And that would have been the
pinnacle of the Jared tale.

Jared reminds us that we don't always have to *create* sticky ideas.
Spotting them is often easier and more useful. What if history teachers
were diligent about sharing teaching methods that worked brilliantly
in reaching students? What if we could count on the volunteers of
nonprofit organizations to be on the lookout for symbolic events or encounters that might inspire other people in the organization? What if
we could count on our bosses to take a gamble on important ideas?
You don't have to admire Subway sandwiches to admire the process of
bringing a great idea to life.

The Art of Spotting

How do we make sure that we don't let a great idea, a potential Jared,
float right under our nose? Spotting isn't hard, but it isn't natural,
either. Ideas don't flag themselves to get our attention. We have to

consciously look for the right ones. So what is it, exactly, that we should look for?

In the introduction of the book, we discussed a study showing that laypeople who'd been trained to use classic ad templates could create ads that were vastly superior to those developed by an untrained group. Just as there are ad templates that have been proven effective, so, too, there are story templates that have been proven effective. Learning the templates gives our spotting ability a huge boost.

Warren Buffett likes to tell the story of Rose Blumkin, a woman who manages one of the businesses that he invested in. Blumkin is a Russian woman who, at age twenty-three, finagled her way past a border guard to come to America. She couldn't speak English and had received no formal schooling.

Blumkin started a furniture business in 1937 with $500 that she had saved. Almost fifty years later, her furniture store was doing $100 million in annual revenue. At age one hundred, she was still on the floor seven days a week. She actually postponed her one-hundredth birthday party until an evening when the store was closed. At one point her competitors sued her for violating the fair-trade agreement because her prices were so much lower. They thought she was selling at a loss in order to put them out of business. Buffett says, "She demonstrated to the court that she could profitably sell carpet at a huge discount and sold the judge $1,400 worth of carpet."

The story of Rose Blumkin isn't from the book *Chicken Soup for the Soul*, but it could be. The *Chicken Soup* series has become a publishing phenomenon, with more than 4.3 million books sold and thirty-seven *Chicken Soup* titles in print, including *Chicken Soup for the Father's Soul*, *Chicken Soup for the Nurse's Soul*, and *Chicken Soup for the NASCAR Soul*.

The *Chicken Soup* books traffic in inspirational stories—stories that uplift, motivate, energize. In that sense, these stories are the opposite of urban legends, which tend to reinforce a cynical, pessimistic, or paranoid view of the world. (Strangers will steal your kidneys! Snapple supports the KKK! McDonald's puts worms in its burgers!)

What's amazing about these stories is that the authors didn't write them—they merely spotted and collected them. We wanted to understand what made these inspirational stories tick. We pored over inspirational stories—hundreds of stories, both from *Chicken Soup* and elsewhere—looking for underlying similarities.

Aristotle believed there were four primary dramatic plots: Simple Tragic, Simple Fortunate, Complex Tragic, and Complex Fortunate. Robert McKee, the screenwriting guru, lists twenty-five types of stories in his book: the modern epic, the disillusionment plot, and so on. When we finished sorting through a big pile of inspirational stories—a much narrower domain—we came to the conclusion that there are three basic plots: the Challenge plot, the Connection plot, and the Creativity plot.

These three basic plots can be used to classify more than 80 percent of the stories that appear in the original *Chicken Soup* collection. Perhaps more surprisingly, they can also be used to classify more than 60 percent of the stories published by *People* magazine about people who aren't celebrities. If an average person makes it into *People*, it's usually because he or she has an inspiring story for the rest of us. If our goal is to energize and inspire others, these three plots are the right place to start. (By the way, if you're a more jaded type of person who finds the *Chicken Soup* series treacly rather than inspirational, you'll still find value in the three plot templates. You can always turn down the volume on the plots a bit.)

THE CHALLENGE PLOT

The story of David and Goliath is the classic Challenge plot. A protagonist overcomes a formidable challenge and succeeds. David fells a giant with his homemade slingshot. There are variations of the Challenge plot that we all recognize: the underdog story, the rags-to-riches story, the triumph of sheer willpower over adversity.

The key element of a Challenge plot is that the obstacles seem daunting to the protagonist. Jared slimming down to 180 pounds is a Challenge plot. Jared's 210-pound neighbor shaving an inch off his waistline is not. We've all got a huge mental inventory of Challenge plot stories. The American hockey team beating the heavily favored Russians in the 1980 Olympics. The Alamo. Horatio Alger tales. The American Revolution. Seabiscuit. The *Star Wars* movies. Lance Armstrong. Rosa Parks.

Challenge plots are inspiring even when they're much less dramatic and historical than these examples. The Rose Blumkin story doesn't involve a famous character. Challenge plots are inspiring in a defined way. They inspire us by appealing to our perseverance and courage. They make us want to work harder, take on new challenges, overcome obstacles. Somehow, after you've heard about Rose Blumkin postponing her one-hundredth birthday party until an evening when her store was closed, it's easier to clean out your garage. Challenge plots inspire us to act.

THE CONNECTION PLOT

Today the phrase "good Samaritan" refers to someone who voluntarily helps others in times of distress. The original story of the Good Samaritan from the Bible is certainly consistent with this definition, but it's even more profound.

The story begins with a lawyer who approached Jesus with a question about how to get to heaven. The lawyer was more interested in testing Jesus than in learning from him. When Jesus asked the lawyer what *he* thought the answer was, the lawyer gave a reply that included the notion "You shall love your neighbor as yourself." Jesus accepted the lawyer's answer. Then the lawyer (perhaps wanting to limit the number of people he's on the hook to love) says, "And who is my neighbor?"

In response, Jesus told a story:

"A man was going down from Jerusalem to Jericho, when he fell into the hands of robbers. They stripped him of his clothes, beat him and went away, leaving him half dead.

"A priest happened to be going down the same road, and when he saw the man, he passed by on the other side. So too, a Levite, when he came to the place and saw him, passed by on the other side.

"But a Samaritan, as he traveled, came where the man was; and when he saw him, he took pity on him. He went to him and bandaged his wounds, pouring on oil and wine. Then he put the man on his own donkey, took him to an inn and took care of him. The next day he took out two silver coins and gave them to the innkeeper. 'Look after him,' he said, 'and when I return, I will reimburse you for any extra expense you may have.'

"Which of these three do you think was a neighbor to the man who fell into the hands of robbers?"

The lawyer replied, "The one who had mercy on him."

Jesus told him, "Go and do likewise."

What's missing from this tale, for modern-day readers, is a bit of context. The Samaritan in the story was not simply a nice guy. He was a nice guy crossing a huge social gulf in helping the wounded man. At the time, there was tremendous hostility between Samaritans and Jews (all the other main characters in the story). A modern-day analogy to the outcast status of the Samaritan might be an "atheist biker gang member." The lesson of the story is clear: Good neighbors show mercy and compassion, and not just to people in their own group.

This is what a Connection plot is all about. It's a story about people who develop a relationship that bridges a gap—racial, class, ethnic, religious, demographic, or otherwise. The Connection plot doesn't have to deal with life-and-death stakes, as does the Good Samaritan. The connection can be as trivial as a bottle of a Coke, as in the famous Mean Joe Greene commercial. A scrawny young white fan encounters a towering famous black athlete. A bottle of Coke links them. It ain't the Good Samaritan, but it's clearly a Connection plot.

Connection plots are also fabulous for romance stories—think of *Romeo and Juliet* (or the top-grossing movie of all time, *Titanic*). All Connection plots inspire us in social ways. They make us want to help others, be more tolerant of others, work with others, love others. The Connection plot is the most common kind of plot found in the *Chicken Soup* series.

Where Challenge plots involve overcoming challenges, Connection plots are about our relationships with other people. If you're telling a story at the company Christmas party, it's probably best to use the Connection plot. If you're telling a story at the kickoff party for a new project, go with the Challenge plot.

THE CREATIVITY PLOT

The third major type of inspirational story is the Creativity plot. The prototype might be the story of the apple that falls on Newton's head, inspiring his theory of gravity. The Creativity plot involves someone making a mental breakthrough, solving a long-standing puzzle, or attacking a problem in an innovative way. It's the *MacGyver* plot.

Ingersoll-Rand is a giant company that makes nonsexy products such as industrial grinders, used in auto shops to sand down auto bodies. Historically, Ingersoll-Rand had been slow at bringing new products to market. One employee, frustrated by the average four-year product life cycle, said, "It was taking us longer to introduce a new product than it took our nation to fight World War II."

Ingersoll-Rand decided to do something about the slow development cycle. The company created a project team whose goal was to produce a new grinder in a year—one quarter the usual time. Standard theories of organizational culture would have predicted a slim chance of success. The grinder team, however, did a lot of things right, including the use of stories to emphasize the group's new attitude and culture. One story, for instance, involved a critical decision about whether to build the new grinder's casing out of plastic or metal. Plastic would be more comfortable for the customer, but would it hold up as well as metal?

The traditional Ingersoll-Rand method of solving this problem would have been to conduct protracted, careful studies of the tensile and compression properties of both materials. But this was the Grinder Team. They were supposed to act quickly. A few members of the team cooked up a less formal testing procedure. While on an off-site customer visit, the team members tied a sample of each material to the back bumper of their rental car, then drove around the parking lot with the materials dragging behind. They kept this up until the police came and told them to knock it off. The verdict was that the new plastic composite held up just as well as the traditional metal. Decision made.

In the history of the Grinder Team, this story has become known as the Drag Test. The Drag Test is a Creativity plot that reinforced the team's new culture. The Drag Test implied, "We still need to get the right data to make decisions. We just need to do it a lot quicker."

The famous explorer Ernest Shackleton faced such enormous odds in his explorations (obviously a classic Challenge plot) that unity among his men was mission-critical. A mutiny could leave everyone dead. Shackleton came up with a creative solution for dealing with the whiny, complaining types. He assigned them to sleep in his own tent. When people separated into groups to work on chores, he grouped the complainers with him. Through his constant presence, he minimized their negative influence. Creativity plots make us want to do something different, to be creative, to experiment with new approaches.

The goal of reviewing these plots is not to help us invent stories. Unless you write fiction or advertisements, that won't help much. The goal here is to learn how to spot the stories that have potential.

When the Jared article hits our desk, we want to spot the crucial elements immediately. *Guy faces huge obstacles and overcomes them — it's a Challenge plot.* Challenge plots inspire people to take on challenges and work harder. If that feeling is consistent with the goal you want to achieve, run with the story; don't tack it on the bulletin board.

If you're running the Grinder Team, and you're trying to reinvent the company culture, then you need to be on the lookout for Creativity plots. When you hear that some of your men dragged metal around a parking lot, you've found something.

Know what you're looking for. You don't need to make stuff up, you don't need to exaggerate or be as melodramatic as the *Chicken Soup* tales. (The Drag Test isn't melodramatic.) You just need to recognize when life is giving you a gift.

Stories at the World Bank

In 1996, Stephen Denning was working for the World Bank, the international institution that lends money to developing countries for infrastructure projects such as building schools, roads, and water-treatment facilities. At the time, he managed the bank's work in Africa — the third-largest area of the bank — and seemed to be on a fast track to the top of the organization.

Then one of his two main mentors retired and the second left. Shortly thereafter he was asked to step down from his Africa position and "look into the issue of information." His superiors asked him to explore the area of knowledge management. Denning said, "Now this was a bank which cared about flows of money, not information. The new assignment was the equivalent of being sent to corporate Siberia."

The task was not just organizationally unattractive, it was daunting. The World Bank knew a lot about how to achieve results in developing nations, but that information was scattered about the

organization. The World Bank conducted projects in dozens of countries all over the world—and while there was a central bureaucracy,
much of the operational know-how was naturally at the local level.
Each project was, in a sense, its own universe. A water-treatment guru
in Zambia might have figured out a great way to handle local political negotiations, but he was unlikely to have the opportunity to share
it with a highway-construction guru in Bangladesh. Neither manager
would know the other existed, unless they happened to be in the
same circle of friends or former colleagues.

A month after accepting his assignment, Denning had lunch with
a colleague who had just returned from Zambia. This colleague was
working on a project to improve health care, particularly for mothers
and children. While he was in Zambia he had met a health-care
worker in Kamana—a small town 360 miles from Zambia's capital—
who was struggling to fight malaria in the community and was trying
to find information on how to combat the disease. The worker had
found a way to log on to the Internet and had discovered the answers
he needed on the website of the Centers for Disease Control (CDC)
in Atlanta. (Keep in mind that this was in 1996, when the Internet
would not have been the obvious first stop for someone in search of
information, especially in Africa.)

Denning says that he didn't give the story much thought at the
time; it was just an interesting anecdote about the resourcefulness of
a colleague. Later, it dawned on him that the Zambia story was a perfect example of the power of knowledge management. Someone in
charge of a vital operation needed information. He went looking for it,
found it, and, as a result, was able to act more effectively. That's the
vision of knowledge management—except that the health-care worker
shouldn't have been forced to conduct a trial-and-error search, ending
at the CDC's website, to get the right information. He should have
been able to tap the knowledge of the World Bank.

Denning began to incorporate the story into conversations with
colleagues, stressing why the World Bank ought to make knowledge

management a serious priority. Weeks later, he had an opportunity to speak to a committee of senior management. He'd have only ten to twelve minutes on the agenda. In that time he'd have to introduce a new organizational strategy and win the group's endorsement. A tall order.

First, Denning set up the problem: the difficulties that the World Bank had experienced in pooling its knowledge and the sorry state of its information systems. Then, rather than doing what most people would have done—i.e., rehashing the discipline of knowledge management and quoting some authorities about the importance of knowledge management for the twenty-first century—Denning did something different. He told the Zambia story.

Immediately after the presentation, two executives raced up to Denning and began to bombard him with all the things he should be doing to get the program off the ground. Denning thought, "This is a very strange conversation. Up till ten minutes ago, these people weren't willing to give me the time of day, and now I'm not doing enough to implement their idea. This is horrible! They've stolen my idea!" And then he had a happier thought. "How wonderful! They've stolen my idea. It's become their idea!"

A few years later, after Denning had left the World Bank, he devoted himself to spreading the lessons he'd learned about storytelling. In 2001, he wrote a very insightful book called *The Springboard*. Denning defines a springboard story as a story that lets people see how an existing problem might change. Springboard stories tell people about possibilities.

One major advantage of springboard stories is that they combat skepticism and create buy-in. Denning says that the idea of telling stories initially violated his intuition. He had always believed in the value of being direct, and he worried that stories were too ambiguous, too peripheral, too anecdotal. He thought, "Why not spell out the message directly? Why go to the trouble and difficulty of trying to elicit the listener's thinking indirectly, when it would be so much simpler if I come straight out in an abstract directive? Why not hit the listeners between the eyes?"

The problem is that when you hit listeners between the eyes they respond by fighting back. The way you deliver a message to them is a cue to how they should react. If you make an argument, you're implicitly asking them to evaluate your argument—judge it, debate it, criticize it—and then argue back, at least in their minds. But with a story, Denning argues, you engage the audience—you are involving people with the idea, asking them to participate with you.

Denning talks about engaging the "little voice inside the head," the voice that would normally debate the speaker's points. "The conventional view of communication is to ignore the little voice inside the head and hope it stays quiet and that the message will somehow get through," Denning says. But he has a different recommendation: "Don't ignore the little voice. . . . Instead, *work in harmony* with it. Engage it by giving it something to do. Tell a story in a way that elicits a second story from the little voice."

In addition to creating buy-in, springboard stories mobilize people to act. Stories focus people on potential solutions. Telling stories with visible goals and barriers shifts the audience into a problem-solving mode. Clearly, the amount of "problem-solving" we do varies across stories. We don't watch *Titanic* and start brainstorming about improved iceberg-spotting systems. But we do empathize with the main characters and start cheering them on when they confront their problems: "Look out behind you!" "Tell him off now!" "Don't open that door!"

But springboard stories go beyond having us problem-solve for the main character. A springboard story helps us problem-solve for ourselves. A springboard story is an exercise in mass customization—each audience member uses the story as a springboard to slightly different destinations.

After Denning told the Zambia story, one of the executives at the meeting took the idea of knowledge management to the president of the World Bank, arguing that it was the future of the organization. Denning was invited to present his ideas to the bank's top leaders, including the president. By the end of the year, the president had announced that knowledge management was one of the bank's top priorities.

The Conference Storybook

We started the chapter with the nurse story, which comes from the researcher Gary Klein. Klein tells another story that provides a good summary of the ground we've covered.

The organizer of a conference once asked Klein's firm to sum up the results of a conference. The organizer wanted a useful summary of the conference—more compact than a transcript and more coherent than an idiosyncratic collection of the presenters' PowerPoint slides.

Klein's firm assigned one person to monitor each of the conference's five parallel tracks. The monitors attended each panel, and each time someone told a story they jotted it down. At the end of the conference, the monitors compared notes and found that, as Klein said, they had compiled a set of stories that were "funny, and tragic, and exciting." The group structured and organized the stories and sent the packet to the conference organizer.

She was ecstatic. She found the packet much more vivid and useful than the typical conference takeaway: a set of dry, jargon-filled abstracts. She even requested funds from her organization to convert the notes into a book. Meanwhile, as a courtesy, she sent the summary notes to all of the conference presenters.

They were furious. They were insulted to have the stories scooped out of their overall structure—they didn't want to be remembered as people who told a bunch of stories and anecdotes. They felt that they'd invested countless hours into distilling their experiences into a series of recommendations. Indeed, their abstracts—which had been submitted to the conference organizers—were filled with tidbits of wisdom, such as "Keep the lines of communication open" and "Don't wait too long when problems are building up."

Klein said, "We want to explain to them how meaningless these slogans are in contrast to stories, such as the one that showed *how* they had kept the lines of communication open during a difficult incident in which a plant was shut down." But the presenters were adamant, and the project was abandoned.

This story is one of our favorites in the book, because the dynamics are so clear. We're not trying to portray the presenters as bad, idea-hating people. Put yourself in their shoes. You've created this amazing presentation, summarizing years of your work, and your goal is to help people master a complex structure that you've spent years constructing. You've erected an amazing intellectual edifice! Then Klein's crew approaches your edifice, plucks a few bricks out of the wall, and tries to pass them off as the sum of all your labors. The nerve!

The problem, of course, is that it's impossible to transfer an edifice in a ninety-minute presentation. The best you can do is convey some building blocks. But you can't pluck building blocks from the roof, which is exactly what you're doing with a recommendation like "Keep the lines of communication open."

Suppose you're a manager at Nordstrom, addressing a conference of your peers. The final slide in your presentation might read, "Lessons from Nordstrom: In retail, outstanding customer service is a key source of competitive advantage." While discussing your fourth slide you might have mentioned, as a humorous aside, the Nordie who gift-wrapped a present bought at Macy's. These jokers from Klein's firm want to keep your gift-wrapping story but drop your punch line. And they're absolutely right.

In the "Simple" and "Unexpected" chapters, we said that good messages must move from common sense to uncommon sense. In contrast, there's nothing *but* common sense in recommendations such as "Keep the lines of communication open" and "Don't wait too long when problems are building up." (Klein comments that these lessons are presumably designed for people who would rather close lines of communication and sit around when they're facing a daunting problem.)

Once again, the Curse of Knowledge has bewitched these presenters. When they share their lessons — "Keep the lines of communication open" — they're hearing a song, filled with passion and emotion, inside their heads. They're remembering the experiences that taught them those lessons — the struggles, the political battles, the missteps, the pain. They are tapping. But they forget that the audience can't hear the same tune they hear.

Stories can almost single-handedly defeat the Curse of Knowledge. In fact, they naturally embody most of the SUCCESs framework. Stories are almost always Concrete. Most of them have Emotional and Unexpected elements. The hardest part of using stories effectively is making sure that they're Simple — that they reflect your core message. It's not enough to tell a great story; the story has to reflect your agenda. You don't want a general lining up his troops before battle to tell a Connection plot story.

Stories have the amazing dual power to simulate and to inspire. And most of the time we don't even have to use much creativity to harness these powers — we just need to be ready to spot the good ones that life generates every day.

WHAT STICKS

S ometimes ideas stick despite our best efforts to stop them. In 1946, Leo Durocher was the coach of the Dodgers. His club was leading the National League, while the team's traditional archrival, the New York Giants, was languishing in the bottom of the standings.

During a game between the Dodgers and the Giants, Durocher was mocking the Giants in front of a group of sportswriters. One of the sportswriters teased Durocher, "Why don't you be a nice guy for a change?" Durocher pointed at the Giants' dugout and said, "Nice guys! Look over there. Do you know a nicer guy than [Giants' manager] Mel Ott? Or any of the other Giants? Why, they're the nicest guys in the world! And where are they? In seventh place!"

As recounted by Ralph Keyes in his book on misquotations, *Nice Guys Finish Seventh*, the metamorphosis of Durocher's quote began a year later. The *Baseball Digest* quoted Durocher as saying, "Nice guys finish in last place in the second division." Before long, as his quip was passed along from one person to another, it evolved, becoming simpler and more universal, until it emerged as a cynical comment on life: "Nice guys finish last." No more reference to the

Giants, no more reference to seventh place—in fact, no more reference to baseball at all. Nice guys finish last.

This quote, polished by the marketplace of ideas, irked Durocher. For years, he denied saying the phrase (and, of course, he was right), but eventually he gave up. *Nice Guys Finish Last* was the title of his autobiography.

One of the most famous misquotations of all time is attributed to the fictional detective Sherlock Holmes. Holmes never said, "Elementary, my dear Watson." This seems hard to believe—the quote is perfectly suited to our schema of Holmes. In fact, if you asked someone to name one Sherlock Holmes quote, this would be it. His most famous quote is the one he never said.

Why did this nonexistent quote stick? It's not hard to imagine what must have happened. Holmes frequently said, "My dear Watson," and he often said, "Elementary." A natural mistake, for someone inclined to quote from a Holmes mystery, would be to combine the two. And, like an adaptive biological mutation, the newly combined quote was such an improvement that it couldn't help but spread. This four-word quotation, after all, contains the essence of Holmes: the brilliant detective never too busy to condescend to his faithful sidekick.

In the "Simple" chapter, we told the story of the 1992 Clinton campaign and Carville's famous proverb, "It's the economy, stupid." We mentioned that this proverb was one of three phrases that Carville wrote on a whiteboard. Here's a trivia question: What were the other two?

The other two phrases were "Change vs. more of the same" and "Don't forget health care." Those phrases didn't stick. So should

Carville have been pleased with the success of "It's the economy, stupid" as an idea? On the one hand, his phrase resonated so strongly that it became a powerful tool in framing the election. On the other hand, he got only one third of his message across!

We bring up these examples because, in making ideas stick, the audience gets a vote. The audience may change the meaning of your idea, as happened with Durocher. The audience may actually improve your idea, as was the case with Sherlock Holmes. Or the audience may retain some of your ideas and jettison others, as with Carville.

All of us tend to have a lot of "idea pride." We want our message to endure in the form we designed. Durocher's response, when the audience shaped his idea, was to deny, deny, deny . . . then eventually accept.

The question we have to ask ourselves in any situation is this: Is the audience's version of my message still core? In Chapter 1 ("Simple"), we discussed the importance of focusing on core messages—honing in on the most important truths that we need to communicate. If the world takes our ideas and changes them—or accepts some and discards others—all we need to decide is whether the mutated versions are still core. If they are—as with "It's the economy, stupid"—then we should humbly embrace the audience's judgment. Ultimately, the test of our success as idea creators isn't whether people mimic our exact words, it's whether we achieve our goals.

The Power of Spotting

Carville, Durocher, and Arthur Conan Doyle were all creators of ideas. They produced ideas from scratch. But let's not forget that it's just as effective to spot sticky ideas as it is to create them.

Think about Nordstrom. You can't very well create from scratch a bunch of stories about sales reps cheerfully gift-wrapping presents from Macy's. But when you come across a real story like that, you've got to be alert to the idea's potential. And this isn't as easy as it sounds.

The barrier to idea-spotting is that we tend to process anecdotes differently than abstractions. If a Nordstrom manager is hit with an abstraction, such as "Increase customer satisfaction scores by 10 percent this quarter," that abstraction kicks in the managerial mentality: How do we get there from here? But a story about a tire-chain-exchanging, cold-car-warming sales rep provokes a different way of thinking. It will likely be filed away with other kinds of day-to-day personal news—interesting but ultimately trivial, like the fact that John Robison shaved his head or James Schlueter showed up late seven days in a row. In some sense, there's a wall in our minds separating the little picture—stories, for instance—from the big picture. Spotting requires us to tear down that wall.

How do we tear down the wall? As a rough analogy, think about the way we buy gifts for loved ones. If we know that Christmas or a birthday is approaching, there's a little nagging process that opens up in our minds, reminding us that "Dad is a gadget guy, so keep an eye out for cool gadgets." It's barely conscious, but if we happen upon a Retractable Roto-Laser-Light on December 8, chances are we'll immediately spot it as a possible fit for Dad.

The analogy to the idea world is maintaining a deeply ingrained sense of the core message that we want to communicate. Just as we can put on Dad Gift Glasses, allowing us to view merchandise from his perspective, we can also put on Core Idea Glasses, allowing us to filter incoming ideas from that perspective. If you're a Nordstrom manager, obsessed with improving customer service, this filter helps you spot the warming-cars episode as a symbol of perfection, rather than as an interesting anecdote.

In the Introduction, we debunked the common assumption that you need natural creative genius to cook up a great idea. You don't. But, beyond that, it's crucial to realize that creation, period, is unnecessary. Think of the ideas in this book that were spotted rather than created: Nordies. Jared. The mystery of Saturn's rings. Pam Laffin, the smoking antiauthority. The nurse who ignored the heart monitor, listened with her stethoscope, and saved the baby's life. If you're a great spotter, you'll always trump a great creator. Why? Because the world will always produce more great ideas than any single individual, even the most creative one.

The Speakers and the Stickers

Each year in the second session of Chip's "Making Ideas Stick" class at Stanford, the students participate in an exercise, a kind of testable credential to show what kinds of messages stick and don't stick. The students are given some data from a government source on crime patterns in the United States. Half of them are asked to make a one-minute persuasive speech to convince their peers that nonviolent crime is a serious problem in this country. The other half are asked to take the position that it's not particularly serious.

Stanford students, as you'd expect, are smart. They also tend to be quick thinkers and good communicators. No one in the room ever gives a poor speech.

The students divide into small groups and each one gives a one-minute speech while the others listen. After each speech, the listeners rate the speaker: How impressive was the delivery? How persuasive?

What happens, invariably, is that the most polished speakers get the highest ratings. Students who are poised, smooth, and charismatic are rated at the top of the class. No surprise, right? Good speakers score well in speaking contests.

The surprise comes next. The exercise appears to be over; in fact, Chip often plays a brief *Monty Python* clip to kill a few minutes and distract the students. Then, abruptly, he asks them to pull out a sheet of paper and write down, for each speaker they heard, every single idea that they remember.

The students are flabbergasted at how little they remember. Keep in mind that only ten minutes have elapsed since the speeches were given. Nor was there a huge volume of information to begin with—at most, they've heard eight one-minute speeches. And yet the students are lucky to recall one or two ideas from each speaker's presentation. Many draw a complete blank on some speeches—unable to remember a single concept.

In the average one-minute speech, the typical student uses 2.5 statistics. Only one student in ten tells a story. Those are the speaking statistics. The "remembering" statistics, on the other hand, are almost a mirror image: When students are asked to recall the speeches, 63 percent remember the stories. Only 5 percent remember any individual statistic.

Furthermore, almost no correlation emerges between "speaking talent" and the ability to make ideas stick. The people who were captivating speakers typically do no better than others in making their ideas stick. Foreign students—whose less-polished English often leaves them at the bottom of the speaking-skills rankings—are suddenly on a par with native speakers. The stars of stickiness are the students who made their case by telling stories, or by tapping into emotion, or by stressing a single point rather than ten. There is no question that a ringer—a student who came into the exercise having read this book—would squash the other students. A community college student for whom English is a second language could easily outperform unwitting Stanford graduate students.

Why can't these smart, talented speakers make their ideas stick? A few of the villains discussed in this book are implicated. The first villain is the natural tendency to bury the lead—to get lost in a sea of information. One of the worst things about knowing a lot, or having access to a lot of information, is that we're tempted to share it all. High school teachers will tell you that when students write research papers they feel obligated to include every unearthed fact, as though the value were in the quantity of data amassed rather than in its purpose or clarity. Stripping out information, in order to focus on the core, is not instinctual.

The second villain is the tendency to focus on the presentation rather than on the message. Public speakers naturally want to appear composed, charismatic, and motivational. And, certainly, charisma will help a properly designed message stick better. But all the charisma in the world won't save a dense, unfocused speech, as some Stanford students learn the hard way.

More Villains

There are two other key villains in the book that the Stanford students don't have to wrestle with. The first is decision paralysis—the anxiety and irrationality that can emerge from excessive choice or ambiguous situations. Think about the students who missed both a fantastic lecture and a great film because they couldn't decide which one was better, or how hard it was for Jeff Hawkins, the leader of the Palm Pilot development group, to get his team to focus on a few issues rather than on many.

To beat decision paralysis, communicators have to do the hard work of finding the core. Lawyers must stress one or two points in their closing arguments, not ten. A teacher's lesson plans may contain fifty concepts to share with her students, but in order to be effective that teacher must devote most of her efforts to making the most critical two or three stick. Managers must share proverbs—"Names, names, and names" or "THE low-fare airline"—that help employees wring decisions out of ambiguous situations.

The archvillain of sticky ideas, as you know by now, is the Curse of Knowledge. The Stanford students didn't face the Curse of Knowledge because the data on crime was brand-new to them—they were more akin to reporters trying to avoid burying the lead on a news story than to experts who have forgotten what it's like not to know something.

The Curse of Knowledge is a worthy adversary, because in some sense it's inevitable. Getting a message across has two stages: the Answer stage and the Telling Others stage. In the Answer stage, you use your expertise to arrive at the idea that you want to share. Doctors study for a decade to be capable of giving the Answer. Business managers may deliberate for months to arrive at the Answer.

Here's the rub: The same factors that worked to your advantage in the Answer stage will backfire on you during the Telling Others stage. To get the Answer, you need expertise, but you can't dissociate expertise from the Curse of Knowledge. You know things that others don't know, and you can't remember what it was like not to know those things. So when you get around to sharing the Answer, you'll tend to communicate *as if your audience were you.*

You'll stress the scads of statistics that were pivotal in arriving at the Answer—and, like the Stanford students, you'll find that no one remembers them afterward. You'll share the punch line—the overarching truth that emerged from months of study and analysis—and, like the CEO who stresses "maximizing shareholder value" to his frontline employees, no one will have a clue how your punch line relates to the day-to-day work.

There is a curious disconnect between the amount of time we invest in training people how to arrive at the Answer and the amount of time we invest in training them how to Tell Others. It's easy to graduate from medical school or an MBA program without ever taking a class in communication. College professors take dozens of courses in their areas of expertise but none on how to teach. A lot of engineers would scoff at a training program about Telling Others.

Business managers seem to believe that, once they've clicked through a PowerPoint presentation showcasing their conclusions, they've successfully communicated their ideas. What they've done is share data. If they're good speakers, they may even have created an enhanced sense, among their employees and peers, that they are "decisive" or "managerial" or "motivational." But, like the Stanford students, the surprise will come when they realize that nothing they've said had impact. They've shared data, but they haven't created ideas that are useful and lasting. Nothing stuck.

Making an Idea Stick: The Communication Framework

For an idea to stick, for it to be useful and lasting, it's got to make the audience:

1. Pay attention
2. Understand and remember it
3. Agree/Believe
4. Care
5. Be able to act on it

This book could have been organized around these five steps, but there's a reason they were reserved for the conclusion. The Curse of Knowledge can easily render this framework useless. When an expert asks, "Will people understand my idea?," her answer will be *Yes*, because she herself understands. ("Of course, my people will understand 'maximizing shareholder value!'") When an expert asks, "Will people care about this?," her answer will be *Yes*, because she herself cares. Think of the Murray Dranoff Duo Piano people, who said, "We exist to protect, preserve, and promote the music of the duo piano." They were shocked when that statement didn't arouse the same passion in others that it did in them.

The SUCCESs checklist is a substitute for the framework above, and its advantage is that it's more tangible and less subject to the Curse of Knowledge. In fact, if you think back across the chapters you've read, you'll notice that the framework matches up nicely:

1. Pay attention: UNEXPECTED
2. Understand and remember it: CONCRETE

3. Agree/Believe: CREDIBLE
4. Care: EMOTIONAL
5. Be able to act on it: STORY

So, rather than guess about whether people will understand our ideas, we should ask, "Is it concrete?" Rather than speculate about whether people will care, we should ask, "Is it emotional? Does it get out of Maslow's basement? Does it force people to put on an Analytical Hat or allow them to feel empathy?" (By the way, "Simple" is not on the list above because it's mainly about the Answer stage—honing in on the core of your message and making it as compact as possible. But Simple messages help throughout the process, especially in helping people to understand and act.)

The SUCCESs checklist, then, is an ideal tool for dealing with communication problems. Let's look at some common symptoms of communication problems and how we can respond to them.

SYMPTOMS AND SOLUTIONS

Problems getting people to pay attention to a message

SYMPTOM: "No one is listening to me" or "They seem bored—they hear this stuff all the time."

SOLUTION: Surprise them by breaking their guessing machines—tell them something that is uncommon sense. (The lead is, There will be no school next Thursday! Nordies gift-wrap packages from Macy's!)

SYMPTOM: "I lost them halfway through" or "Their attention was wavering toward the end."

SOLUTION: Create curiosity gaps—tell people just enough for them to realize the piece that's missing from their knowledge. (Remember Roone Arledge's introductions to college football games, setting the context for the rivalry.) Or create mysteries or puzzles that are slowly solved over the course of the communication. (Like the professor who started each class with a mystery, such as the one about Saturn's rings.)

Problems getting people to understand and remember

SYMPTOM: "They always nod their heads when I explain it to them, but it never seems to translate into action."

SOLUTION: Make the message simpler and use concrete language. Use what people already know as a way to make your intentions clearer, as with a generative analogy (like Disney's "cast member" metaphor). Or use concrete, real-world examples. Don't talk about "knowledge management"; tell a story about a health worker in Zambia getting information on malaria from the Internet.

SYMPTOM: "We have these meetings where it seems like everyone is talking past each other" or "Everyone has such different levels of knowledge that it's hard to teach them."

SOLUTION: Create a highly concrete turf where people can apply their knowledge. (Think of the venture-capital pitch for a portable computer where the entrepreneur tossed his binder onto the table, sparking brainstorming.) Have people grapple with specific examples or cases rather than concepts.

Problems getting people to believe you or agree

SYMPTOM: "They're not buying it."

SOLUTION: Find the telling details for your message—the equivalent of the dancing seventy-three-year-old man, or the textile factory so environmentally friendly that it actually cleans the water pouring through it. Use fewer authorities and more antiauthorities.

SYMPTOM: "They quibble with everything I say" or "I spend all my time arguing with them about this."

SOLUTION: Quiet the audience's mental skeptics by using a springboard story, switching them into creative mode. Move away from statistics and facts toward meaningful examples. Use an anecdote that passes the Sinatra Test.

Problems getting people to care

SYMPTOM: "They are so apathetic" or "No one seems fired up about this."

SOLUTION: Remember the Mother Teresa effect—people care more about individuals than they do about abstractions. Tell them an inspiring Challenge plot or Creativity plot story. Tap into their sense of their own identities, like the "Don't Mess with Texas" ads, which suggested that not littering was the Texan thing to do.

SYMPTOM: "The things that used to get people excited just aren't doing it anymore."

SOLUTION: Get out of Maslow's basement and try appealing to more profound types of self-interest.

Problems getting people to act

SYMPTOM: "Everyone nods their heads and then nothing happens."

SOLUTION: Inspire them with a Challenge plot story (Jared, David and Goliath) or engage them by using a springboard story (the World Bank). Make sure your message is simple and concrete enough to be useful—turn it into a proverb ("Names, names, and names").

John F. Kennedy versus Floyd Lee

"I believe that this nation should commit itself to achieving the goal, before this decade is out, of landing a man on the moon and returning him safely to the earth." Those were John F. Kennedy's words in May 1961. An inspiring message for an inspiring mission. It was a single idea that motivated a nation to a decade of work—and an eventual, historic, unforgettable success.

But here's the thing: You're not JFK.

And neither are we. We don't have an ounce of his charisma or power. We are less concerned with traveling to the moon than with, say, remembering our wallets when we leave home in the morning. So, if being JFK was what it took to make an idea stick, this would be a depressing book indeed.

JFK isn't the standard. In fact, he's the aberration. Keep in mind that the same chapter where we first mentioned the "Man on the Moon" speech also contains a reference to the Kentucky Fried Rat. Our heads are not entirely in the clouds.

Sticky ideas have things in common, and in this book we've reverse-engineered them. We've studied preposterous ideas: the kidney thieves and their ice-filled bathtub. We've studied brilliant ideas: Ulcers are caused by bacteria. We've studied boring ideas made interesting: the flight-safety announcement. We've studied interesting ideas made boring: Oral rehydration salts that could save the lives of thousands of kids. We've seen ideas related to newspapers, accounting, nuclear war, evangelism, seat belts, dust, dancing, litter, football, AIDS, shipping, and hamburgers.

And what we've seen is that all these ideas—profound and mundane, serious and silly—share common traits. Our hope is that, now that you understand these traits, you'll be able to apply them to your own ideas. *They laughed when you shared a story instead of a statistic. But when the idea stuck . . .*

The SUCCESs checklist is intended to be a deeply practical tool. It's no accident that it's a checklist and not an equation. It's not hard, and it's not rocket science. But neither is it natural or instinctive. It requires diligence and it requires awareness.

This book is filled with normal people facing normal problems who did amazing things simply by applying these principles (even if they weren't aware that they were doing it). These people are so normal that you probably won't even recognize their names when you see them. Their names aren't sticky, but their stories are.

There was Art Silverman. He was the guy who stopped a nation from eating obscenely unhealthy movie popcorn. He laid out a full day's worth of fatty foods next to a tub of popcorn and said, "This is how much saturated fat is in this snack." A normal person with a normal job who made a difference.

There was Nora Ephron's journalism teacher. Poor guy, we didn't even mention his name. He told his class, "The lead is 'There will be no school next Thursday.'" And in that one sentence he rewrote his students' image of journalism. He inspired Ephron—and doubtless many others—to become journalists. A normal person with a normal job who made a difference.

What about Bob Ocwieja? No chance you remember his name. He's the Subway franchise owner who served sandwiches to a fat guy every day and spotted a great story in the making. Because of Ocwieja the hugely successful Jared campaign was discovered and launched. A normal person with a normal job who made a difference.

Then there was Floyd Lee, the leader of the Pegasus mess hall in Iraq. He defined his role as being about morale, not food service. He got the same supplies as everyone else, but soldiers flocked to his tent and his pastry chef started describing her desserts as "sensual." A normal person with a normal job who made a difference.

And there was Jane Elliott. Her classroom simulation of racial prejudice is still etched in the minds of her students more than twenty years later. It's not a stretch to say that she came up with an idea that *prevented* prejudice, like a vaccine. A normal person with a normal job who made a difference.

All these people distinguished themselves by crafting ideas that made a difference. They didn't have power or celebrity or PR firms or advertising dollars or spinmeisters. All they had were ideas.

And that's the great thing about the world of ideas—any of us, with the right insight and the right message, can make an idea stick.

STICKY ADVICE

I. TALKING STRATEGY

Since the release of *Made to Stick*, we've had the chance to work with a lot of organizations, and we've been surprised to find that their external communications are usually far more sophisticated than their internal communications. Compare a typical customer with a typical employee. Companies spend millions trying to understand the Typical Customer. He is studied and analyzed. His whims are plotted and charted. Messages are laboriously tailored to his concerns and delivered to him via convenient media.

Meanwhile, the Typical Employee receives a bland (but cheerful) monthly e-mail newsletter, which an unlucky HR employee hacked together in ninety minutes.

We are being facetious, of course, but the trend is unmistakable: Customer communication is taken very seriously, and employee communication isn't. And that's a tremendous opportunity for organizational leaders. Employees need to understand what your organization stands for, where it's headed, and what will make it successful. In other words, they need to be able to "talk strategy." And if they can talk strategy back to you, you'll benefit from insights that would otherwise be untapped and invisible.

To see why the ability to talk strategy can be so effective, consider Cranium, the company that manufactures the hit board game Cranium and many other products. Whit Alexander, the co-founder of Cranium, recalls a time when he called a Chinese manufacturing partner to describe a concept for a new plastic game piece. The piece would be purple and made of multiple parts that would need to be glued together. His partner balked. "It's not CHIFF," he said. Alexander was astonished. His supplier, halfway across the globe, had just corrected him using Cranium's own strategic language. And the supplier was absolutely right.

CHIFF is an acronym that stands for "Clever, High-quality, Innovative, Friendly, Fun." The CHIFF concept defines Cranium's strategic differentiation in the extremely competitive board-game market. CHIFF informs decisions across the organization—from branding to package design and the content of individual questions. (Example: A suggested question for the game asked how many justices were on the Supreme Court. It was rejected for being insufficiently clever and fun to be CHIFF. So it was rewritten: "In which of these sports could the members of the U.S. Supreme Court field a regulation team, with no justices left on the 'bench'?")

The Chinese manufacturer had chastised Alexander for his kludgy idea for a game piece. Glued together? That's not particularly innovative or high-quality, the feel of the piece would be all wrong. The manufacturer came back with design so smooth and novel that during a game players would hold spare pieces in their hand, turning them over and over just for tactile pleasure. Not only had the manufacturer improved the quality he had also made a game piece fun. Alexander was impressed.

This is a game-board manufacturing success story. More important, though, it is a *strategy* success story. The executives of Cranium developed a way to communicate a crucial element of the company's strategy—the competitive advantage that makes it better than its competitors—in a useful, comprehensible way. "CHIFF" is simply a clear, actionable statement of strategic differentiation. Cranium employees, suppliers, and channel partners all use CHIFF to make hundreds of on-the-ground decisions that defend Cranium's competitive differentiation.

Let's face it, there is no clearer proof that a strategy has been communicated properly than when a manufacturing supplier, in another country, with a different native language, uses it to correct the founder of the company.

CHIFF works because it respects the principles that make ideas "sticky"—understandable, memorable, and effective in changing thought or behavior. And these principles for creating sticky ideas can be used to transform the way strategy is communicated within a firm.

Talking Strategy

A strategy is, at its core, a guide to behavior. It comes to life through its ability to influence thousands of decisions, both big and small, made by employees throughout an organization. A good strategy drives actions that differentiate the company and produce financial success. A bad strategy drives actions that lead to a less competitive, less differentiated position. A lot of strategies, though, are simply inert. Whether they are good or bad is impossible to determine, because they *do not drive action*. They may exist in pristine form in a PowerPoint document, or in a "strategic planning" binder, or in speeches made by top executives. But if they don't manifest themselves in action they are inert, irrelevant. They're academic.

It's not a lack of effort or good intentions that renders a strategy inert. Every executive *wants* his team to understand. But there are three nasty barriers that make strategic communication more difficult. We'll discuss them and offer suggestions for overcoming them.

Barrier 1: The Curse of Knowledge

If there's one concept we wish we had emphasized more in *Made to Stick*, it's the Curse of Knowledge. We see its effects everywhere. And, as in all the domains we discussed in the book, the Curse of Knowledge afflicts leaders when they try to communicate a strategy to the rest of an organization. It leads executives to talk about strategy as though they themselves were the audience. It tempts them to use language that is sweeping, high-level, and abstract: *The most efficient manufacturer of semiconductors! The lowest-cost provider of stereo equipment! World-class customer service!*

Often, leaders aren't even aware that they're speaking abstractly.

When a CEO urges her team to "unlock shareholder value," that challenge *means something vivid to her*. As in the Tappers and Listeners game, there's a song playing in her head that the employees can't hear. What does "unlocking shareholder value" mean for how I treat this particular customer? What does being the "highest-quality producer" mean for my negotiation with this difficult vendor?

Now, leaders can't unlearn what they know. But they can thwart the Curse of Knowledge by "translating" their strategies into concrete language. For instance, Trader Joe's is a specialty food market that carries inexpensive but exotic food. At Trader Joe's, you might purchase some Moroccan simmer sauce for $2.53 or a quart of red-pepper soup for $1.99. Trader Joe's describes its target customer as an "unemployed college professor who drives a very, very used Volvo." The image is a simplification, obviously—at any given moment, there are probably zero of these "target customers" in Trader Joe's. What the "unemployed college professor" image does for Trader Joe's is this: It ensures that everyone in the organization has a common picture of the customer.

A crucial element of every strategy is deciding which markets and customers a company will serve. The "unemployed college professor" speaks directly to this issue. Trader Joe's could have referred to its customers as "people who are of high socioeconomic status and are quality-conscious but also budget-conscious, and who value variety and new experiences." But this adjective-filled statement doesn't provide as clear an image as the unemployed college professor. Would the professor like the red-pepper soup? Yep. The Curse of Knowledge has been thwarted.

Stories work particularly well in dodging the Curse of Knowledge, because they force us to use concrete language. For instance, FedEx has an award called the Purple Promise, which honors employees who keep FedEx's delivery promise that packages will "absolutely, positively" arrive overnight. The Purple Promise award honors stories like these: In St. Vincent, a tractor-trailer accident blocked the main road going into the airport. Together, a driver and a ramp agent tried every possible alternate route to the airport, but they were stymied by traffic jams. Eventually, having run out of options, they struck out on foot, carrying every package the last mile to the airport, which ensured an on-time departure. In New York, after a delivery truck broke down and the replacement van was running late, the FedEx driver initially delivered a few packages on foot, but then, despairing of finishing her route on time, she managed to persuade a driver from a competitor to take her on her last few deliveries.

These are not just interesting stories. They are tangible demonstrations—in vivid, concrete, on-the-ground terms—of the company's competitive advantage, which is to be the most reliable shipping company in the world. Like CHIFF, these stories can work to inform decisions across the organization. A top sales executive can use the New York story to convey, "This is how seriously we take reliability." A new delivery driver can use the story as a guide to behavior: "My job is not to drive a route and go home at 5 P.M.; my job is to get packages delivered any way I can." An operations person can use the story to make better decisions about maintenance contracts—for example, it's worth negotiating for the fastest possible maintenance cycles on delivery trucks.

A good strategy should guide behavior, and a story can work better in this role than the standard boilerplate missionspeak. At Costco, as described in the book *Around the Corporate Campfire*, by Evelyn Clark, people talk about "salmon stories." Jim Sinegal, the co-founder of Costco, said, "In 1996 we were selling between $150,000 and $200,000 of salmon fillets company-wide every week at $5.99 a pound. Then our buyers were able to get an improved product with belly fat, back fins, and collarbones removed at a better price. As a result, we reduced our retail price to $5.29. So they improved the product and lowered the price."

But the buyers weren't finished. They subsequently negotiated for salmon at an even better price that had the pin bones and skin removed. They lowered the price on this higher-quality salmon to $4.99 a pound. Later, because the lower prices were driving large volumes of sales, Costco began to place big orders directly with Canadian and Chilean salmon farms, which drove the retail price down to $4.79. The point? Costco stands for the relentless pursuit of ever-increasing quality at ever-decreasing prices. "Salmon stories," like the elements of CHIFF, provide a brilliant way to communicate the company's competitive advantage.

Sinegal says, "We've used that story so much as a teaching tool that I've had other buyers in the company, such as a clothing buyer in Canada, come up to me and say, 'I've got a salmon story to tell you.' "

Two paragraphs back, you came across the sentence "Costco stands for the relentless pursuit of ever-increasing quality at ever-decreasing prices." Note that the sentence works as a summary of the salmon story—it's punctuation on the end of the sentence. But here's the counterintuitive part: It doesn't stand alone very well without the story. Saying an abstract sentence like that one, without the related story, is the same as being the Tapper in the Tapper and Listener game. "Ever-increasing quality at ever-decreasing prices" is something that is powerful and profound to an executive *who has internalized years of salmon stories*, but it's sort of dry and vague to someone who doesn't have access to those same experiences. (How do we decrease prices? What if you can't decrease the prices and maintain the same level of profitability?)

Stories that speak to an organization's strategy have two parts. There's the story itself, and there's the moral of the story. It's nice to have both. If you have to choose between the two, though, choose the story. Because the moral is implicit in the story, but *the story is not implicit in the moral*. And the story—with its concrete language, specific protagonists, and real-world setting—is more likely to guide behavior.

Both stories and concrete language help leaders dodge the Curse of Knowledge, and everyone in the organization benefits from a shared understanding of the strategy.

Barrier 2: Decision paralysis

Most people in an organization aren't in charge of formulating strategy; they just have to understand the strategy and use it to make decisions. But many strategies aren't concrete enough to resolve a well-established psychological bias called decision paralysis.

Psychologists have uncovered situations where the mere existence of choice, even choice among several good options, seems to paralyze us in making decisions. (We discuss one example in the "Simple" chapter, on page 25). In *The Paradox of Choice,* Barry Schwartz discusses many other examples of decision paralysis. Imagine two tables in a grocery store where you can taste different kinds of jam. One table has twenty-four kinds of jam, and the other has six. Both tasting tables were popular with customers. But when the sales of jam were tallied, there was a shock: The table with only six jars generated ten times as many sales as the other table! (People simply couldn't decide which jar, among twenty-four, to buy.) Employees of companies with 401(k) plans also experience decision paralysis. For every additional ten mutual funds offered as investment choices by the plan, the employees *reduce* their retirement saving by 1 percent. Decision paralysis even affects the domain of love. When singles attended a speed-dating session where they met six other people, they formed more relationships than they did when they met twelve.

If decision paralysis affects retailing and finance and dating, you can feel pretty confident that it's affecting your employees, too. Think about the sources of decision paralysis in your company. Every organization must make choices among attractive options: Customer service versus cost minimization. Revenue growth versus maximizing profitability. Quality versus speed to market. People development versus the needs of the quarter. Mix together lots of these tensions—an atmosphere full of potential opportunities and risks and uncertainties and incomplete information—and you've got a recipe for paralysis.

Furthermore, many classic strategy statements, such as the quest to be the "low-cost provider," simply don't speak to many of these trade-offs—for instance the trade-off between quality and speed to market. Now, leaders could solve decision paralysis by encoding *everything* into a rule: *Try all available medications before proceeding to surgery!* Many companies do, in fact, adopt this approach—witness the three-inch-thick binders given to new employees to explain "company policy." But you can never generate enough rules to encompass all the decisions that must be made by your employees. The world is complex, and it evolves. Yet rules forbid anyone to adapt to the world except the leaders who are write the rules.

How can strategy liberate employees from decision paralysis? When people are able to talk about strategy, they're more likely to make good decisions than when strategy exists only as a set of rules. Frontline employees want to do the right thing. Most of them find it quite easy to decide between the right thing and the wrong thing. The problem is deciding between the right thing and the right thing.

The hardest decisions, after all, are the ones where we must decide between two good options. Consider the Costco salmon story. If you're selling scads of salmon at $5.99 per pound, and subsequently you secure a supply higher-quality salmon at a lower price, what do you do? You know that there's enough demand for the salmon to exhaust your supply at the $5.99 price point. So do you maintain the price (or even raise it) to deliver a better bottom line for shareholders? Or do you cut the price to maintain your focus on value for customers? This is a choice between two good options. To make such a choice, you need an index of priorities, and the salmon story provides it. The salmon story is a statement of competitive advantage that drives home the message that Costco's priority is the customer over the shareholder. (Or, to be more precise, customer value over short-term shareholder profits.)

Organizations, in formulating their strategies, must grapple not just with competitive advantage but with their internal capabilities. What capabilities do we need in order to grow? What skills will our employees need to successfully please customers, and how will we get better at serving our customers over time? An example of strategic language that speaks to internal capabilities comes from Thomas Alva Edison, the inventor of the phonograph and the lightbulb. Edison was not a lone inventor; he created the first industrial R&D lab in Menlo Park, New Jersey. The researchers in his labs were called "muckers." The term comes from two slang phrases of the time—"to muck in" was to work together as mates, and "to muck around" was to fool around. Why was this a good way for Edison's researchers to talk strategy?

In any entrepreneurial organization, there's a natural tension between efficiency and experimentation. Innovation requires experimentation and freedom, and it necessarily involves dead ends and wasted time and errors—all of which, in turn, will reduce efficiency. Edison's environment, then, is ripe for decision paralysis: How do we decide between efficiency and experimentation? Efficiency promises reduced costs, better margins, and more orders. Experimentation promises new products and other opportunities. How do you choose in the myriad daily situations where the conflict will arise? (E.g., "Is it okay to spend the next hour of my time fooling around in the lab?")

The term "muckers" is a strategy statement masquerading as a nickname. It makes it clear that, given the tough choice between efficiency and experimentation, you choose experimentation. Why? Because you're a mucker. Muckers don't obsess over Gantt charts. Muckers muck. And muckers muck because that is precisely the organizational capability that will make Menlo Park successful. Talking strategy in a thoughtful way can relieve the burden of decision paralysis.

Barrier 3: Lack of a common language

In the classic 1950s models of communication, a "sender" communicates with a "receiver." The metaphor suggests that the message passed is a kind of package—wrapped up on one side and unwrapped on the other. There is certainly a lot of communication that operates in this way—professors lecturing to their students, ministers preaching to their congregations, etc. Should strategic communication work this way?

Absolutely not. Good strategic communication is like Esperanto. It facilitates communication among people who have different native languages and carves out turf that people can share. Employees rely on leaders to define the organization's game plan. Leaders rely on employees to tell them how the game is going. For this dialogue to work, both sides must be able to understand each other. This is easier said than done.

Strategy is often articulated in a way that makes it hard for employees to talk back to leaders. For instance, suppose Cranium's stated strategy had been "To be the No. 1 provider of engaging table-top entertainment." Now, imagine that you are the Chinese manufacturer, and that you are displeased with the design of the new game piece. On what grounds do you state your objection? The strategy is so high-level, so abstract, that it would make you feel foolish to talk back. What are you going to say? "Using this glued-together piece will threaten our No. 1 provider position"? Doubtful.

The scrappy Savings & Loans Credit Union, based in Adelaide, Australia, has developed a common strategic language. Internally, the company defines its strategy this way: "We don't want to be first, but we sure as hell don't want to be third." The meaning: They want the company to be a fast-follower. They'll stand back and let the first mover take the risk and grab the glory of innovation, then they'll come in right behind and copy it, while making the copy crisper than the original. For instance, a competitor offered a credit card that paid part of its commission to an environmental group. The card was a flop, but, meanwhile Savings & Loans had ginned up its own card affiliated with the local children's hospital, which was an instant hit—

proceeds from the card funded a $2.5 million renovation of the Emergency Department.

The strategy is clear, and it's easy to see how it informs behavior across the firm. Marketers should be constantly scanning the environment for good ideas. HR needs to find new employees who are good, quick executors, not creative pioneers. The executives need to use incentives to reward people who are improvers, not inventors. The strategy motto is a one-liner that brings clarity to an environment muddied with choices.

Just as important, it provides a way for front-liners to quibble with executives. Let's say the president is pushing for a new initiative in mobile banking; he's convinced that's where the market is heading, and Savings & Loans needs to stay competitive. But wait a second, says a teller: We don't want to be first. Why not wait for some of our competitors to experiment with mobile banking, and we can monitor closely what's working and what's not.

If everyone in your organization has the same understanding of its strategy, people can disagree constructively. As an analogy, if you're playing darts and your friend consistently aims too high, you can give useful feedback. But it's the obvious location of the bull's-eye that makes your comment possible. What if you and your friend don't agree on where it is? In that case, your communication will be unproductive and irritating for both of you—and if you were playing "business" rather than darts, the person with more power would win the discussion. A common strategic language allows everyone to contribute.

Making strategies stick: Three principles

The three barriers to talking strategy—the Curse of Knowledge, decision paralysis, and the lack of a common strategic vocabulary—emerge for different reasons, but they can be overcome in similar ways. Cranium's CHIFF overcomes all three. It communicates how top managers see the brand in a way that overcomes the Curse of Knowledge. It guides people in selecting among competing choices, which overcomes decision paralysis. And it establishes vocabulary that allows everyone in the organization to communicate on the same turf; it even helps a Chinese supplier to argue credibly with the company's founder.

The trick to talking strategy is making strategic ideas sticky. Here are a few tips for making your strategy stick with people:

1. *Be concrete.* The beauty of concrete language—language that is specific and sensory—is that everyone understands your message in a similar way. Trader Joe's "unemployed college professor" provides a common understanding; "upscale but budget-conscious customer" does not.

2. *Say something unexpected.* If a strategy is common sense, don't waste your time communicating it. (If it's common sense, why bother?) It's critical, though, for leaders to identify the *uncommon sense* in their strategies. What's new about the strategy? What's different? Edison's muckers concept was uncommon sense—in an era when hard work involved farming from dawn until dusk, Edison was telling people to goof around at work.

3. *Tell stories.* A good story is better than an abstract strategy statement. Remember, you can reconstruct the moral from the story, but you can't reconstruct the story from the moral. Think of the power packed into the FedEx Purple Promise award stories, or Costco's salmon stories. If your company doesn't have stories that convey your strategy, that should be a warning flag about your strategy—it may not be sufficiently clear to influence how people act. (Otherwise, you'd have some stories to tell.)

Avoiding inert strategies

The conventional wisdom is that leaders should spend a lot of their time presenting and discussing strategy. The most common refrain in strategic communication is repetition, repetition, repetition. Keep repeating the strategy, again and again, until it finally sinks in. Here's the problem: Repetition doesn't prevent the Curse of Knowledge or encourage two-way communication. Indeed, sticky ways of talking strategy, such as salmon stories, don't need much repetition; innumerable psychology studies tell us that it's much easier to remember concrete language and stories.

There's a well-established canon of knowledge about what makes a good strategy, and in this article we haven't contributed anything to it. Rather, we are proposing that leaders treat strategy as a two-step process: Step 1 is determining the right strategy. Step 2 is communicating it in a way that allows it to become part of the organizational vocabulary. Both are necessary.

Unfortunately, many organizations stop at Step 1. Or they implement Step 1 and follow up with 150 executive speeches broadcasting a vision that is impossible for employees to remember and use. If strategies are to be living and active — if they are to become embodied in the actions of employees and outside partners — they *must* be woven into day-to-day conversations and decisions.

A strategy that is built into the way an organization talks cannot be inert. If your frontline employees can talk about your strategy, can tell stories about it, can talk back to their managers and feel credible doing so, then the strategy is doing precisely what it was intended to do: guide behavior.

II. TEACHING THAT STICKS

As a teacher, you're on the front lines of stickiness. Every single day, you go to work and try to make ideas stick. Let's face it, your mission is not easy. Few students burst into the classroom, giddy with anticipation for the latest lesson on punctuation, polynomials, or Pilgrims. How can you reach them?

In this section, we'll give you more detail about how to apply the six traits of stickiness to your teaching. (A quick note: This article assumes that you've read, or at least skimmed, the rest of the book. We won't reintroduce the basic concepts. By the way, if you want to forward free sticky resources to a colleague who *hasn't* read the book, simply visit www.madetostick.com/teachers.)

There are very practical ways of making your teaching stickier. For instance, every Earth Science class talks about the earth's magnetic field. But one teacher decided to add a bit of mystery. She asked the students, "Did you know that if you'd been holding a compass 25,000 years ago, and you were walking north according to the compass, you'd be headed straight for the South Pole?" That's an example of making an idea more unexpected using a knowledge gap. [See pages xxx—xxx for more on knowledge gaps.]

We'll take the six traits of stickiness, one by one, and show how a little focused effort can make almost any idea stickier. And a sticky idea is one that's more likely to change how your students think and act.

Simple

Andrew Carl Singer taught a class on digital signal processing at the University of Illinois at Urbana-Champaign. It's a complex subject, and it's easy to get lost in the mathematics. So he worked hard to find the core of his class. He began by asking himself a simple question:

When a student from the University of Illinois interviews at a company and says, "I took digital signal processing from Professor Singer," what are the three things he needs to know in order to get the job *and* make the University of Illinois proud to have its graduate working in this field?

This is one of the hardest responsibilities of being a teacher. You've got more things to teach your students than they could ever remember. So which concepts are most important? And how can you use your class time to make sure those points stick? Professor Singer said that by focusing on the core ideas of the course, "I whitted away the extraneous details—ones that served to separate the A^{+++} students from the A^{++} students but weren't so relevant for the rest of the class." He identified several core concepts that he wanted *every* student to learn during the semester. Then he drew a picture that served as a reminder of these core messages. It depicted a process where sounds, such as musical recordings, are sampled and become a digital file. Then the digital file is manipulated and played out through a digital-to-analog converter. He said, "By showing this picture to the class at the beginning of the term and referring to it often, I found that I could keep the class on track with the core messages I wanted everyone to learn. And I also used the core message myself—in deciding which material to keep in the course and which to leave out."

Once you've found the core of your lesson, you'll need to explain it as simply as you can. To make explanations simpler, you should *anchor* them in concepts that students already know. By anchoring, you use the knowledge they already have as a platform for new learning. In the late nineteenth century, when the automobile was introduced, it was often called a "horseless carriage." Automobile makers were anchoring in the concept of a "carriage," which was common knowledge. As another example, in the "Simple" chapter, we discussed the classic Bohr model of an atom. Teachers often explain it like this: "Electrons orbit the nucleus the way that planets orbit the sun." They're anchoring the Bohr model in knowledge the students already have. Using an analogy is an easy way to anchor a new concept. Bjorn

Holdt, a high school teacher in South Africa who teaches a Java programming class, was having a hard time communicating the concept of "variables." So he came up with an analogy: "Variables are just like cups. They are containers that hold some information." Each student was given a different type of cup. Glass mugs were able to store only numbers. Beer mugs were allowed to store only text. Coffee mugs could store only "true" and "false." Contents were never allowed to be mixed—for instance, you couldn't put a number in a coffee mug. (This limitation illustrated a procedure called "type-safe programming.") Holdt reported that this analogy, helped students understand the concept of a variable more quickly and retain it longer. He said that he was frequently able to untangle misunderstandings by explaining things in terms of the coffee cup or the glass mug.

To make an idea simple, then, first find the core of your lesson, then anchor it in knowledge that your students already have.

[REMINDERS: "Simple" concepts from the book that are useful for teachers: Generative analogies (pp. 60–62). Complexity through schemas (pp. 53–57). The inverted pyramid (pp. 31–33).]

Unexpected

William B. Yeats once said, "Education is not filling a bucket, but lighting a fire." That's a great sentiment, but how do you light the fire of your students to learn about, say, mammalian physiology? Well, you might take a hint from a book we recently spotted in the bookstore that had this title: "Why Do Men Have Nipples?" We suspect that ten seconds ago you weren't pondering mammalian physiology.

But when you see this question and realize that you don't have a ready explanation, it makes you wonder. It sparks curiosity, and that's the beginning of a fire.

In the "Unexpected" chapter, we discuss George Loewenstein's gap theory of curiosity, which says that curiosity comes from a gap between what we know and what we want to know. Teachers can make powerful use of this technique. For instance, a physics teacher in Colorado asked his students, "Have you ever noticed that in the winter your car tires look a little flat? So where did the air go?" The book *Freakonomics* also makes great use of curiosity gaps: "Why do so many drug dealers live with their moms?"

Curiosity can provide the fuel for a series of lessons. The San Diego Zoo teaches a summer program in which junior high school students learn to do DNA analysis. Maggie Reinbold, the designer of the program, introduced the topic with a mystery worthy of a *CSI* episode: An animal has been sneaking into the food bin at the petting zoo and eating the animals' food stores. The goats, deprived of their vittles, are losing weight. (And you do not want your goats getting anorexic.) The students must investigate and figure out which animal is doing the thieving.

Two nights earlier, the food-thieving culprit left a few threads of black hair on the feeding station. Unfortunately, this narrows down the suspects only a little. The lineup of black-haired animals includes a goat, a pig, a sheep, and a horse. Only DNA analysis can reveal the truth about the thief. Over the course of the week, Reinbold used this mystery to teach her students a whole mini-course in molecular biology. Students used dissecting microscopes to extract some cells for DNA analysis. They learned about the Nobel Prize–winning Polymerase Chain Reaction (PCR) procedure that can be used to turn a few copies of DNA into billions of copies, and then they put on their white lab coats and consulted with zoo researchers about how to conduct a PCR analysis on the zoo's machine. They used gel electrophoresis to compare the DNA pattern of the thief with DNA patterns of pigs, goats, sheep, and horses. After enough legwork, they discover that the villain was . . . Ed the Pony. (But don't expect a tearful confession.)

That's the value of curiosity in a nutshell: It can hold kids' attention for a week as they tackle serious science. To make it work in your lessons, use knowledge gaps and the power of mystery.

[REMINDERS: "Unexpected" concepts from the book that are useful for teachers: Curiosity gaps (pp. 84–85). Professor Cialdini's mystery of Saturn's rings (pp. 80–82). Nora Ephron's journalism teacher (pp. 75–76).]

Concrete

In math, students often struggle with the notion of a "function." What exactly is a function, and what is meant by its strange "f(x)" notation, which looks like nothing else that students have seen before?

It seems so abstract, so mysterious. So Diana Virgo, a math teacher at the Loudoun Academy of Science in Virginia, gives students a more real-world experience with functions. She brings a bunch of chirping crickets into the classroom and poses a question: What will happen to the crickets' chirping as the temperature changes? Will it get faster or slower? And might the crickets' reaction be so predictable that we can actually graph a function that *predicts* how fast they'll chirp? Our function would be like a little machine: You feed in a temperature (say, 85 degrees) and out pops the rate of chirping (say, sixty chirps per minute).

So the class runs the experiment: The crickets chirp. The students count the chirps. Virgo changes the temperature. The crickets, undoubtedly puzzled by the weather, chirp differently. The students count again. And soon the class has gathered a bunch of data that can be plugged into a software package, which generates the predictive function. It turns out that the hotter it is, the faster the crickets chirp—and it's predictable! Suddenly, the idea of a function makes sense—it's been grounded in reality. Students have personally experienced the entire context—where functions come from, how they're constructed, and how they can be used. (As a side note, Virgo also wants her students that human judgment is always indispensable. For instance, if you plug into the function the temperature "1000 degrees," it'll predict a really, really fast rate of chirping! Sadly, though, at 1,000 degrees crickets don't chirp at all.)

The cricket function is an example of making a concept concrete—avoiding abstraction and conceptual language and grounding an idea in sensory reality. It's the difference between reading about a wine ("bold but balanced") and tasting it. The more sensory "hooks" we can put into an idea, the better it will stick. An eighth-grade teacher named Sabrina Richardson helped students "see" punctuation by using macaroni. Richardson described her exercise:

The students were given cards with sentences that were missing punctuation like quotation marks, periods, exclamation points, commas, apostrophes. The students were divided into groups of two and three and were given baggies that contained elbow macaroni, small macaroni shells, and ritoni. The students were asked to place the pieces of macaroni in the correct place in the sentence. For example, they were given the sentence:

Jackie shouted Gwen come back here

The students had to use the elbow macaroni as commas and quotation marks and a small macaroni shell as a period. They could combine the ritoni and the small macaroni shell for an exclamation point. I knew that a lot of my students were confused about whether the comma went inside or outside the quotation marks, so this gave all of them a chance to "see" the correct way to punctuate quotations. Once they were finished, they knew the sentence would read: Jackie shouted, "Gwen, come back here!"

Concrete, sensory experiences etch ideas into our brain—think of how much easier it is to remember a song than a credit card number, even though a song contains much more data!

[REMINDERS: "Concrete" concepts from the book that are useful for teachers: Math instruction in Asia (pp. 104–06). The Velcro theory of memory (pp. 109–11). Jane Elliott's elementary-school simulation of prejudice (pp. 111–13)]

Credible

Amy Hyett, an American literature teacher at Brookline High School in Boston, teaches a unit on transcendentalism. She says that when students read Thoreau, and learn how much time he spent alone in the wilderness, they have a common reaction: Er, why would he do that? So, in the spirit of building empathy, she gives them an unorthodox assignment: Spend thirty minutes alone in nature. No cell phone. No iPod. No pet companions. No Game Boy. Just you and the great outdoors.

Hyett says, "It's quite amazing, because almost every student has an illuminating experience. They are surprised by how much the experience moves them. Even the most skeptical students come away with a deeper understanding of transcendentalism and nature."

For an idea to stick, it needs to be credible. YouTube–era students don't find it credible that hanging out outside, alone, could be conducive to great thinking. So how do you combat their skepticism? You let them see for themselves. Sometimes you have to see something, or experience it, to believe it. For instance, you might not believe that adding Mentos candy to a two-liter bottle of soda would cause a volcanic eruption that sends soda spewing ten to fifteen feet from the bottle. But you'd believe it if you saw it. (In the meantime, just Google it for a laugh.) Lots of science-lab experiments operate on this principle: *See for yourself.* (Notice, too, that labs are pedagogically useful for other reasons: They are often unexpected—"Look, the chemicals turn bright blue when mixed!" And they are always concrete—instead of talking about a phenomenon, you're seeing it or producing it.)

Another technique for making ideas credible is to use statistics—but perhaps not in the way you'd expect. It's difficult to make a statistic stick. Numbers tend to slide easily in one ear and out the other. But the relationships illustrated by statistics can be quite sticky. Tony Pratt, a fourth-grade teacher in the New Orleans Recovery School District, was teaching his students the basics of probability, and as an example he told them that they had a really, really small probability of winning the lottery. The odds are one in millions. But this statistic is so extreme that it fuzzes our brains. Our brains can't easily distinguish between "one in millions" and "one in tens of thousands," even though there's an enormous gap there! So Pratt grounded the probability in a relationship. He said, "You're more likely to be struck by lightning than to win the lottery." That amazed the students—it gave them an intuition for just how rare it is to win. In fact, several of them rushed home to tell their families.

One student, Jarred, relayed his story: "I saw my uncle buying lottery tickets last night. I told him that he was more likely to be struck by lightning than he was to win the lottery and that buying lottery tickets was a bad idea because of probability."

"What did he say?"

"He told me to get the F—— out of his face."

Some people are more resistant to sticky ideas than others.

[REMINDERS: "Credible" concepts from the book that are useful for teachers: The NBA and AIDS education (pp. 162–63). The bacteria-chugging scientist (pp. 130–32). Using the human-scale principle (pp. 143–46).]

Emotion

Bart Millar, an American history teacher at Lincoln High School in Portland, Oregon, was having a hard time getting his students to care about the Civil War. "We talked about the weaponry, the tactics, the strategy, and so on. The students were respectful, but not much beyond that," he said.

Determined to do better, he went to the National Archives Web site and downloaded photos of battlefield surgeons and their surgical tents. He presented these to his students and asked them to imagine the sounds of war: the explosions, the rustle of uniforms, the occasional eerie quiet. And the smells of war: dust, gunpowder, blood, excrement. This activity, which brought sensory information into a "dry" subject, was beautifully concrete. But Millar had one more surprise in store for the students.

In a corner of the room was a table covered with a tarp. Millar whisked away the tarp to reveal two stopwatches, two thick-looking bones, and two handsaws. The bones were cow legs procured from a local butcher that approximated the weight and thickness of a human femur. Two student volunteers were asked to play the role of a battlefield surgeon, forced to amputate a soldier's leg in the hope of saving his life. Their mission: Saw through bone forcefully and quickly—after all, at the time there was very little anesthesia

Millar says, "The entire lesson only took about fifteen minutes, but ten years later students who stop in to say hi still talk about that lesson." And it's not hard to see why: He found a way to make his students care, to give them a peek into the brutal realities of war.

That's what emotion does for an idea—it makes people care. It makes people *feel something*. In some science departments, during the lesson on "lab safety," instructors will do something shocking: They'll take some of the acid that the students will be handling and use it to dissolve a cow eyeball. A lot of students shudder when they see the demonstration. They *feel* something. (It should also be noted that some students, mostly male, think it's "cool.") Lab safety "dos and don'ts" don't grab you in the gut, but a dissolving eyeball sure does.

And that's the role of emotion in making ideas sticky: to transform the idea from something that's analytical or abstract or theoretical and make it hit the students in the gut (or the heart).

[REMINDERS: "Emotional" concepts from the book that are useful for teachers: The dilution of "sportsmanship" (pp. 174–77). Why study algebra? (pp. 192–95). Voters who vote against their self-interest (pp. 187–91).]

Story

Have you ever noticed, when you teach, that the moment you start sharing a personal story with your students, they instantly snap to attention? You understand the value of stories. But some teachers don't insert many stories into their lessons, because they're worried that they don't have gripping stories to tell, or that they aren't good story-tellers. So maybe it's worth identifying which kinds of stories are effective in making ideas stick. The answer is this: virtually any kind.

The stories don't have to be dramatic, they don't have to be captivating, and they don't have to be very entertaining. The story form itself does most of the heavy lifting — even a boring story will be stickier than a set of facts. Several times in the book, we've seen the power of a story to keep students engaged — remember the "Safe Night Out" entrepreneurial story, used to teach accounting? (pp xxx–xxx) It was so effective that it made students more likely to major in accounting. Or recall Cialdini's story of the race to solve the mystery of Saturn's rings (pp. 80–82). Just a few pages back, we discussed the tale of the petting-zoo food thief. None of these stories were Oscar material, but they were irresistible to students.

Stories can be useful for discipline as well as academics. Greg Kim, a ninth-grade English teacher at Eagle Rock High School, used a story to reach an unruly student, whom we'll call John. John was a well-meaning student who just couldn't seem to stop socializing or horsing around in class. Kim talked to him several times and tried to explain that his behavior was disrupting the class and endangering his grade. Often, John would take these talks to heart and change his behavior — for a few days. Making matters worse, on the rare days that he did behave well, John would say, "Aren't you proud of me? I was good today."

Kim said, "I tried to talk to him about consistency, and how he needed to be focused every day. But John looked at me, confused. . . . In his mind, being good sometimes was being good always." Kim struggled with the problem of how to get John to understand the need for consistent behavior. He tried analogies like "one step forward two steps back." But all he got from John was a blank look.

Later, Kim was discussing the situation with another teacher who had taught John in English class the previous year. The teacher had similar problems with John, and, indeed, the only time John had shone was when he wrote a personal narrative about how he'd lost thirty pounds. Suddenly, Kim realized what he should do:

> The next day I spoke to John about his behavioral inconsistency and compared it to a friend of mine who had struggled with weight loss. The friend had decided to go on a diet and exercise regimen to lose weight. The first day, he was good. He ate right and exercised, but the second day he broke his diet and didn't exercise. The next day he was good, but the following two days he was bad again. And so it went, on and on. I told John that my friend would beg for my approval by letting me know he was good on the days that he was, but weeks later he had somehow gained weight. I told John this story and asked if he knew what the problem was. He laughed and said the answer was obvious. With a big smile, John said, "He didn't stick to his diet every day." I stared at him and watched the realization engulf him, and his smile became thoughtful.
>
> This conversation was about three weeks ago, and while John isn't perfect every day, the ratio has reversed and he is consistently focused most every day.

John couldn't "see" his behavior, couldn't understand why it needed to change, until he was confronted with a story that made him see things in a different way. Continual nagging didn't change him—a story did. Stories have a unique power to engage and inspire. How can you harness that power to make your lessons stick?

[REMINDERS: "Story" concepts from the book that are useful for teachers: See the second paragraph of this section above. Also, stories as flight simulators (pp. 207–17). The three kinds of inspiring stories (pp. 224–31).]

The Curse of Knowledge

Let's not forget the villain of the book, the Curse of Knowledge, which says that once you know something, it's hard to imagine *not* knowing it. And that, in turn, makes it harder for you to communicate clearly to a novice. It's a tough problem to avoid—every year, you walk into class with another year's worth of mental refinement under your belt. You've taught the same concepts every year, and every year your understanding gets sharper. If you're a biology teacher, you simply can't imagine anymore what it's like to hear the word "mitosis" for the first time, or to lack the knowledge that the body is composed of cells. You can't unlearn what you already know.

That's where these tools of stickiness can help. Stickiness is a second language of sorts. When you open your mouth to communicate, without thinking about what's coming out of your mouth you're speaking your native language: Expertese. But students don't speak Expertese. They do speak Sticky, though. Everyone speaks Sticky. In a sense, it's the universal language. The grammar of stickiness— simplicity, storytelling, learning through the senses—enables anyone to understand the ideas being communicated.

What Sticks

Making ideas stickier isn't hard. It just takes a bit of time and focus. The six principles of stickiness that we've discussed can be used as a checklist—imagine the checklist written on a Post-it note, to the side of your desk as you outline a lesson. "Okay, for tomorrow's lesson I've got to compare sedimentary and igneous rock. How can I make this Simple? Do students have some knowledge I can anchor in? How can I make it Concrete? Can I get a sample of the kinds of rock to show them? How can I tell a Story? Can I find a story of an archaeologist who used knowledge of the rock layers to solve an interesting problem?" You get the idea.

A group of teachers at the Loudon Academy of Science—Linda Gulden, Jennifer Lynn, and Dan Crowe—did exactly this in revising their oceanography unit. They weren't happy with the way things had gone in the past, so they put a lot of energy into revamping it. Here's the new lesson plan:

In the first class, they start with a mystery: "Let's say you put a message in a bottle, drive out to the coast, and throw it as far as you can into the ocean. Where will the bottle end up?" They let students make their guesses. ("The waves will bring it right back to shore." "It'll end up in Antarctica." "It'll sink.") But they don't provide an answer (since there *isn't* a clear answer).

Then they begin to explore this same mystery in a more dramatic form. Students read a fascinating article about a cargo ship that hit a severe storm in January 1992 and lost a container overboard, somewhere in the Pacific Ocean. The container broke apart and released its contents: 28,800 floating duckies, turtles, beavers, and frogs. Years later, we know where many of these animal floaties ended up. Many hundreds of them beached near Sitka, Alaska, about 2,200 miles away—some made it there within six months, some *twelve years* later. By tracing the paths that these rubber duckies swam, we learn a lot about the way ocean currents work.

In other classes, the teachers help the kids do some hands-on experimentation. They set up tanks of water with different levels of salinity and different temperatures, and let them see how those variables change the water current. In essence, the students are able to create their own ocean currents.

Finally, they pivot to the critical role that oceans play in global climate. They start with a question: What determines the weather of a city, like New York City? Inevitably, students say it depends on latitude—the closer to the equator the city is, the warmer it is, and the closer to the poles it is, the colder it is. There is much truth in that, but there are huge discrepancies: For instance, New York City and Madrid are at roughly the same latitude, but it snows every winter in

New York City and it doesn't snow in Madrid. What's the difference? That opens the topic of how ocean currents influence climate.

In closing, notice that these teachers have developed a teaching plan that uses all the elements of sticky ideas.

- Simple: Anchoring in students' knowledge of weather (New York vs. Madrid).
- Unexpected: Where will the bottle end up? Where did the duckies end up? Why is Madrid's weather different than New York's?
- Concrete: The message in a bottle, the rubber duckies, the hands-on tanks of water, the mention of specific cities.
- Credible: See for yourself, using this tank, how temperature affects water current.
- Emotional: Think of the hope, mystery, and anxiety involved in tossing an important message into the sea and wondering where it will go.
- Story: The tale of thousands of rubber duckies that fell overboard—and the journey they took around the world.

Our hats are off to these teachers. We hope we've reinforced what you're doing that is already sticky, and that we've inspired you to try something new. May your ideas stick!

III. UNSTICKING AN IDEA

Since *Made to Stick* came out, many anxious people have asked us, "How do I unstick a sticky idea?" They want to unstick a rumor about their company or a false perception of a particular product. They want to unstick whispered mistruths about political candidates. Once, we were even asked, "How would you unstick Paris Hilton?"

Our answer on that last one was a bit slow in coming. We finally admitted, "You can't." There's no Goo Gone for ideas. Sticky ideas stick. There are millions of people who've come to follow, willingly or unwillingly, the antics of a party-girl heiress. There's no magic sticky incantation that will make us divert our attention to alternative energy, or some other worthy topic. Our best advice, on the Paris Hilton matter, was: Just wait it out. As we age, the memories will fade, and perhaps those neurons will die off entirely. (With any luck, they'll go before the "dress ourselves" neurons.)

But the question—*How do I unstick an idea?*—nagged at us. So we dug into the relevant academic research. It was a long and frustrating search, because there's not much research tackling this topic. But we did find one promising lead that was about sixty-five years old.

During World War II, social scientists had a keen patriotic interest in rumor control. About two-thirds of the rumors during were "wedge-drivers," accusations that provoked anger at various social groups (blacks, Jews, the Brits). These rumors were false and socially destructive, so the government wanted to fight back aggressively. One tactic that seemed to work against wedge-drivers was to redirect the anger and make people mad at the rumormongers. For instance, the rumor-control people would put up posters of Nazi spies spreading rumors to gullible dupes. This primed listeners to react angrily when someone spread a rumor: *You're undermining the American war effort by spreading Nazi untruths!*

At first, this work in wartime propaganda seemed pretty removed from the concerns of our readers, who want their ideas to stick in business or in school. But then it dawned on us: Trying to unstick an idea is a bad strategy. The World War II rumor-control people weren't trying to unstick an idea. They were shifting the turf and propagating a different, competing idea. Instead of arguing that the rumors themselves were baseless, they argued: *The Nazis are trying to trick you. Are you going to fall for that?*

This suggests that we shouldn't try to unstick ideas. We should fight sticky with stickier, meet Scotch tape with duct tape.

For decades, McDonald's fought rumors that it used earthworms as filler in its burgers. At first, the company tried to unstick the idea. In 1978, McDonald's officials had denounced the rumors as "completely unfounded and unsubstantiated." (Quotes taken from *Newsweek* via Snopes.com, the mecca of urban-legend debunking.) Guess which idea was stickier: "earthworms in your meat patties" or "unfounded and unsubstantiated"?

By 1992, Ray Kroc, McDonald's most famous CEO, had come up with a better approach. He said, "We couldn't afford to grind worms into meat. Hamburger costs a dollar and a half a pound, and night crawlers cost six dollars!" That's nice; Kroc is fighting sticky with sticky. Notice the elements of credibility (dollars per pound) and unexpectedness (*We can't afford to serve you earthworms.*) He might even have gone a step further and made a joke about it: "If someone ever tries to sell you a WormBurger, you should worry about them secretly filling it with beef."

Another case of fighting sticky with sticky came during the late 1990s, when e-mailed rumors about nasty computer viruses circulated constantly. According to these rumors, if you clicked the wrong link, or opened the wrong e-mail, you'd destroy your computer. One day, a young systems operator, fed up with the dozens of bogus warnings he received every day, wrote a parody of the rumors:

Warning: if you receive an e-mail with "Goodtimes" in the subject line, DO NOT OPEN IT!!!!! Goodtimes will rewrite your hard drive. It will also scramble any disks that are even close to your computer. It will recalibrate your refrigerator's coolness setting so all your ice cream goes melty. It will demagnetize the strips on your credit cards and use subspace field harmonics to scratch your CDs. It will give your ex your new phone number. It will mix Kool-Aid into your fish tank. It moves your car randomly around parking lots so you can't find it.

The parody became a viral hit, as popular as the rumors it mocked. Bill Ellis, a folklorist at Penn State Hazleton, has documented that, as this parody spread, the apocalyptic virus warnings faded away. The parody cleverly provided people with a schema of an overhyped warning. Afterward, if you received more e-mails that fit the schema—full of overheated language and dire warnings—you knew to laugh rather than get worried. The young systems operator fought a sticky idea with a stickier idea.

But sometimes the best way to fight a sticky idea is not with a message at all, even a stickier one. Sometimes what you need is a sticky action. Consider the dawn of the automobile era. As described in Hayagreeva Rao's book *Market Rebels: How Activists Make or Break Radical Innovations*, the gasoline-powered car was greeted, at first, with skepticism and outright fear. People called it a "devilish contraption." It spawned rabid opposition. The Farmer's Anti-Automobile Society of Pennsylvania, for example, demanded that cars traveling at night on country roads "must send up a rocket every mile, then wait ten minutes for the road to clear. If a driver sees a team of horses, he is to pull to one side of the road and cover his machine with a blanket or dust cover that has been painted to blend into the scenery." One technologist of the time scoffed at the idea that gasoline engines would ever be widely adopted: "You can't get people to sit on an explosion."

That's a sticky idea: simple, concrete, emotional. If you were an entrepreneurial automaker, how would you combat it? Well, the dumb thing to do would be to try to "unstick it" with a message: Go ahead, try telling potential customers, "Don't worry, you're actually sitting on a *contained explosion.*" Oh, and all the top automotive authorities say your fears are "unfounded and unsubstantiated."

Auto enthusiasts chose to act. They created a series of "reliability races" in which automobile inventors would bring their autos together and have them compete on endurance, fuel economy, and hill-climbing ability. Reliability contests were one part product testing and one part festival. The first contest took place in 1895, and by 1912 they had been discontinued, because cars were an accepted social reality. What happened in between was that the automakers gave thousands of people the chance to see firsthand the promise of automobiles—to see that there was nothing to fear. (In fact, the acclaim Henry Ford received from his performance in the reliability contests enabled him to launch the Ford Motor Company in 1903.)

Note that the auto enthusiasts didn't try to argue their way out of the fears; they acted their way out. They chose a demonstration that was Unexpected (*Until today I thought cars were dangerous and unreliable*); Concrete (*Did you see it take that hill?*); Emotional (*I can see myself becoming one of those liberated drivers*); and Credible (*I saw it all with my own eyes!*).

So how do you unstick an idea? First of all, be realistic. It took seventeen years for reliability races to establish public trust in the automobile. The rumor about earthworms in McDonald's hamburgers still circulates in some places, despite Ray Kroc's brilliant response. Sticky ideas endure, and, as we've seen in the book, that can be a great thing. It can also be a real nuisance if you're working against a sticky idea that's false.

Our advice is simple: Fight sticky ideas with stickier ideas. We hope we've given you some useful tools for making your ideas sticky. And if you want to unstick Paris Hilton, maybe you should be looking for another fame-hungry heiress to take her place? (We're not sure heiress races will do the trick.)

What Sticks?

Kidney heist. Halloween candy. Movie popcorn.

Sticky = understandable, memorable, and effective in changing thought or behavior.

SIX PRINCIPLES: SUCCESs.

SIMPLE UNEXPECTED CONCRETE CREDIBLE EMOTIONAL STORIES.

THE VILLAIN: CURSE OF KNOWLEDGE. *It's hard to be a tapper. Creativity starts with templates: Beat the Curse with the SUCCESs checklist.*

1. Simple

FIND THE CORE.

Commander's Intent. Determine the single most important thing: "THE low-fare airline." *Inverted pyramid:* Don't bury the lead. *The pain of decision paralysis. Beat decision paralysis through relentless prioritization:* "It's the economy, stupid." Clinic: Sun exposure. *Names, names, names.*

SHARE THE CORE.

Simple = core + compact. Proverbs: sound bites that are profound. Visual proverbs: The Palm Pilot wood block. How to pack a lot of punch into a compact communication: (1) Using what's there: Tap into existing schemas. The pomelo. (2) Create a high concept pitch: "Die Hard on a bus." *(3) Use a generative analogy: Disney's* "cast members."

2. Unexpected

GET ATTENTION: SURPRISE.

The successful flight safety announcement. Break a pattern! Break people's guessing machines (on a core issue). The surprise brow: a pause to collect information. Avoid gimmicky surprise—make it "postdictable." "The Nordie who . . ." "There will be no school next Thursday." Clinic: Too much on foreign aid?

HOLD ATTENTION: INTEREST.

Create a mystery: What are Saturn's rings made of? Screenplays as models of generating curiosity. The Gap Theory of Curiosity: Highlight a knowledge gap. *Use the news-teaser approach: "Which local restaurant has slime in the ice machine?"* Clinic: Fund-raising. *Priming the gap: How Roone Arledge made NCAA football interesting to nonfans. Hold long-term interest: the "pocketable radio" and the "man on the moon."*

3. Concrete

HELP PEOPLE UNDERSTAND AND REMEMBER.

Write with the concreteness of a fable. (Sour grapes.) Make abstraction concrete: The Nature Conservancy's landscapes as eco-celebrities. Provide a concrete context: Asian teachers' approach to teaching math. Put people into the story: accounting class taught with a soap opera. Use the Velcro theory of memory: The more hooks in your idea, the better. Brown eyes, blue eyes: a simulation that "cured" racial prejudice.

HELP PEOPLE COORDINATE.

Engineers vs. manufacturers: Find common ground at a shared level of understanding. Set common goals in tangible terms: Our plane will land on Runway 4-22. Make it real: The Ferraris go to Disney World. Why concreteness helps: white things versus white things in your refrigerator. Create a turf where people can bring their knowledge to bear: The VC pitch and the maroon portfolio. Clinic: Oral Rehydration Therapy. *Talk about people, not data: Hamburger Helper's in-home visits and "Saddleback Sam."*

4. Credible

HELP PEOPLE BELIEVE.

The Nobel-winning ulcer insight no one believed. Flesh-eating bananas.

EXTERNAL CREDIBILITY. Authority and antiauthority. *Pam Laffin, smoker.*

INTERNAL CREDIBILITY.

Use convincing details. *Jurors and the Darth Vader Toothbrush. The dancing seventy-three year old.*

Make statistics accessible. *Nuclear warheads as BBs. The Human Scale principle. Stephen Covey's analogy of a workplace to a soccer team.* Clinic: Shark attack hysteria.

Find an example that passes the Sinatra Test. *"If you can make it there, you can make it anywhere." Transporting Bollywood movies: "We handled Harry Potter and your brother's board exams." A business-friendly environmentalist and the textile factory that actually purified the water that fed it—and yielded fabric that was edible.*

Use testable credentials. *"Try before you buy." Where's the beef? Snapple supports the KKK?! Coaches: It's easier to tear down than to build up: Filling the Emotional Tank. NBA rookie orientation: "These women all have AIDS."*

5. Emotional

MAKE PEOPLE CARE.

The Mother Teresa principle: If I look at the one, I will act. People donate more to Rokia than to a huge swath of Africa. The Truth anti-

smoking campaign: What made kids care was not health concerns but anticorporate rebellion.

USE THE POWER OF ASSOCIATION.

The need to fight semantic stretch: the diluted meaning of "relativity" and why "unique" isn't unique anymore. Transforming "sportsmanship" into "honoring the game."

APPEAL TO SELF-INTEREST (AND NOT JUST BASE SELF-INTEREST).

Mail-order ads — "They laughed when I sat down at the piano. . . ." WIIFY. Cable television in Tempe: Visualizing what it could do for you. Avoid Maslow's basement: our false assumption that other people are baser than we are. Floyd Lee and his Iraq mess tent: "I'm in charge of morale."

APPEAL TO IDENTITY.

The firemen who rejected the popcorn popper. Understand how people make decisions based on identity. (Who am I? What kind of situation is this? And what do people like me do in this kind of situation?) Clinic: Why study algebra? *Don't mess with Texas: Texans don't litter. Don't forget the Curse of Knowledge — don't assume, like the defenders of the duo piano, that others care at the same level that you do.*

6. Stories

GET PEOPLE TO ACT.

STORIES AS SIMULATION (TELL PEOPLE HOW TO ACT).

The day the heart monitor lied: how the nurse acted. Shop talk at Xerox: how the repairman acted. Visualizing "how I got here": simulating problems to solve them. Use stories as flight simulators. Clinic: Dealing with problem students.

STORIES AS INSPIRATION (GIVE PEOPLE ENERGY TO ACT).

Jared, the 425-pound fast-food dieter. How to spot inspiring stories. Look for three key plots: *Challenge (to overcome obstacles), Connection (to get along or reconnect), Creativity (to inspire a new way of thinking).* Tell a springboard story: *a story that helps people see how an existing problem might change. Stephen Denning at the World Bank: a health worker in Zambia. You can extract a moral from a story, but you can't extract a story from a moral. Why speakers got mad when people boiled down their presentations to stories.*

What Sticks.

USE WHAT STICKS.

Nice guys finish last. Elementary, my dear Watson. It's the economy, stupid. The power of spotting. *Why good speaking skills aren't necessarily good sticking skills: Stanford students and the speech exercise. A final warning about the Curse of Knowledge.*

Remember how SUCCESs helps people to:

Pay attention	Unexpected
Understand and remember	Concrete
Believe and agree	Credible
Care	Emotional
Act	Stories

Simple helps at many stages. Most important, it tells you *what* to say.

Symptoms and solutions: For practical guidance, see pages 247–49.

John F. Kennedy versus Floyd Lee: How normal people, in normal situations, can make a profound difference with their sticky ideas.

Introduction: What Sticks?

4   **"Comprehensive community building":** Tony Proscio, "In Other Words: A Plea for Plain Speaking in Foundations," Edna McConnell Clark Foundation, 2000.

6   **The Truth About Movie Popcorn:** A good account of the popcorn story is in Howard Kurtz, "The Great Exploding Popcorn Exposé," *Washington Post*, May 12, 1994, C1.

13   **Who Spoiled Halloween?:** The story of the contaminated Halloween candy legend is told in Joel Best and Gerald T. Horiuchi, "The Razor Blade and the Apple: The Social Construction of Urban Legends," *Social Forces* 32 (1985): 488–99. Joel Best is one of a group of sociologists who study the "construction" of social problems. Social concerns about various problems such as drunk driving, drug abuse, or poisoned Halloween candy do not always match the underlying incidence of problems, and sociologists have tried to understand how social problems become defined as "problems." For another interesting read on this topic, see Joel Best, *Random Violence: How We Talk About New Crimes and New Victims* (Berkeley: University of California Press, 1999).

19   **the Curse of Knowledge:** The Curse of Knowledge concept comes from C. F. Camerer, G. Loewenstein, and M. Weber, "The Curse of Knowledge in Economic Settings: An Experimental Analysis," *Journal of Political Economy* 97 (1989): 1232–54. The Curse of Knowledge increases as people gain more expertise. Pamela Hinds asked experts (salespeople at a cellular company) to

predict how long novice cell-phone users would take to learn to perform various tasks (e.g., storing a greeting on voice mail or saving some messages and deleting others). Experts dramatically underestimated the amount of time it would take novice users to accomplish the tasks (i.e., they estimated that it would take thirteen minutes to perform functions that actually took thirty-three minutes), and their estimates did not improve when they were specifically asked to think about the problems they encountered while they were originally learning. See Pamela J. Hinds, "The Curse of Expertise: The Effects of Expertise and Debiasing Methods on Predicting Novice Performance," *Journal of Experimental Psychology: Applied* 5 (1999): 205–21. See also brilliant work in psychology by Boas Keysar, Linda E. Ginzel, and Max H. Bazerman, "States of Affairs and States of Mind: The Effect of Knowledge on Beliefs," *Organizational Behavior and Human Decision Processes* 64 (1995): 283–93. Ironically, the Curse of Knowledge has been well documented in economic and market settings, where people should have the greatest incentives to try to overcome it (see http://curse-of-knowledge .behaviouralfinance.net/). If you can't overcome the Curse of Knowledge when it's costing you lots of money, it's going to be even harder to detect and overcome it in day-to-day situations.

19 **In 1990, Elizabeth Newton:** L. Newton, "Overconfidence in the Communication of Intent: Heard and Unheard Melodies," Ph.D. diss., Stanford University, 1990.

22 **In 1999, an Israeli research team:** Jacob Goldenberg, David Mazursky, and Sorin Solomon, "The Fundamental Templates of Quality Ads," *Marketing Science* 18 (1999): 333–51. The Pictorial Analogy template features extreme analogies rendered visually. For instance, a Nike ad is shot from the perspective of someone jumping from a tall building. A group of firemen are on the street below, preparing to cushion the jumper's fall with an oversized Nike sneaker. The tagline reads, "Something soft between you and the pavement." The majority of the winners are composed of Pictorial Analogy and Extreme Consequences. The other templates were Extreme Situations (in which a product is shown performing under unusual circumstances or in which a product's attribute is exaggerated to the extreme), Competition (in which a product is shown winning in competition with another product, often in an unusual usage situation), Interactive Experiments (where listeners interact with the product directly—see "Testable Credentials" in Chapter 4), and Dimensionality Alteration (e.g., a time leap that shows the long-run implications of a decision).

1. Simple

29   **Herb Kelleher ... once told:** James Carville and Paul Begala, *Buck Up, Suck Up, and Come Back When You Foul Up* (New York: Simon & Schuster, 2002), 88. This is one of the most interesting books we've found about the dynamics of political campaigns, and there's a chapter on how to communicate in a political campaign that echoes several of the principles we cover in this book: tell stories ("facts tell but stories sell"), be emotional, and be unique (their version of "Unexpected").

31   **A healthy 17-year-old heart:** Jonathan Bor, "It Fluttered and Became Bruce Murray's Heart," *Syracuse Post-Standard*, May 12, 1984.

31   **JERUSALEM, Nov. 4:** Barton Gellman, "Israeli Prime Minister Yitzhak Rabin Is Killed," *Washington Post*, November 5, 1995. Chip Scanlon has a great collection of online columns describing the tradecraft of journalism, including one that contains the two headlines here: www.poynter.org/column.asp?id= 52&aid=35609.

31   **the inverted pyramid arose:** Rich Cameron, "Understanding the Lead and the Inverted Pyramid Structure Are Staples of Journalism 101 Classes," *The Inverted Pyramid*, 2003. See www.cerritosjournalism.com, in the section entitled "101 — Newswriting."

33   **"It was simple":** Carville's advice to remember the basics is from Mary Matalin and James Carville, *All's Fair: Love, War, and Running for President* (New York: Random House, 1994), 244. The Clinton interchange leading up to the "If you say three things, you don't say anything" quote is on page 175.

34   **In 1954, the economist L. J. Savage:** Leonard J. Savage, *The Foundations of Statistics* (New York: Wiley, 1954).

35   **Amos Tversky and Eldar Shafir:** The study about the Christmas vacation in Hawaii study is in Amos Tversky and Eldar Shafir, "The Disjunction Effect in Choice Under Uncertainty," *Psychological Science* 3 (1992): 305–9. The lecture/foreign film/library study is found in Donald A. Redelmeier and Eldar Shafir, "Medical Decision Making in Situations That Offer Multiple Alternatives," *Journal of the American Medical Association* 273 (1995): 302–6. The phenomenon of decision paralysis is pronounced even for professionals. Redelmeier and Shafir show that doctors will delay in prescribing any treatment when they are forced to choose among multiple good treatments.

38   **Sun Exposure: Precautions and Protection:** Message 1 of the Sun Exposure Idea Clinic is from http://ohioline.osu.edu/hyg-fact/5000/5550.html.

47   **Cervantes defined proverbs:** The discussion of proverbs is based on Paul

Hernandi and Francis Steen, "The Tropical Landscapes of Proverbial: A Crossdisciplinary Travelogue," *Style* 33 (1999): 1–20.

50 **"The real barrier to the initial PDAs":** Tom Kelley, *The Art of Innovation: Lessons in Creativity from IDEO, America's Leading Design Firm* (New York: Doubleday Currency, 2001).

51 **J FKFB INAT OUP:** The letter/acronym exercise demonstrates the classic principle of "chunking" from cognitive psychology. Working memory is sufficient to hold only about seven independent pieces of information. (See George Miller's classic description in "The Magical Number Seven, Plus or Minus Two," *Psychological Review* 63 (1956): 81–97. In the first exercise, the chunks are letters, and most people can hold about seven of them. In the second, the chunks are pre-stored acronyms; people can remember around seven acronyms even though they each contain multiple letters. By taking advantage of preexisting chunks of information, we can cram more information into a limited attentional space.

54 **Psychologists define schema:** Schemas are part of the standard tool kit of cognitive and social psychology. For an interesting discussion of schemas in social perception, see Chapters 4 and 5 of Susan T. Fiske and Shelley E. Taylor, *Social Cognition*, 2nd ed. (New York: McGraw-Hill, 1991). For an interesting summary of cognitive psychology research on schemas, see Chapter 2 of David C. Rubin, *Memory in Oral Traditions: The Cognitive Psychology of Epic, Ballads, and Counting-out Rhymes* (Oxford: Oxford University Press, 1995).

An analogy is a good way of helping people access the knowledge in a schema. Educational psychologists have published a number of papers on the value of analogies in learning new material, particularly Richard Mayer. In a 1980 paper, he helped students learn to program the language of a database. One group of students was given analogies for the structure of the computer: "The long-term storage function of the computer was described as a file cabinet; the sorting function was described as an in-basket, save basket, and discard basket on an office desk." When students were confronting *easy* problems, the analogies didn't matter much, but when the problems became more complex, students who had been given analogies were about twice as good as the others. See R. Mayer, "Elaborate Techniques That Increase the Meaningfulness of Technical Text: An Experimental Test of the Learning Strategy Hypothesis," *Journal of Educational Psychology* 72 (1980): 770–84.

Metaphor is another way of allowing people to access the knowledge in a schema. George Lakoff has, in a number of books, shown how deep metaphors structure the way that we understand and talk about the world (e.g., George Lakoff and Mark Johnson, *Metaphors We Live By* [Chicago: University of Chicago Press, 1980]). For example, we talk about and think of love as a journey (Look at *how far we've come.* We're *at a crossroads.* We're *off track.*) Lakoff has been better than anyone else at recognizing the pervasive ways in which such metaphors affect our communication, but metaphors need not be deep or pervasive to be useful in conveying a message; they just need to be shared by the relevant audience, as in the discussion of "high concept" in Hollywood.

60   **Good metaphors are "generative":** D. A. Schon, "Generative Metaphor: A Perspective on Problem-Solving in Social Policy," in *Metaphor and Thought*, 2nd ed., edited by A. Ortony, (Cambridge: Cambridge University Press, 1993).

60   **Disney calls its employees "cast members":** The examples from Disney are from: Disney Institute, *Be Our Guest: Perfecting the Art of Customer Service* (New York: Disney Editions, 2001).

2. Unexpected

63   **A flight attendant named Karen Wood:** It's no accident that Karen Wood was a flight attendant on Southwest Airlines. See Kevin Freiberg and Jackie Freiberg, *Nuts! Southwest Airlines' Crazy Recipe for Business and Personal Success* (Austin, Tex.: Bard Press, 1996), 209–10.

68   **"the surprise brow":** Paul Ekman and Wallace V. Friesen, *Unmasking the Face: A Guide to Recognizing Emotions from Facial Clues* (Englewood Cliffs, N.J.: Prentice-Hall, 1975). The role of surprise is an understudied topic in psychology, because it falls in the cracks between psychological disciplines. Cognitive researchers who study attention and learning find it too emotional; social psychologists who study emotions such as anger, fear, and disgust find it too cognitive. Yet you could make the case that surprise is the most important emotion because of its role in controlling attention and learning.

70   **"PHRAUG and TAYBL":** Bruce W. A. Whittlesea and Lisa D. Williams, "The Discrepancy-Attribution Hypothesis II: Expectation, Uncertainty, Surprise, and Feelings of Familiarity," *Journal of Experimental Psychology: Learning, Memory, and Cognition* 27 (2001): 14–33.

73   **The Nordie who ironed:** Jim Collins and Jerry I. Porras, *Built to Last: Successful Habits of Visionary Companies* (New York: HarperBusiness, 1994), 118.

75   **Journalism 101:** Ephron's account is in Lorraine Glennon and Mary Mohler, *Those Who Can . . . Teach! Celebrating Teachers Who Make a Difference* (Berkeley, Calif.: Wildcat Canyon Press, 1999), 95–96.

77   **Americans persist in thinking:** Message 1 from the foreign aid Clinic is from www.ipjc.org/journal/fall02/nick_mele.htm.

78   **Polls suggest that most Americans:** See surveys conducted by the Program for International Policy Attitudes (PIPA) at the University of Maryland.

78   **All of sub-Saharan Africa:** As of 2001, sub-Saharan Africa and the entire region of Asia each received a little more than $1 billion per year. Assuming that there are 280 million Americans, twelve soft drinks at a bargain price of $.33 equals $1.1 billion. One movie per year at $8 per movie ticket equals $2.24 billion.

80   **How do we *keep* people's attention?:** Arousing people's interest and keeping it are topics that have been discussed frequently among educational psychologists who want to keep kids engaged in textbooks. Many of their findings are consistent with the topics we consider in this book: Kids are more engaged when texts evoke action and images (Concrete) or emotions (Emotional) or when something is novel (Unexpected, though in our view novelty is more likely to attract interest than to sustain it). Other topics go beyond what we discuss here. For example, kids are more engaged when material is personalized (e.g., they pay more attention to math problems that feature their names or the names of their friends), though this customization strategy is hard to apply in general. But most of the research in educational psychology has been limited in that it focuses only on sentence- or paragraph-level characteristics of texts rather than on broader questions, such as how do you get readers to read whole sections, chapters, or books. Cialdini's observations on mystery and Loewenstein's gap theory of curiosity would add a great deal to this important area of research. For a review of educational research, see Suzanne Hidi, "Interest and Its Contribution as a Mental Resource for Learning," *Review of Educational Research* 60 (1990): 549–71.

80   **A few years ago, Robert Cialdini:** Cialdini wrote his article for psychology professors, but it's excellent advice for all teachers. See Robert B. Cialdini, "What's the Best Secret Device for Engaging Student Interest? The Answer Is in the Title," *Journal of Social and Clinical Psychology* 24 (2005): 22–29.

83   **McKee says, "*Curiosity*":** Robert McKee, *Story: Substance, Structure, Style and the Principles of Screenwriting* (New York: ReganBooks, 1997). McKee also has good insight into the difference between gimmicky surprise and surprise that leads to resolution in movies: "We can always shock filmgoers by cutting to something it doesn't expect to see or away from something it expects to continue." But he says that "true surprise" happens when a legitimate gap is suddenly revealed between what we expect and what actually happens.

The legitimacy comes from a rush of insight, revealing some truth that was previously hidden.

84 **In 1994, George Loewenstein:** George Loewenstein, "The Psychology of Curiosity: A Review and Reinterpretation," *Psychological Bulletin* 116 (1994): 75–98. This is a brilliant article that reviews decades of psychological research.

91 **Heretofore, television has done:** The Roone Arledge story is from his autobiography, *Roone: A Memoir* (New York: HarperCollins, 2003). The quote from the memo is on page 32.

93 **In the rubble of Tokyo:** The Sony history is from John Nathan, *Sony: The Private Life* (Boston: Houghton Mifflin, 1999).

96 **"If people *like* curiosity":** Loewenstein, "Psychology of Curiosity," 86.

3. Concrete

99 **"Business Buzzword Generator":** The buzzword generator was invented by W. Davis Folsom at the University of South Carolina–Aiken. See http://highered.mcgraw-hill.com/sites/0072537892/student_view0/business_jargon_exercise.html.

100 **Concreteness helps us avoid these problems:** The advantages of concrete ideas show up across psychology. Concrete ideas are more memorable. Perhaps the most interesting summary of this evidence is from a book by David Rubin, a cognitive psychologist at Duke University who has spent years trying to understand how aspects of culture—epic sagas, ballads, and children's rhymes—propagate from person to person and generation to generation. His book *Memory in Oral Traditions* is a masterful summary of work across the humanities and psychology. Concrete elements are the most likely to survive transmission from one person to another because they are the easiest to understand and remember. See David C. Rubin, *Memory in Oral Traditions: The Cognitive Psychology of Epic, Ballads, and Counting-Out Rhymes* (Oxford: Oxford University Press, 1995).

Concrete ideas are also more understandable. In education research, Mark Sadoski, Ernest Goetz, and colleagues have published a number of interesting papers illustrating that concrete ideas are more understandable, memorable, and, as a side benefit, more interesting. See Mark Sadoski, Ernest T. Goetz, and Maximo Rodriguez, "Engaging Texts: Effects of Concreteness on Comprehensibility, Interest, and Recall in Four Text Types," *Journal of Educational Psychology* 92 (2000): 85–95.

107 **Yale researcher Eric Havelock:** E. A. Havelock, *Preface to Plato* (Cambridge, Mass.: Harvard University Press, 1963).

107 **Two professors from Georgia State University:** Carol W. Springer and A. Faye Borthick, "Business Simulation to Stage Critical Thinking in Introductory Accounting: Rationale, Design, and Implementation," *Issues in Accounting Education* 19 (2004): 277–303.

111 **Brown Eyes, Blue Eyes:** The description of Jane Elliott's antiprejudice simulation is taken from a PBS *Frontline* documentary, "A Class Divided." It's one of the most frequently requested programs in the station's history, winning an Emmy for Outstanding Informational, Cultural, or Historical Programming in 1985. It can be seen on the Web at www.pbs.org/wgbh/pages/frontline/shows/divided/etc/view.html.

112 **Studies conducted ten and twenty years later:** Phil Zimbardo, *Psychology and Life*, 12th ed. (Glenview, Ill.: Scott, Foresman, 1985), 634.

114 **A researcher named Beth Bechky:** B. A. Bechky, "Crossing Occupational Boundaries: Communication and Learning on a Production Floor," Ph.D. diss., Stanford University, 1999.

116 **The 727 must seat 131 passengers:** Jim Collins and Jerry I. Porras, *Built to Last: Successful Habits of Visionary Companies* (New York: HarperBusiness, 1994), 93.

116 **The Ferraris Go to Disney World:** The Stone-Yamashita work with HP is based on Victoria Chang and Chip Heath, "Stone-Yamashita and PBS: A Case at the Graduate School of Business," Stanford University Graduate School of Business case study SM119 (2004).

120 **Kaplan and Go Computers:** This example is from a great book by Jerry Kaplan: *Start-Up: A Silicon Valley Adventure* (Boston: Houghton Mifflin, 1995). It's one of the best accounts we've read about the day-to-day uncertainty and struggle of being an entrepreneur and building a company. And it's very funny.

121 **My audience seemed tense:** Ibid., 25–26.

122 **Their investment valued:** Kaplan's company, later named Go Computers, ultimately failed because the technology of its time wasn't sufficient to support pen-based computers. Nonetheless, the idea of pen-based computing was so sticky—the "pocketable radio" of its generation—that several other firms in addition to Kaplan's arose and attracted venture capital dollars (and skilled engineering talent) to pursue the technology.

124 **Diarrhea is one of the leading killers:** Message 1 of the Oral Rehydration Therapy Clinic is from PSI, a Washington, D.C., nonprofit organization that

is doing innovative work on health for low-income populations. See www
.psi.org/our_programs/products/ors.html.

125 **"Do you know"**: Message 2 of the Oral Rehydration Therapy Clinic is by
James Grant, who, during his time at UNICEF, made changes that have
been credited with saving the lives of more than 25 million children. Vacci-
nation rates increased, for example, from 20 percent to 80 percent. This remarkable story is told in David Bornstein, *How to Change the World: Social
Entrepreneurs and the Power of New Ideas* (Oxford: Oxford University Press,
2004). See page 248 for the quote.

128 **"Saddleback Sam"** Rick Warren, *The Purpose-Driven Church* (Grand
Rapids, Mich.: Zondervan, 1995): 169. Warren's book explains the organizing
principles of one of the largest and fastest-growing churches in the country.

4. Credible

131 **"simply didn't have the demeanor"**: Daniel Q. Haney, "News That Ulcers
Are Caused by Bacteria Travels Slowly to MDs," *Buffalo News*, February 11,
1996.

132 **"It tasted like swamp water"**: Manveet Kaur, "Doctor Who Discovered
'Ulcer Bugs,'" *New Straits Times*, August 13, 2002, 6.

132 **an important theme in modern medicine**: Laura Beil, "A New Look at Old
Ills: Research Finds Some Chronic Diseases May Be Infectious," *The Record*
(Northern New Jersey), March 24, 1997.

133 **But if we're skeptical about**: Naturally sticky ideas are a great source of insight about the process of persuasion, and researchers who study persuasion
in psychology would benefit from studying them. Traditional studies of persuasion in psychology have sidestepped the issue of credibility by creating a
bunch of arguments, having people rate them for credibility, then using the
ones that are rated as having high or low credibility. With the exception of a
number of studies on the impact of authority, researchers have avoided trying
to understand what makes messages credible. Yet rumors and urban legends
regularly evolve features that ascribe credibility to bizarre claims. The
"testable credentials" idea that we discuss in the chapter, for example, has
been a feature of dozens of urban legends, yet it has not been discussed by the
research literature on persuasion.

133 **Around 1999, an e-mail message**: The flesh-eating banana legend is discussed at www.snopes.com/medical/disease/bananas.asp.

135 **Pam Laffin, the Antiauthority**: The story of Pam Laffin is described in Bella

English, "Sharing a Life Gone Up in Smoke," *Boston Globe*, September 20, 1998.

135 **"I started smoking to look older"**: From the website of the U.S. Centers for Disease Control and Prevention, www.cdc.gov/tobacco/christy/myth1.htm.

136 **The Doe Fund sent a driver**: We thank Spencer Robertson for this example.

138 **"acquire a good deal"**: Jan Harold Brunvand, *The Vanishing Hitchhiker: American Urban Legends and Their Meanings* (New York: W. W. Norton & Company, 1981), 7. This book is largely responsible for creating the urban legends craze in the United States. For years, folklorists had been writing articles about the folklore of modern people, but this book by Brunvand was accessible enough that everyone started hearing about urban legends—and they were *shocked* to hear that different versions of their local stories were being told by everyone else in the nation.

138 **By making a claim tangible**: There is a running debate in the psychology literature on the impact that vivid details have on memory and credibility. In our view, the evidence is confusing because researchers have not been careful about distinguishing details that support or distract from a *core* message. People inevitably focus on and remember vivid details. When the vivid details support the core message, it is more memorable and convincing, but irrelevant vivid details can also distract people from the core and make a message less memorable and convincing (thus the concern, in educational psychology, about "seductive details"). A good summary of the issues can be found in Ernest T. Goetz and Mark Sadoski, "Commentary: The Perils of Seduction: Distracting Details or Incomprehensible Abstractions?" *Reading Research Quarterly* 30 (1995), 500–11.

138 **In 1986, Jonathan Shedler and Melvin Manis**: Jonathan Shedler and Melvin Manis, "Can the Availability Heuristic Explain Vividness Effects?" *Journal of Personality and Social Psychology* 51 (1986), 26–36.

145 **"If, say, a soccer team"**: The Covey example is from an excerpt from his book reprinted in *Fortune*, November 29, 2004, 162.

149 **A SHARK   A DEER**: We thank Tim O'Hara for the idea for the comparison in Message 2 of the Shark Attack Hysteria Clinic.

153 **Edible Fabrics**: William McDonough, 2003 Conradin Von Gugelberg Memorial Lecture on the Environment, Stanford University, February 11, 2003; www.gsb.stanford.edu/news/headlines/2003_vongugelberg.shtml. See also Andrew Curry, "Green Machine," *U.S. News & World Report*, August 5, 2002, 36.

158 **"The Emotional Tank"**: "Emotional Tank" is from Jim Thompson, *The Double-Goal Coach: Positive Coaching Tools for Honoring the Game and De-*

veloping Winners in Sports and Life (New York: HarperCollins, 2003). The exercise is described on page 63. This book is a must-read for anyone who coaches kids' sports.

159 **But in the United States:** The statistics in the Our Intuition Is Flawed Clinic about various causes of death are from the 2001 Statistical Abstract of the United States.

162 **A few weeks before the NBA:** The NBA rookie orientation is described in a great article by Michelle Kaufman, "Making a Play for Players," *Miami Herald*, October 5, 2003.

163 **At the NFL's orientation:** See Grant Wahl and L. Jon Wertheim, "Paternity Ward," *Sports Illustrated*, May 4, 1998, 62.

5. Emotional

165 **In 2004, some researchers at Carnegie Mellon:** Deborah A. Small, George Loewenstein, and Paul Slovic, "Can Insight Breed Callousness? The Impact of Learning About the Identifiable Victim Effect on Sympathy," working paper, University of Pennsylvania, 2005.

168 **This chapter tackles the emotional component:** This chapter focuses on the power of emotions to make people *care*, but research suggests that emotional ideas are also more *memorable*. Emotions increase memory for an event's "gist or center." Memory researchers talk about "weapon focus"— people who have been robbed or who have witnessed crimes often remember the perpetrator's gun or knife with great clarity but remember little else (Reisberg and Heuer, below). People remember the central emotional theme of an event and other things that are closely related in space or causal structure. Thus, highlighting the emotional content of an idea may be one way to focus people on a core message. See Daniel Reisberg and Friderike Heuer, "Memory for Emotional Events" in *Memory and Emotion*, ed. Daniel Reisberg and Paula Hertel (Oxford: Oxford University Press, 2004).

Mark Sadoski and colleagues have found that emotional aspects of texts are rated as more important (Sadoski, Goetz, and Kangiser, 1988) and are recalled much better (Sadoski and Quest, 1990). Interestingly, the latter article is among several research studies that have found that things are more emotional when they are easy to visualize. Making things concrete not only helps make them understandable, it makes them emotional and helps people care. Mark Sadoski and Z. Quest, "Reader Recall and Long-term Recall for Journalistic Text: The Roles of Imagery, Affect, and Importance," *Reading Research Quarterly* 25 (1990), 256–72. Mark Sadoski, Ernest T. Goetz, and

Suzanne Kangiser, "Imagination in Story Response: Relationships Between Imagery, Affect, and Structural Importance," *Reading Research Quarterly* 23 (1988), 320–36.

170 **"We felt that [the Truth ads]":** "Smoke Signals," *LA Weekly*, November 24–30, 2000 (also found at www.laweekly.com/ink/01/01/offbeat.php).

170 *American Journal of Public Health:* The comparison of the "Truth" and "Think. Don't Smoke" campaigns is in Matthew C. Farrelly, et al, "Getting to the Truth: Evaluating National Tobacco Countermarketing Campaigns," *American Journal of Public Health* 92 (2002), 901–7.

171 **associating themselves with emotions:** This principle has been well-known since Ivan Pavlov won the Nobel Prize for teaching dogs to salivate in response to a bell. A fun discussion of the power of association is found in the chapter on "Liking" in Robert Cialdini's book *Influence: The Psychology of Persuasion* (New York: Quill, 1993). Cialdini opens with the dilemma of the weatherman in a rainy city who regularly receives hate mail because viewers associate him with the news he delivers; he also discusses research on the "luncheon technique" that showed people were more likely to endorse political statements that they first heard while eating lunch. Cialdini's book is the classic study on influence and one of the best books in the social sciences.

171 **"*Rashomon* can be seen as":** C. Vognar, "Japanese Film Legend Kurosawa Dies at 88," *Dallas Morning News*, September 7, 1998, 1A.

172 **In 1929, Einstein protested:** Einstein's comments about the way people used the term *relativity* is from David Bodanis, $E = mc^2$: *A Biography of the World's Most Famous Equation* (New York: Walker & Company, 2000). Quotes are on pages 84 and 261.

173 **Research conducted at Stanford and Yale:** Chip Heath and Roger Gould, "Semantic Stretch in the Marketplace of Ideas," working paper, Stanford University, 2005. In this paper, Chip and Roger also showed that extreme synonyms for the word *good* (e.g., *fantastic* or *amazing*) are increasing in use faster than synonyms that are less extreme (*okay* or *pretty good*), and that extreme synonyms for *bad* (*awful* versus *bad*) show the same pattern. Either semantic stretch is happening or the world is becoming simultaneously much better and much worse.

175 **Sportsmanship was once a powerful idea:** Jim Thompson, *The Double-Goal Coach: Positive Coaching Tools for Honoring the Game and Developing Winners in Sports and Life* (New York: HarperCollins, 2003). Chapter 4 talks about the problems with sportsmanship and the idea of Honoring the Game.

177 **In 1925, John Caples:** The classic book on mail-order advertising is John

Caples, *Tested Advertising Methods*, 5th ed., revised by Fred E. Hahn (Paramus, N.J.: Prentice Hall, 1997). Mail-order ads are frequently schlocky, but, as we say in the text, they're one of the few places where advertisers get immediate, measurable feedback about what is and isn't working. That means that there's often a lot of wisdom to be gained in understanding why they look the way they do—someone has tested every attribute.

179 **Jerry Weissman, a former TV producer:** Jerry Weissman, *Presenting to Win: The Art of Telling Your Story* (New York: Financial Times Prentice Hall, 2003). The quote is on page 18.

180 **"Don't say, 'People will enjoy' ":** Caples/Hahn, *Tested Advertising*, 133.

180 **Cable TV in Tempe:** W. Larry Gregory, Robert B. Cialdini, and Kathleen M. Carpenter, "Self-Relevant Scenarios as Mediators of Likelihood Estimates and Compliance: Does Imagining Make It So?" *Journal of Personality and Social Psychology* 43 (1982): 89–99.

183 **In 1954, a psychologist named Abraham Maslow:** Abraham Maslow, *Motivation and Personality* (New York: Harper, 1954).

183 **Subsequent research suggests that the hierarchical:** See any introductory book in psychology. Every textbook author prints a picture of Maslow's hierarchy because it's a great graphic, then confesses that the hierarchical aspect of his theory didn't quite work.

184 **Imagine that a company offers:** The bonus and new job-framing studies are from Chip Heath, "On the Social Psychology of Agency Relationships: Lay Theories of Motivation Overemphasize Extrinsic Rewards," *Organizational Behavior and Human Decision Processes* 78 (1999): 25–62.

186 **Dining in Iraq:** The Floyd Lee story is from a marvelous article by Julian E. Barnes, "A Culinary Oasis," *U.S. News & World Report*, December 6, 2004, 28.

187 **The Popcorn Popper and Political Science:** The popcorn popper story is from Caples/Hahn, *Tested Advertising*, 71.

188 **When faced with affirmative action:** Donald Kinder, "Opinion and Action in the Realm of Politics," in *Handbook of Social Psychology*, ed. Daniel T. Gilbert, Susan T. Fiske, and Gardner Lindzey, 4th ed. (London: Oxford University Press, 1988), 778–867. The extended quote is from page 801.

190 **A related idea comes from James March:** James March describes the two patterns of making decisions—consequence versus identity—in Chapters 1 and 2 of James G. March, *A Primer on Decision Making* (New York: Free Press, 1994). Economic analysis, in particular, assumes that all decisions are made on the basis of consequences, so it makes incorrect predictions in a

number of arenas where identity is important; most economists would be surprised that the "Don't Mess with Texas" campaign would work without imposing fines for littering.

192 **In a 1993 conference on "Algebra":** Message 1 in the Idea Clinic is from Joseph G. Rosenstein, Janet H. Caldwell, and Warren G. Crown, *New Jersey Mathematics Curriculum Framework* (New Jersey: New Jersey Department of Education, 1996).

194 MESSAGE 3: Dean Sherman's response and an extended discussion of this question among algebra teachers can be found at http://mathforum.org/t2t/thread.taco?thread=1739.

195 **Dan Syrek is the nation's leading:** Seth Kantor, "Don't Mess With Texas Campaign Scores Direct Hit with Ruffian Litterers," *Austin American-Statesman*, August 4, 1989, A1.

196 **"We call him Bubba":** Allyn Stone, "The Anti-Litter Campaign in Texas Worked Just Fine," *San Francisco Chronicle*, November 28, 1988, A4.

197 **Too-Tall Jones steps toward:** The Dallas Cowboys spot is described in Robert Reinhold, "Texas Is Taking a Swat at Litterbugs," *New York Times*, December 14, 1986.

198 **The Department of Transportation originally:** Marj Charlier, "Like Much in Life, Roadside Refuse Is Seasonally Adjusted," *The Wall Street Journal*, August 3, 1989.

6. Stories

204 **The nurse was working:** The story about the blue-black baby is found in Gary Klein, *Sources of Power: How People Make Decisions* (Cambridge, Mass.: MIT Press, 1998), 178–79.

206 **stories make people act:** As in previous chapters, this chapter highlights one virtue of stories—encouraging action—but we could have discussed others. Stories also help people understand and remember. It's hard to tell an abstract story, so stories inherit all the virtues of the Concrete, but they also serve as Simple (core and compact) ways of integrating lots of information. Research on jury decision-making shows that jurors rely heavily on stories to decide on their verdicts. Jurors confront masses of facts, presented in a scrambled sequence with substantial gaps in the record, filtered through the obvious personal biases of witnesses. How do they deal with this complexity? It turns out they spontaneously construct a story (or stories) to account for this welter of information, then match their personal story with the stories told by the prosecution and the defense and choose whichever side tells a story that

best matches their own. In one study in this area, Nancy Pennington and Reid Hastie showed that verdicts shifted depending on how easily jurors were able to construct a story, even when identical information was presented. When the defense presented evidence in the order of an unfolding story but the prosecution presented evidence out of story order, only 31 percent of jurors voted to convict the defendant. When exactly the same information was presented but the defense presented witnesses out of order and the prosecution presented witnesses in story order, 78 percent of the jurors voted to convict. Jurors felt most confident in their decision when both sides presented in story order; people like to understand both stories, to see the evidence clearly in their mind, and then decide. See Nancy Pennington and Reid Hastie, "Explanation-based Decision Making: Effects of Memory Structure on Judgment," *Journal of Experimental Psychology: Learning, Memory & Cognition* 14 (1988): 521–33.

Stories also improve credibility. Researchers Melanie Green and Timothy Brock point out that attitudes formed by direct experience are more powerful, and stories give us the feeling of real experience. They show that people are more likely to be persuaded by a story when they are "transported" by it — when they feel more wrapped up in their mental simulation. See Melanie C. Green and Timothy C. Brock, "The Role of Transportation in the Persuasiveness of Public Narratives," *Journal of Personality and Social Psychology* 79 (2000): 701–21.

207 **The new XER board configuration:** Julian E. Orr, *Talking About Machines: An Ethnography of a Modern Job* (Ithaca, N.Y.: Cornell University Press, 1996). The dicorotron story is on page 137.

209 **"John *put on* his sweatshirt":** This study is among dozens of studies that support the importance of mental simulation. For a review, see Rolf A. Zwaan and Gabriel A. Radvansky, "Situation Models in Language Comprehension and Memory," *Psychological Bulletin* 123 (1998): 162–85. Not only do people mentally simulate space, they also simulate time. In a story about people entering a movie theater, respondents are more likely to recognize a reference to "the projectionist" if only ten minutes have elapsed in the story than if six hours have elapsed, even if both references are just a few sentences away on the page from the line about the movie theater.

210 **no such thing as a passive audience:** The best overview of the "active reader" research is provided by Richard Gerrig, a researcher in the field. See *Experiencing Narrative Worlds: On the Psychological Activities of Reading* (New Haven, Conn.: Yale University Press, 1988). Gerrig says that Samuel Coleridge was wrong to describe our ability to appreciate stories as the "suspension

of disbelief," because his quote implies that the default state of humans is skeptical disbelief. In fact, the real state is the opposite. It's *easy* to get wrapped up in a story; it's *hard* to evaluate arguments skeptically, disbelieving them until they are proven. One of our favorite illustrations of the power of simulation is Gerrig's research on stories with well-known endings. When people are in the middle of a story, they often get so wrapped up in the simulation that they momentarily act as though they'd forgotten an obvious ending. Watch out for that iceberg, *Titanic!*

212 **Why does mental simulation work?:** The tapping, Eiffel Tower, lemon juice, and other examples are from Mark R. Dadds, Dana H. Bovbejerg, William H. Redd, and Tim R. H. Cutmore, "Imagery in Human Classical Conditioning," *Psychological Bulletin* 122 (1997): 89–103.

213 **A review of thirty-five studies:** James E. Driskell, Carolyn Copper, and Aidan Moran, "Does Mental Practice Enhance Performance?" *Journal of Applied Psychology* 79 (1994): 481–92.

215 **Dealing with Problem Students:** Message 1 is from a tip sheet, "Tips for Dealing with Student Problem Behaviors," from the Office for Professional Development, Indiana University–Purdue University Indianapolis. See www.opd.iupui.edu/uploads/library/IDD/IDD6355.doc. Message 2, by Alison Buckman, was originally posted to http://research.umbc.edu/~korenman/wmst/disruptive_students2.html.

219 **When Fogle registered:** Ryan Coleman, "Indiana U. Senior Gains New Perspective on Life," *Indiana Daily Student*, April 29, 1999.

221 **In 1999, Subway's sales:** Performance statistics for Subway, Schlotzky's, and Quiznos are from Bob Sperber, "In Search of Fresh Ideas," *Brandweek*, October 15, 2001, M54.

225 **Blumkin is a Russian woman:** Rose Blumkin is described by Warren Buffett in his 1983 shareholder letter (see www.berkshirehathaway.com/letters/1983.html).

226 **These three basic plots:** These results are from Chip's research at Stanford. After studying urban legends for a while — stories that frequently specialize in creating negative emotions such as fear, anger, or disgust — he asked whether there were stories that circulated because they produced positive emotions. The *Chicken Soup for the Soul* stories were the obvious place to start. The research on the frequencies of the three plots was done by giving raters the classification system but no other information about the hypotheses of the research. Even though raters worked independently, pairs of raters who saw the same stories showed strong agreement on classifications.

Another Stanford study suggests that these three plots are a good way to ensure that your stories are more inspiring. Students were given the assignment of finding a true story that would inspire their classmates, either from their own lives or from some public source. Later, their fellow students rated the stories on their ability to inspire—to make them feel proud, excited, and determined. Stories that featured one of the three plots were much more likely to wind up in the top half of the stories. Of the stories that wound up in the top 10 percent, all had one or more of the three plots.

Another study showed that each plot drives a specific form of activity. People read through a selection of stories, one per day, and recorded how they felt after reading each story. Challenge plots made people want to set higher goals, to take on new challenges, to work harder and persist longer. Connection plots made people want to work with others, to reach out and help them, and to be more tolerant. Creativity plots made people want to do something different, to be creative, to experiment with new approaches. Thus, the right stories not only tell us how to act, they operate as a kind of psychological battery pack, giving us the energy to take action. Notably, none of these stories was more likely to drive "feel good" activity. People weren't more likely to was to do something to enjoy themselves—to listen to good music, watch television, or eat a good meal; instead, they wanted to go out and accomplish something. Thus these stories drive productive action, not passive self-involvement.

227 **In response, Jesus told a story:** The Good Samaritan story is from the New International Version of the Bible, Luke 10:25–37.

229 **Ingersoll-Rand:** The story of the Grinder Team is told in Chapter 6 of Tom Peters, *Liberation Management* (New York: Knopf, 1992).

231 **Stories at the World Bank:** This section is based on two excellent books by Stephen Denning. His first book, about the role of storytelling in organizations, is *The Springboard: How Storytelling Ignites Action in Knowledge-Era Organizations* (Boston: Butterworth-Heinemann, 2001). There are dozens of books available that talk about the role of storytelling in organizations and organizational culture; *The Springboard* is the best book on the subject, and among the best business books of any kind. A follow-up book that describes a number of story plots other than springboard stories is *The Leader's Guide to Storytelling: Mastering the Art and Discipline of Business Narrative* (San Francisco: Josey-Bass, 2005), The "corporate Siberia" quote is from a talk by Stephen Denning at IDEO, June 9, 2005.

233 **"This is a very strange conversation":** Denning, *The Leader's Guide*, 63.

233 **"Why not spell out the message"**: Denning, *The Springboard*, 80.

234 **"little voice inside the head"**: Denning, *The Leader's Guide*, 62.

235 **Klein tells another story**: The story of the failed conference summaries is from Klein, *Sources of Power*, 195–96.

Epilogue: What Sticks

238 **As recounted by Ralph Keyes**: Ralph Keyes, *Nice Guys Finish Seventh: False Phrases, Spurious Sayings and Familiar Misquotations* (New York: Harper-Collins, 1992). This book is filled with interesting examples of how proverbs evolve and change as they spread in society.

Several people gave feedback on our initial proposal, which needed a lot of work. We thank the following people for helping us create a document that was compelling enough to pass the first essential test: Doug Crandall, James Dailey, Ben Ellis, John Lin, Tom Prehn, Chloe Sladden, and Craig Yee.

When we finished the first half of the book, we were very excited and anxious to get some feedback. So we sent it to a bunch of friends and colleagues, who humored us and sent along written feedback. They also saved you, the reader, from lots of unconvincing and uninteresting anecdotes, like the one about the Charm Bracelet Punchline, so you owe them some gratitude as well. Here is the roll call of good people: Daryl Anderson, E. Joseph Arias, Deena Bahri, Amy Bryant, Mark and Chelsea Dinsmore, Julie Balovich, Danny Fitelson, Alfred Edmond, Michael Erisman, Chris Ertel, Erika Faust, Craig Fox, Emmet Gaffney, Lisa Gansky, Liz Gerber, Julio Gonzalez, Eric Guenther, Steven Guerrero, Susanna Hamner and Byron Penstock, Tod and Susan Hays, Fred and Brenda Heath, Ian Hill, Joe Lassiter, Alex Kazaks, Brian Kelly, Paul Marshall, George Miller, Shara Morales, Michael Morris, Derek Newton, Justin Osofsky, Jeff Pfeffer, Bill Sahlman, Andrew and Katie Solomon, Melissa Studzinski, Mark Schlueter, Paul Schumann, Steven Slon, Amy and Walter Surdacki, Bob Sutton, Mike Sweeney, Anthony Trendl, Ed Uyeshima, Steve and Trae Vassallo, Rachel Ward, Keith Yamashita. Thank you all—you gave us the feedback we needed when it was most useful.

Here is a hodgepodge of thank yous for people who helped us in distinctive ways. Thank you to Noah Weiss, who spent hours combing obsure sources for interesting examples in the early stages, and to Maggie Cong-Huyen, who picked up where he left off. Special thanks to Jeff Saunders for pointing out Commander's Intent. Thanks to Chip's students in several years of OB 368 classes, who helped refine and test this framework. Thanks to Chip's collaborators who helped work out many of these ideas: Adrian Bangerter, Chris Bell, Jonah Berger, Sanford Devoe, Nate Fast, Alison Fragale, Emily Sternberg, Scott Wiltermuth. Thanks to the following people who read the book and helped collect examples for the international editions: Eugine Chong, Hide Doi, Atsuko Jenks, Hyun Kim, Motoki Korenaga, Andreas Kornstaedt, and Noriko Masuda.

Now for the paragraph of people whose work inspired us. You didn't have anything to do with this book, and yet you had a lot to do with this book. A fan letter to: Edward Tufte, Don Norman, Malcolm Gladwell, James Carville, Stephen Denning, Robert McKee, Andy Goodman, Jim Thompson, Steven Tomlinson, Edward Burger, George Wolfe, David Placek, Keith Yamashita, Jacob Goldenberg, George Loewenstein, Robert Cialdini, Mark Schaller, David Rubin, Jan Brunvand, and many others that we're going to kick ourselves for not including by press time.

To our agents Don Lamm and Christy Fletcher, we are deeply grateful to you for making this experience possible. And thank you to Mark Fortier, for spreading the word about the book.

It is obligatory to thank your publisher. According to what we've heard from other authors, you usually have to say thanks through gritted teeth. This is our first book, and in the process of getting it to market, we were supposed to accumulate a lot of publishing horror stories. We were supposed to feel underappreciated and undersupported. Random House has been an utter failure on this front. The people at Random House have been such a joy to work with, so unexpectedly and unnecessarily nice, that it's hard to know where to begin. Thanks to: Debbie Aroff, Avideh Bashirrad, Rachel Bernstein, Nicole Bond, Evan Camfield, Gina Centrello, Kristin Fassler, Jennifer Hershey, Stephanie Huntwork, Jennifer Huwer, London King, Sally Marvin, Dan Menaker, Jack Perry, Tom Perry, Kelle Ruden, Robbin Schiff, and Carol Schneider. And Sanyu Dillon, my goodness, how can we adequately express our appreciation for all that you've done? Unbelievable.

And a huge, engraved, foil-embossed, calligraphied thank you to our amazing editor, Ben Loehnen. Our parents will read this book once, if we're lucky. (An aside: Our dad has a Quantity Theory of Literature, which says that it's not worth reading a book with fewer than four hundred pages. We're relying purely on connections to get a read out of him.) Meanwhile, Ben has read this thing probably a dozen times without ever breaking down, at least in front of us. Ben, you are endlessly patient, thoughtful, insightful, and supportive. Okay, this is starting to sound like we're signing your yearbook. (Stay cool!) But, really, we know we gave you a lot to stomach at times. Like our duct tape campaign.

Now to our family, who put up with us. We owe you this heartfelt thank you, which really has nothing to do with this book and everything to do with your support of us in all that we do. This section just gives us a great opportunity to put it in black and white. Thanks, Mom and Dad, for giving us co-authors. Thanks, Susan. Thanks, Emory. Thanks, sister Susan. Thanks, Tod, Hunter, and Darby.

We hope you enjoy the book. We had fun writing it.

ABOUT THE TYPE

This book was set in Electra, a typeface designed for Linotype by W. A. Dwiggins, the
renowned type designer (1880–1956). Electra is a fluid typeface, avoiding the contrasts
of thick and thin strokes that are prevalent in
most modern typefaces.

How to change things

sw!tch

when change is hard

Chip & Dan Heath

Switch

9781847940322 (paperback)
9781448108213 (ebook)

We all know that change is hard. It's unsettling, it's time-consuming, and all too often we give up at the first sign of a setback.

But why do we insist on seeing the obstacles rather than the goal? This is the question that bestselling authors Chip and Dan Heath tackle in their compelling and insightful new book. They argue that we need only understand how our minds function in order to unlock shortcuts to switches in behaviour. Illustrating their ideas with scientific studies and remarkable real-life turnarounds – from the secrets of successful marriage counselling to the pile of gloves that transformed one company's finances – the brothers Heath prove that deceptively simple methods can yield truly extraordinary results.